The Architecture of Blame and Praise

The Architecture of Blame and Praise

An Interdisciplinary Investigation

DAVID SHOEMAKER

Great Clarendon Street, Oxford, OX2 6DP,
United Kingdom

Oxford University Press is a department of the University of Oxford.
It furthers the University's objective of excellence in research, scholarship,
and education by publishing worldwide. Oxford is a registered trade mark of
Oxford University Press in the UK and in certain other countries

© David Shoemaker 2024

The moral rights of the author have been asserted

All rights reserved. No part of this publication may be reproduced, stored in
a retrieval system, or transmitted, in any form or by any means, without the
prior permission in writing of Oxford University Press, or as expressly permitted
by law, by licence or under terms agreed with the appropriate reprographics
rights organization. Enquiries concerning reproduction outside the scope of the
above should be sent to the Rights Department, Oxford University Press, at the
address above

You must not circulate this work in any other form
and you must impose this same condition on any acquirer

Published in the United States of America by Oxford University Press
198 Madison Avenue, New York, NY 10016, United States of America

British Library Cataloguing in Publication Data

Data available

Library of Congress Control Number: 2024934376

ISBN 9780198915836

DOI: 10.1093/9780198915867.001.0001

Printed and bound in the UK by
Clays Ltd, Elcograf S.p.A.

Links to third party websites are provided by Oxford in good faith and
for information only. Oxford disclaims any responsibility for the materials
contained in any third party website referenced in this work.

To Parker and Cohen

Contents

Preface	ix
List of Tables	xvii
Introduction: Materials	xix

PART ONE: SYMMETRY

1. Asymmetries	3
2. Functions	12
3. Hazards	46
4. Forms	54
5. Emotions	63

PART TWO: NORMATIVITY

6. Grounds	81
7. Fitmakers	97
8. Directions	122
9. Sanctions	140
Conclusion: The Architecture of Blame and Praise	160

References	167
Index	179

Preface

This book was inspired by four events. First, about fifteen years ago I read the paper "Variantism about Responsibility," by Joshua Knobe, Robert Woolfolk, and my now-colleague John Doris. It (finally) opened my eyes to a new way of doing philosophy, empirically informed to the hilt, applying a slew of results in social psychology and experimental philosophy studies to various stalemates in good old a priori philosophical theorizing about moral responsibility, theorizing in which philosophers nevertheless claimed that their (clear and distinct?) intuitions spoke for all. The authors posed a dilemma to responsibility theorists who claimed to be working in the Strawsonian tradition: either you respect and embrace people's *actual* (empirically investigated) attitudes and practices about blame and praise, in which case it turns out you're going to have some really messy asymmetries on your hands (and so you won't have a unified—invariant— theory), or you reject what the folk think (as unclear and indistinct?), in which case you ain't no Strawsonian, and you're going to wind up being a serious revisionist—on the basis of some pretty highfalutin and speculative metaphysical speculations—about our actual attitudes and practices.

I was excited about this new direction in moral psychology, and intrigued by their results, so I enthusiastically joined in on the game, conducting a series of X-Phi studies with David Faraci about actual blaming and praising reactions people had to those who were raised in moral ignorance, those who did the wrong thing while thinking it the right thing (e.g., Susan Wolf's JoJo), and those who did the right thing while thinking it the wrong thing (e.g., Huck Finn). Our results added more to the pile of evidence seemingly supporting the "asymmetry" between blame and praise found by other social and moral psychologists. There seemed no denying it.

And yet, to our credit, Faraci and I were a bit hesitant to jump fully on board the asymmetry train. Indeed, in two of our three papers on the topic, we offered possible alternative explanations of the data that were compatible with there still being a symmetry between blame and praise. But that's all it was: a hypothesis.

The second event inspiring this book was, perhaps oddly, my writing in recent years about humor and morality. In my new book *Wisecracks*, for instance, I write a lot about mockery, and part of my aim is to defend it against uninformed moralists (a lot of whom are philosophers), people who want to rid the world of it. In reading through some fascinating linguistics and psychological literature, a picture emerged in which mockery is thoroughgoing, and incredibly valuable, in our interpersonal lives. It is, I wrote as an aside at the time, probably an underappreciated form of *blame*. But that's all I said about that.

X PREFACE

The third event was seeing presented live, and then having the honor of editing, a groundbreaking paper by David Brink and Dana Nelkin at the first New Orleans Workshop on Agency and Responsibility (NOWAR), in 2011, called "Fairness and the Architecture of Responsibility," which eventually wound up being published in the first volume of a series I've edited for over twelve years, *Oxford Studies in Agency and Responsibility*. This paper (along with a remarkable [slightly earlier] paper by John Fischer and Neal Tognazzini, called "The Physiognomy of Responsibility") laid out an actual design plan, an *architecture*, of responsibility that aimed to capture all of its various forms, flavors, and features. I have borrowed their emphasis on architecture for the title and structure of this book, although it will be clear pretty early on that they and I have very different foci and results.

The final inspiration—and most immediate spark—came after I presented an early version of a lot of the material that has wound up in Part One of this book at a meeting of the Moral Psychology Research Group at Duke in June 2022. I got some great feedback, including from Steve Stich, who noted wryly that the presentation had "covered a lot of ground." When I mentioned this remark to my colleague Shaun Nichols, who had also been in attendance, he laughingly responded, "That's what happens when you're actually presenting a book!" I realized he was right. I started writing it down the following day.

This book represents the culmination of what I've recently realized that much of my career has been driving at, namely, a long attempt to excise a certain kind of metaphysics from normative domains in which it doesn't belong, in which it hasn't belonged, and in which it has been the source of all sorts of problems and stalemates. In my early work, stemming from my dissertation at UC Irvine, I started to develop a view according to which our person-related attitudes and practices are grounded independently of the metaphysics of personal identity, despite what many (most) in the field have assumed. And since 2007 or so, I have been advocating for the "normative turn" in responsibility theorizing, a turn away from taking the metaphysics of free will (demanding a robust sort of control or sourcehood) to be the essential necessary condition of responsibility, and a turn towards starting with and focusing on our actual responsibility attitudes and practices to see what their grounding consists in more directly. This book is my final statement on the matter: Our actual responsibility attitudes and practices need no grounding whatsoever in the metaphysics of free will or desert. If I'm right, this is a gamechanger. We can finally finalize the divorce between metaphysics and responsibility that P. F. Strawson initiated in 1962 in "Freedom and Resentment," and we can get on with the task of directly examining the proper—thoroughly normative—grounds of those attitudes and practices.

I have many people to thank for their help as I wrote this book. First, I want to thank audiences where I presented early versions of some of this material, starting in 2021, at a University at Buffalo Romanell workshop, a Bogota Workshop on

PREFACE xi

Praise, a Cornell moral psychology brown bag, a Leeds colloquium, (and into 2022) a Syracuse colloquium, the aforementioned MPRG Duke meeting, (and into 2023) a Wayne State University conference on agency and responsibility, a Bratislava conference on Modal Metaphysics(!), a University of Stockholm practical seminar, the New Orleans Workshop on Agency and Responsibility (NOWAR), and the Agency and Responsibility Research Group (ARRG!). There were great questions at each of these events that helped me make the material much better, or so I hope.

I am incredibly fortunate to have the friends and (some of) the colleagues that I do, both in this field and in the broader fields of ethics and moral psychology. Many individuals provided helpful comments on either drafts or verbally presented versions of a lot of this material. Those who contributed the most get their own little blurbs:

- Where I once idolized him from afar, now I get to go on hikes and drink IPAs with him: the towering **John Doris**. He was the earliest inspiration for my thinking about the ostensible asymmetries of blame and praise, and he's had excellent things to tell me about narcissism and desert. He's also one of the very few people who scares my pit bull Mack.
- He basically hired me in an early job of mine, and after we parted ways from that job we actually became the best of friends. He's brilliant, one of the canniest philosophical minds I know: **David Sobel**. On a spectacular winter hike in nearby Connecticut Hills Nature Preserve in January 2023, Sobel helped me to see many new lights in the material in Chapter 9 on desert and economic games.
- There are forces of nature and then there are *Forces of Nature*. **Jada Twedt Strabbing** is of the latter ilk. If she were merely the persistent and sharp questioner that she is, she'd be philosophically annoying, a Socratic gadfly. But her persistence and sharpness are coupled with such a joy, warmth, friendliness, and sincere desire to help the work, that somehow there aren't even any *pro tanto* reasons for annoyance left when she's done. She helped me sharpen up the material in Chapter 9 on desert, as well as some of the material in Chapter 7 on blaming corporations.
- There are students and then there are students. **Geoff Weiss** is both. He was a grad student of mine at Tulane, and then moved with me (well, not *with* me) to Cornell in 2021. He has provided me with many sharp comments on all aspects of the manuscript. Oh, and he's writing a soon-to-be-bestselling dissertation on the unthinkable, so you need to start planning your lives around that.
- I'd describe them in hilarious terms too, if only I knew who they were. Oxford University Press commissioned **three anonymous reviewers** for this book, and they were all helpful in different ways. The book is immeasurably better for their efforts.

xii PREFACE

- In the previous bullet point, I lied. Only two of the reviewers remained anonymous. The third revealed himself to be the suave and debonair **Gunnar Björnsson**. Gunnar outdid all the other reviewers (who were no slouches) by leaps and bounds, writing fifteen single-spaced pages of comments, most of which I have tried to incorporate or respond to in the final version (and the rest of which I ignored because they were just too hard to respond to).
- From 2016 to 2019 or so, I had the great pleasure of writing a paper with another suave and debonair fellow, **Manuel Vargas**. It was called "Moral Torch Fishing: A Signaling Theory of Blame." It's where we first sort of stumbled upon a functionalist account of blame and ran with it, cutting against the constitutivist theories that were all the rage at the time. When we first presented it, everyone hated it: philosophers hated it because they were all (almost) constitutivists, and they thought we gave their theories short shrift; (moral) psychologists hated it, because they found it to be trivially and obviously true; and biologists hated it, because they thought we got the science wrong. So we knew we had a winner on our hands. I have since come to believe that we could have expressed ourselves far more clearly in spots, so as to head off wrongheaded objections, and I also now think the original theory's focus on blame was too narrow, and the discussion of costly signaling didn't capture its actual role. I have thus presented a much altered—clarified, expanded, and defended—version of that paper in Chapter 2 (which is in all-new language and shape). But I am deeply grateful to Manuel for working with me on the original project, as well as for providing me with great comments on the new version.
- There had already been a very few other functionalist theories of blame on the scene before Manuel's and my paper was published. One of them was by the crackling **Coleen Macnamara**. Coleen was generous enough to make time to talk me through a number of issues she had with my new version of the functionalist theory, and I have tried to respond to her incisive remarks herein.
- Among those other early functionalist theorists was my now dear friend and colleague **Shaun Nichols**. Shaun's fame is worldwide, for good reason. He does impressively wide-ranging interdisciplinary and empirically informed philosophy, and he has counseled me repeatedly since 2021 on a number of issues that I take up in this book. He also provided me with incredibly helpful comments on my functionalism chapter, comments that finally got me to see the light on a number of fronts. He has also been my Sazerac pal and record buddy on many a Tuesday night over the past several years, and during that time together, we've also co-written a book on personal identity that you should keep an eye out for in the next few years.

- I'm a lucky man. Not only are some of my colleagues at Cornell excellent philosophers and friends, but one person who has long retired from Cornell is also an excellent philosopher and friend, the legendary **Carl Ginet**. I try to get to lunch with Carl several times a year, and he always wants to read some philosophy beforehand to discuss it together. Carl wanted to read an early version of this entire manuscript, and we discussed it over a couple of lunches. His keen mind always zeroes in on the right sort of worries, so I've been at pains to make sure I address them all. I'm very grateful for his comments and for his friendship.
- A final detailed shout-out to my former colleague, longtime friend, and occasional nemesis, the King of Ethics, **Doug Portmore**. Doug and I have had many conversations, some heated, over many years, about many, many aspects of moral philosophy. We had one such (heated) conversation on the rooftop of an Oslo hotel in 2019, about self-blame, which considerably sharpened my arguments in Chapter 8. Fortunately, neither of us "fell" over the side. We had another (email) conversation about my chapter on desert (Chapter 9), and even more conversations at the 2023 NOWAR about guilt, fit, desert, and much more. I learn something every time I talk to Doug, and his generosity in providing comments on written work is pretty amazing.

Many others made smaller but key contributions to my thinking on this project. **Eddy Nahmias** offered a crucial question at the MPRG meeting about compliments that led me to introduce the sting/buzz feature of blame/praise. **Thomas Nadelhoffer** asked a series of excellent questions at the ARRG talk for which I also had to make adjustments. **John Martin Fischer**—the man, the myth, the legend—asked me some good and helpful questions at a small workshop on responsibility in Portland in August 2022 that I had to adjust for, as did **Dana Nelkin, Randy Clarke, Andrew Eshleman**, my wonderful colleague **Derk Pereboom,** and the already mentioned Coleen Macnamara and Manuel Vargas. **Santiago Amaya**, as he is wont to do, asked me some very difficult questions about my work, but in the most polite and friendly tone and terms possible, at the online "Bogota" conference in 2021 and also at the Duke MPRG. And I had a great Uber and dinner discussion with **Holly Kantin** about mockery of the innocent and desert.

I taught a seminar on responsibility in the Fall of 2022 at Cornell. The grad students, as well as the faculty who sat in, were tremendous. I learned a ton from them, and because I was writing this book during the teaching of that class, I was able to try out various ideas in it with them in real time. It was one of the greatest teaching pleasures of my life, and somehow I wrote a draft of about two-thirds of the present book during that semester, so it was also one of the most fertile writing periods of my life. The discussion in Chapter 7, defending a Quality of Will

xiv   PREFACE

(QW) theory of angry blame's fitmaker, is particularly indebted to that group of students and faculty. They included **Monima Chadha, Bobbi Cohn, Santiago Garcia Jaramillo, Maria Camila Castro Maldonado, Julia Markovits, Itay Melamed, Joseph Orttung, Z. K. Payne, Dominic Sprigg, Anni Sun, Gus Turyn, Migdalia Arcila Valenzuela, Geoff Weiss, Hannah Winckler-Olick**, and **Guyu Zhu**.

I was very fortunate to have a workshop on this book organized by the wonderful people at the Lund/Gothenburg Responsibility Project, where I've been fortunate to spend a lot of professional time over the past eight or nine years of the project. The impetus came from the project's director, the incomparable **Paul Russell**, and it was organized and led by **Daniel Telech** and **Patrick Todd**, to whom I owe many intellectual debts. In attendance and contributing insightfully and helpfully throughout that looooong and productive day were **Anton Emilsson, Hadi Fazeli, Marianna Leventi, Robert Pál-Wallin, András Szigeti, Alexander Velichkov**, and **Marta Johansson Werkmäster**. I'm also grateful to Paul Russell for a very productive discussion on a lot of the material in Part Two over a delightful and coffee-drenched lunch.

A final professional debt of gratitude is owed to **Peter Momtchiloff**, the long-term editor in chief of OUP philosophy. Indeed, Peter *was* OUP to me, as he was their editor for the entire duration of my time as a professional philosopher. Peter first approved my proposal for an edited book series, *Oxford Studies in Agency and Responsibility*, which started in 2013. He was the editor for my previous monograph, *Responsibility from the Margins* (2015). And he was an enthusiastic supporter of this book; indeed, his enthusiasm sped this project along, from my writing an initial draft in the Fall of 2022 to my final submission of the manuscript in December 2023. As many now know, Peter retired from OUP at the same time (coincidence?). We in the philosophical community will miss him, as he really did make OUP philosophy great, and it was a major pleasure to work with him for the years I was lucky enough to do so.

Final thanks go to my family, and in particular to my wife, Marie Lantz, who has been my rock steady, my steady rock, of a kind one can only dream of having.

OK, now your eyes can glaze over. What follows are required acknowledgments of permissions to use some previously published material in this book.

- Some of the material in Chapters 5 and 8 is from my article "The Trials and Tribulations of Tom Brady: Self-Blame, Self-Talk, Self-Flagellation," in Andreas Brekke Carlsson, ed., *Self-Blame and Moral Responsibility* (Cambridge: Cambridge University Press, 2022), pp. 28–47. Reprinted with permission.
- Some of the material in Chapter 9 is from my article "Blame and Punishment," in D. Justin Coates and Neal A. Tognazzini, eds., *Blame: Its*

Nature and Norms (New York: Oxford University Press, 2013), pp. 100–18. Reprinted with permission.

- Some of the material in Chapter 7 is from my article "Blameworthy but Unblamable: A Paradox of Corporate Responsibility," originally published by *The Georgetown Journal of Law and Public Policy* 17 (Special Issue 2019): 897–917.
- Approximately two paragraphs in Chapter 5 are from my article "The Forgiven," in Brandon Warmke, Dana Kay Nelkin, and Michael McKenna, eds., *Forgiveness and its Moral Dimensions* (New York: Oxford University Press, 2021), pp. 29–56. Reprinted with permission.
- Some material in Chapter 7 is from my article "Threatening Quality of Will," published on-line in *The Journal of Moral Philosophy* in December 2023. Reprinted with permission.

Newfield, NY, USA
December 30, 2023

List of Tables

5.1	The partial architecture of blame and praise	77
C.1	The first sketch of an architecture of blame and praise (descriptive)	161
C.2	The complete architecture of blame and praise	166

Introduction

Materials

What does it mean and take for us to be *responsible* for what we do, believe, feel, or are? The answer that many philosophers give begins with some version of the following:

> **Motto**: To be a responsible agent is to be an apt candidate for responses such as blame and praise.[1]

What **Motto** suggests is that the best way to understand what it is to *be* responsible is to investigate what it is to be open or vulnerable to being aptly *held* responsible, and the most familiar way in which we hold each other responsible is through responses like blame and praise. Consequently, to understand responsible agency, we have to understand blame and praise.[2]

But we don't. Or at least so I aim to argue. Here's the gist. Philosophers have, over the past fifteen years or so, gotten very excited about blame, investigating what it is, what it targets, the pain it may or may not cause, whether it's deserved, who has standing to do it, how to be a hypocrite in doing it, and much more. A lot of this work has been excellent and insightful. But there's a serious problem: Blame is incredibly capacious. We blame all sorts of agents for all sorts of reasons:[3] I can

---

[1] See, e.g., Fischer 1986: 12; McKenna 2012: 7–8; Arpaly and Schroeder 2014: 160 (albeit with special explanation and ultimately a treatment compatible with mine in various respects); Mason 2019b: 1.

[2] Of course, philosophers being philosophers, there are also some who reject **Motto**. For them, the question of responsible agency is merely a matter of the relation that obtains between agents and various actions or attitudes that can properly render those actions or attitudes *attributable* to their agents (see, e.g., Scanlon 1998; Smith 2005 and 2012). Once an action or attitude is properly attributable to someone, that person is only then open to various responses, depending on what additional conditions are met, such as whether the agent was culpable, or whether the action/attitude was good or bad. But even these philosophers admit to a close, if not constitutive, connection between responsible agency and blame or praise, for these responses are still, for them, those to which all and only responsible agents are indeed rendered susceptible, once those other conditions are met, and those responses are also their leading data points for the construction of their theories, i.e., their theories are ultimately supposed to be in reflective equilibrium with our blame/praise responses (see, e.g., Smith 2005).

[3] I'm restricting the relevant sort of blame to agents, but we blame plenty of non-agential things too, including blaming a faulty electrical connection for draining my car's battery, blaming a noisy A/C unit for drowning out a student's question, and blaming fossil fuels for climate change. These latter are merely causal attributions, although there are actually interesting and difficult questions here

blame Archduke Ferdinand's assassin for starting World War I, blame Trump for intensifying partisan divide, blame my dead father for my crippling fear of commitment, blame my roommate for not letting me know my secret crush called me last week, blame my favorite baseball team's manager for not pulling his tiring pitcher in time, blame my favorite musical artist for a lackluster new album, blame BP for despoiling the Gulf of Mexico, blame my spouse for forgetting to pick up the milk she'd promised to get at the grocery, and blame myself for blaming others too much. We also blame in all sorts of different ways, by getting angry, yelling, expressing disappointment, criticizing, correcting, scolding, finger-wagging, unfriending, gossiping about, stopping talking to, protesting, ceasing to trust, withdrawing friendly feelings, and much else.

There is, then, a serious unity problem: What could possibly unite all of these disparate attitudes, activities, and reasons under a single umbrella, *blame*? Indeed, is it even unified *at all*?

Here's a second problem: Hardly any of the philosophical work has been about *praise*. Theorists have simply assumed that, once they figure out what blame is and what it tells us about responsible agency, those results will simply carry over to what is assumed to be its symmetrical positive counterpart, praise. So, for example, if blame primarily communicates anger at wrongdoing, then praise primarily communicates [*some positive emotion*] at right-doing. Or if deserved or fitting blame requires certain modal or control capacities in the target (so that, for example, the agent could have avoided being blamed), then apt praise must require those same capacities. Or if one's hypocrisy undermines one's standing to blame certain others, then so too it undermines one's standing to praise certain others.

But this assumption, so far as I can see, rests on nothing but blind faith. Indeed, as I'll show, there actually seem to be numerous *asymmetries* in our ordinary conceptions of blame and praise, so many that to simply assert that they are symmetrical counterparts may well be, um, irresponsible. Part One of the book aims to lay out, discuss, and then dissolve these purported asymmetries, a project which will replace philosophers' blind faith in the symmetry with actual evidence, albeit in ways that no one has previously anticipated.

I will detail all of the seeming asymmetries in Chapter 1 (there are at least ten), but here's just one teaser: Blame typically demands some pretty heavy-duty responses from its targets, such as apology, guilt, remorse, and recompense, and the reasons for blame don't really dissolve unless it gets what it demands; praise, however, typically demands *nothing* from its targets, other than a simple "Thanks!" (and it doesn't even *demand* that!), so no real reasons for its "dissolution" are necessary.

---

about how to draw non-arbitrary distinctions between blame for agents and non-agents, questions which are insightfully explored in Chislenko 2021. Because I'm interested ultimately in blame/praise as it pertains to responsible agency, as in **Motto**, I'll focus exclusively on agential, or interpersonal, blame/praise.

These two general problems point to an alarming fact: If understanding blame and praise is the key to understanding responsibility and we are nowhere near agreement on either their nature or their relation to each other, then it's no surprise that we are nowhere near agreement on the nature of responsible agency.

My aim in this book is to lay out the comprehensive architecture of blame and praise, so that we can at least get clear on what holding ourselves and others responsible amounts to, in all of its various guises. This result should thus get us one step closer to agreement—or at least to a diagnosis of the source of our disagreements—about the nature of responsible agency. That, I think, will be significant philosophical progress.

To get there I will take seriously and wrestle with not only philosophical discussions about blame (and what little there is on praise) but also work on blame and praise in psychology—developmental, social, and moral—which many philosophers have unfortunately overlooked. Indeed, some psychologists have been well aware of, and have theorized about, some of the seeming asymmetries that I will discuss. For instance, according to the Good True Self theory, developed by Joshua Knobe, George Newman, Paul Bloom, and other colleagues, we tend to view others as being essentially good "deep down inside," so that when people have and express beliefs and desires that we deem bad, we tend to view those beliefs and desires as less attributable to those people than we would if we viewed their beliefs and desires as good. For liberals who view homosexuality to be perfectly morally permissible, a young religious man's resisted homosexual desires are deemed more attributable to him than his beliefs about its wrongness, whereas for conservatives, the opposite is more or less true (see, e.g., Newman, De Freitas, and Knobe 2015).

There is also a massive literature in experimental economics on strategic interaction in various economic games (e.g., the dictator, trust, and ultimatum games), where how people respond is construed as punishment or reward, themselves construed as forms of blame or praise. From these interactions we can learn about our retributive nature, as well as how various sanctions or rewards can serve incentivizing or educative functions. Again, these features of blame and praise are often overlooked or ignored by a priori philosophers.

Given my interest in articulating the whole wide world of blame and praise—what counts, how we do it, how it varies in different contexts, what it's for, what it targets, and much more—this sort of empirical work must be brought to bear. But it is by nature incomplete, as it lacks any story about what renders blame and praise apt. There's a normative gap between blame/praise and their *worthiness*. My aim in Part Two is to fill in this gap in the empirical literature. We can't, after all, just take all of our responses to one another at face value. In our everyday lives we often easily recognize that some of these responses are inapt. Blaming a benefactor for benefiting you would be a mistake, for instance, as would praising your beloved daughter's killer for killing her. More familiarly, it might be that we *should* blame some charming wrongdoers more than we do, or we *should* praise those who have worked hard at their craft more than we do those who stumble their way into excellence. We get no such "shoulds" from the empirical research, but if our ultimate goal is to gain fuller understanding of the nature of blame and praise, so as to gain a fuller understanding of the nature of responsible agency, we can't do so without weeding out "bad" responses and identifying what count as "good" ones.

So the psychologists and economists correctly recognize various blame/praise responses and note some seeming asymmetries between praise and blame that philosophers tend to miss, but they are also, as it were, too permissive in what they allow into the picture, and they don't (by design) tell us about the nature and grounding of blame, praise, and responsibility generally, which is what the philosophers are aiming to explicate. Both approaches capture some of the right elements but overlook others. My aim here is to pluck the best from both worlds, bringing philosophers and empirical researchers into conversation with one another, with the ultimate aim of articulating the complete architecture of blame and praise as they pertain to responsible agency, one that will, hopefully, satisfy the desires of all. In so doing, I'll work my way through the following issues.

* * * * *

In Chapter 1 ("Asymmetries"), I motivate my overall project by documenting what seem to be a lot of asymmetries in our ordinary conceptions of blame and praise, many more than have been noticed even by the psychologists who have been theorizing about some asymmetries. These seeming asymmetries threaten the possibility of generating any unified or coherent story about the nature of either holding responsible or responsible agency. I explore two possible rejoinders— one revisionary, one descriptive—before setting the stage for the third approach, one that will take up the remainder of Part One. It requires, first, that we come up with an account of just what the proper target of our investigation truly is.

In Chapter 2 ("Functions"), I provide that target, starting with the question, "What *are* blame and praise, precisely?" Most philosophical theorists have, first, attempted to answer this question only about blame, and then done so, second, by giving primarily constitutive accounts, appealing variously to specific emotions, attitudes, or types of expression as what constitutes blame. I will argue instead, first, that blame *and praise* are (continuous) responses within a recognizable and stable *system*, one that is not, second, unified in terms of any individual bit of constitutive content. Rather, the only unified story we can get about the nature of this whole system of blame and praise is to ask and answer the question, "What is it *for*?" That is, we have to ask not about the constitutive content of individual contributors to the system but about the system's *function*, as well as what role those contributors play relative to that function. In doing so, I build on, clarify, radically expand, amend, and defend a functionalist theory of the blame/

praise system that Manuel Vargas and I first sketched in 2021 ("Moral Torch Fishing: A Signaling Theory of Blame").

In Chapter 3 ("Hazards"), with my new understanding of the function of blame and praise in hand, I will begin exploring ways to dissolve some of the purported asymmetries between them. I start by revealing some of the unappreciated hazards shared by both blame and praise, found in their over- and under-deployment. It might seem obvious how over-blame can be dangerous, as it can generate serious psychological damage in its targets, which itself can lead to self-harm or worse. But under-blame is dangerous too, as it may generate a sense of entitlement in those who are allowed to get away with wrongdoing. However, as it turns out, both over- and under-*praise* are psychologically dangerous too, as they can generate a pretty nasty personality disorders (nasty for those who have the disorder and nasty for those who have to deal with them). But examining this disorder also reveals some surprisingly important information about blame and praise. There's a sense in which those with this disorder simply can't "accept" blame (they deny that it's applicable to them), but they also crave and totally accept "praise." All of this information actually threatens to introduce yet more asymmetries, but it also points the way toward an overarching *symmetry*, I will argue.

Chapter 4 ("Forms") reveals the way there by leaning on the two very different forms blame and praise may take. I'll show that there's a kind of "blame" that's previously been unrecognized, a kind of blame that's perfectly symmetrical with the kind of praise that seemed asymmetrical with blame before. This revelation is the key to revealing a more general symmetrical structure to blame and praise.

Indeed, as we'll see, there are two different types of blame and praise, one that's acknowledgment-seeking, the other that's not. There is much here to unpack, and that's my job in Chapter 5 ("Emotions"). I will get there by talking about various emotions. Blame and praise can of course be unemotional. You may eviscerate me with a dryly cutting criticism, and I may induct you into the watch repairer's hall of fame by praising all of your accomplishments in a way that puts you (and me!) to sleep. Nevertheless, emotions are often felt and expressed in blame and praise. My aim in this chapter will be to enumerate and explicate them. Blame's most familiar emotional paradigm is anger, but many have misunderstood anger's nature and relevance, both for blame and for responsible agency. Further, there's a positive counterpart to blaming anger that has been insufficiently theorized: gratitude. This is a kind of praise that is, in its way, acknowledgment-seeking (as is blaming anger), although what it seeks of one's benefactor is to feel a kind of pleasure, namely, *gratification*. But there are other emotions in the blame and praise mix. On the former side, there's disappointment, contempt, disdain, condemnation, and hurt feelings. On the latter side, there's admiration, shared pride, and warm feelings. Each reveals something interesting about responsible agency, namely, that it involves multiple capacities and conditions, that we should be *pluralists* about responsibility. Once we become pluralists, we'll be able to see the multiple symmetries between blame and praise.

These symmetries raise new questions about their *grounds*. The job in Part One is to describe the nature of the many types of blame and praise. The job in Part Two is to provide an account of what renders each of them apt or inapt. Suppose, for example, that you're a colleague who has asked me to pick you up at a certain time at the airport, which is a good 30 miles away from me, on one of my very busiest days. I nevertheless agree to do so. When I arrive, you aren't there. You don't respond to my calls or texts. After two hours, I bag it and go home. That evening you finally text me: You'd decided to stay an extra day and had been scuba diving all afternoon. Can I come and pick you up instead tomorrow? Well, let's just say I'll be peeved. I may have some harsh words for you, and it's quite unlikely that I'll come back tomorrow to pick you up. I'm surely blaming you, and my blame seems quite apt. But what renders it so?

Further, when you sense my anger, you may feel some pained emotion; that is, my anger may *sting* you. Now ordinarily, I need moral justification to deliberately cause someone pain, emotional or otherwise. What moral justification might I have here? Many philosophers think this is the precise point where we need to appeal to *desert*: You deserve my blame, they want to say, and perhaps you do so insofar as you met whatever (robust?) conditions for free will that desert demands. Other philosophers appeal only to *fit*: My blame, they say, is simply an appraisal of what you did as a slight of some kind, and it is apt (and needs no moral justification) just to the extent that you indeed slighted me. Both desert and fit are backward-looking considerations: they offer reasons rendering blame apt grounded entirely in what you did. But other philosophers appeal to forward-looking considerations, suggesting that my blame is rendered apt only insofar as it'll be an effective way to get you to change your ways, to stop taking advantage of people like this.

These are all theoretical questions drawn from consideration of blame alone. Complications are introduced yet again when we start seeing similar questions arising for praise. As it turns out, sometimes we praise people (our children, our students) for forward-looking reasons, as a way to provide them with positive incentives to do good things and/or to educate them. But sometimes we praise people exclusively for backward-looking reasons, as when I compliment, through gritted teeth, my athletic nemesis for her decisive victory against me (I surely don't want to incentivize her to beat me again!). Are these matters of desert as well? Merely of fit? Of something else? And is moral justification needed for praise too?

These are all hard questions. The symmetrical architecture I sketch in Chapters 4 and 5 will enable us to begin answering them in Chapter 6 ("Grounds"), although the full answer won't be provided until Chapter 9. I will start with purely private blaming attitudes, and I'll defend a view according to which all that's needed to ground them normatively is fittingness, not desert. I will do the same for the new form of blame and praise I revealed in Chapter 4.

Chapter 7 ("Fitmakers") continues the normative investigation by examining what precisely makes various forms of blame or praise fitting. When I fittingly blame or praise you for some action or attitude, I'm doing so in *virtue* of something. What is this *something*? In this chapter I lay out the fittingness conditions of our emotional blame/praise responses. I have previously argued (and still believe) that their fit is a function of the blamed or praised agent's quality of will (QW), as long as "quality of will" is understood pluralistically to refer to qualities of *character, judgment,* or *regard* (Shoemaker 2015). But QW theories have been taken to be otiose—or worse—by a lot of recent work in moral philosophy and moral psychology. Starting with investigation into implicit bias, many now think that agents can be blameworthy for certain of their stereotyping attitudes, beliefs, and treatment of others, *even if they have the purest of wills.* Those who commit microaggressions, those who believe stereotypical things about people even for good evidential reasons, or those who automatically associate certain non-white or non-male faces with negative qualities—these may all be blameworthy activities and attitudes, say the many, regardless of their agents' qualities of will. Indeed, such objections are sometime buttressed by pointing to what seem to be blameworthy *institutions* and *corporations* that nevertheless lack any qualities of will. The U.S. healthcare system may be racist, for instance, or BP might be blameworthy for befouling the Gulf Coast. My main aim in Chapter 7 will be to thwart these threats to the QW theory, either by blocking the purported connection between blameworthiness and non-bad-will in the examples given, or by dissolving those examples' purported anti-quality-of-will implications.

To this point in the book, I will have focused almost exclusively (as do most theorists) on blame and praise that's directed at *others*. One might think that the normativity of other-blame and -praise will simply carry over directly to the self-directed versions. But they don't. Chapter 8 ("Directions") starts with a fascinating puzzle that brings out this point. As it turns out, while of course there are cases of hypocritical blame of others, rendering it inapt, in a way, there's no such thing as hypocritical self-blame. The reason is quite surprising, derived from a mistake many philosophers and psychologists have long touted, namely, that self-blame is *guilt.* But it's not. What self-blame consists in—in its apt forms—will be the topic of this chapter. What I'll reveal in addition is the nature of self-praise, which also differs from various types of other-praise. I'll draw heavily here from fascinating work on the phenomenon of "self-talk," which has been studied extensively in various exercise and athletic-performance sciences.

The final substantive chapter (Chapter 9: "Sanctions") will be about the painful blaming treatments we occasionally inflict on one another, as well as their normative grounds. My focus in the book is on blame and praise in our interpersonal lives, the ways in which we informally respond to one another for successes or failures relative to a variety of normative standards. But for many people, talk of blame, at least, is or ought to be closely connected to talk of *punishment*, which is paradigmatically doled out by various authoritative institutions like the state, and which raises questions about the relations between interpersonal and criminal blame (and responsibility). They are, I'll argue, starkly different. Nevertheless, a lot of work in psychology and experimental economics has assumed an extremely thin interpersonal notion of punishment regardless, illustrated by how people respond to one another in various economic games (I will call these, more neutrally, *sanctions*). I will bring together these different literatures and, in so doing, articulate different kinds and conditions of blaming sanctions, as well as their ultimate interrelations, differences, and justifications. My ultimate (and quite controversial) aim will be to offer a complete backward-looking account of the aptness of many blaming sanctions that nevertheless needs no justifying appeal to *desert*. In doing so, I will emphasize the very close relation between interpersonal sanctions and the enforcement of rules in various kinds of games and sports.

The concluding chapter will tie together all of the strands of the previous chapters to reveal a clear, unified, and complicated-but-symmetrical architecture of blame and praise. My hope is that once this architectural design has been made clear, the many disciplines that have been studying blame and praise from radically different angles might actually be brought together, generating genuine theoretical progress by enabling us to finally speak to one another and collaborate in a common language going forward.

The Architecture of Blame and Praise: An Interdisciplinary Investigation. David Shoemaker, Oxford University Press.
© David Shoemaker 2024. DOI: 10.1093/9780198915867.001.0001

PART ONE
SYMMETRY

1
Asymmetries

As I noted in the Introduction, the guiding assumption of most philosophers working on responsibility has been **Motto**:

To be a responsible agent is to be an apt candidate for responses such as blame and praise.

Built into **Motto** is the even deeper assumption that blame and praise are wholly symmetrical counterparts, the negative and positive versions of the same general kind of thing, namely, ways of *holding responsible*. When a responsible agent has done something bad, she's an apt candidate for blame; when she's done something good, she's an apt candidate for praise. Blame is the label for our set of negative responsibility responses, and praise is the label for our set of positive responsibility responses.

We've seen tons of philosophical work on blame over the last fifteen to twenty years, but hardly any on praise.[1] Instead, it's been taken to be obvious that, since praise is essentially blame's positive correlate, then once we figure out the nature of blame, our results will immediately deliver to us on a platter the nature of praise. And blame is much more exciting anyway.[2] For one thing, there's the long-standing (presumed) link between blame and free will: How could it ever be apt to blame someone for whom determinism has rendered free will impossible? More generally, blame is just dangerous: It can really hurt, so it cries out for moral justification. But praise doesn't much motivate concerns about free will, as who really cares if a praiseworthy deed was determined? Furthermore, praise doesn't hurt, so moral justifications for it are unnecessary (see, e.g., Watson 2004: 284).[3] As Dana Nelkin writes, "It is notable that we don't speak of the unfairness of

---

[1] This situation in philosophy is changing, perhaps rapidly, with the onset of new articles by Stout (2020), Telech (2021 and 2022), Jeppsson and Brandenburg (2022), and Bingeman (Forthcoming).

[2] I wrote a review of George Sher's excellent 2006 book *In Praise of Blame* for the *Australasian Journal of Philosophy* back in the day. The book is exclusively about blame, and at the end of my review, I suggested that Sher's follow-up book be *In Praise of Praise*, which was underexplored. When I met George in person, he remembered the review, and he pseudo-jokingly remarked that he'd never write such a book, saying, "Praise? How *boring*." (It turns out that Daniel Telech's dissertation of 2018 was indeed titled *In Praise of Praise*.)

[3] Although, again, some of the recent writing on praise stresses that there are moral considerations—such as comparative fairness or respect—that are in fact in play for praise. See, e.g., Telech and Tierney 2019, Jeppsson and Brandenburg 2022, and Bingeman Forthcoming.

4 THE ARCHITECTURE OF BLAME AND PRAISE

lacking an opportunity to avoid acting well and so missing out on [praise's] benefit" (Nelkin 2011: 33).

But simply on the basis of such remarks we should start to get worried, for how could blame and praise be symmetrical counterparts if only one cries out for moral justification or free will?

As it turns out, there are actually many more seeming asymmetries between praise and blame, so many that it may be quite difficult to see them as being responses to the same thing at all—responsible agency, purportedly. My general aim in this chapter is to document these apparent asymmetries before, in the next several chapters, dissolving them so as to reveal the true—but heretofore unrecognized—overall symmetry between blame and praise. Once we recognize what's going on, we will have in place the crucial foundation of our blame/praise architecture.

A quick note before proceeding: My focus in this chapter and most others will be on blame and praise directed at *others*. Self-directed praise and blame, as we will see in Chapter 8, are actually quite different in many significant respects than their other-directed versions, and they bring their own heretofore unrecognized wrinkles into the praise/blame architecture. So I'll hold off till then to discuss them.

Ten Asymmetries

In what follows, I aim to explore our ordinary conceptions of blame and praise in their most familiar, paradigmatic forms. Blame, as it's ordinarily understood, is thought to be a directed, angry response to wrongdoing, a response captured succinctly in the stinging phrase (with all its religious echoes), "Damn you!" Praise, as it's ordinarily understood, is most typically an admiring or encouraging response to someone doing something well, a response captured most succinctly by the phrase "Good job!" Praise in its most familiar form is a kind of *compliment*. There are thus ten seeming asymmetries between these two conceptions.[4]

1. *Demands*: As we tend to construe it, blame typically demands, calls for, or invites some kind of response from the blamed party, often a rather robust and difficult suite of responses: guilt, remorse, apology, repair, compensation,

---

[4] Nathan Stout has recently laid out two asymmetries between praise and blame that he takes to motivate a new "ethics of praise," to be investigated independently of blame. The first is that, while blame is apt for intentionally doing the wrong thing for bad reasons, there's no symmetrical standard for praise, as sometimes doing the right thing for the right reasons is praiseworthy (saving a drowning child), but sometimes it's not (keeping a promise). The second asymmetry is that blame seems to require emotions (e.g., anger), whereas praise doesn't. (See Stout 2020: 216–17.) While the first may be less a metaphysical asymmetry than an epistemic gap, the second is indeed an apparent asymmetry (in our ordinary conceptions), and I include it in my list.

and more.[5] In its most familiar form, my angry blame of you demands most directly and dramatically that you recognize and appreciate how it is that you made me feel from my perspective (that is, it demands *empathic acknowledgment*).[6] Only once you've met that demand can we get back on equal footing with one another, as the reasons for continued blame no longer exist.[7]

Praise, on the other hand, typically demands *nothing* of its recipients. My praise for your excellent meal or putt expects—not demands—nothing more than a simple "Thanks!" If you don't respond to my praise, you may be an asshole, but I have no claim whatsoever on your saying "Thanks," and my praise is fully discharged without it.

2. *Desert*: The blamed party, many tend to think, has to deserve it for blame to be just (see, e.g., Clarke 2023). Blaming your toddler for her insufficient empathy with the plight of the homeless is surely undeserved, we tend to say, as is blame for the slowness of someone in a wheelchair or blame for someone's ugly "beauty" mark or mismatched eyes. Desert is a mighty metaphysical conundrum, to be sure, but nevertheless we often talk about it as a crucial condition on apt blame.

Desert, however, is unnecessary for—and indeed irrelevant to—many cases of apt praise. I may well praise you for your beautiful beauty mark, or for your bewitching eyes, for your lighthearted gait or your highly discriminating sense of smell. When we offer such praising compliments, no one says, "He didn't deserve that!"

3. *Emotions*: Blame's paradigmatic form, as I noted earlier, typically includes an emotion, most often a kind of directed anger. We tend to see wrongdoing through an angry emotional lens, whether the wrongdoing targets us, a loved one, or even a stranger. It rouses us, and it typically motivates some kind of confrontation, an urge to get in the face of the wrongdoer and give him or her what for.

Praise, on the other hand, typically includes no (or not much) emotional content, and there's certainly no particular emotion that comes to mind when we think about praise. We can easily praise one another dispassionately, as when I drily compliment your choice of wine at a dinner party.[8]

4. *Attitudes*: Blame is thought to be fundamentally attitudinal (see, e.g., Sher 2006b; Arpaly and Schroeder 2014: 159; Brink and Nelkin 2022), and so is

---

[5] See Watson 2004: 219–88; Darwall 2005: ch. 4; Shoemaker 2007; Macnamara 2013a (for the "call-and-response" version); and Telech 2021 (for the "inviting" version).

[6] See Fricker 2016 and Shoemaker 2015 and 2021 for much more on this demand for acknowledgment. I'll say even more about it in Chapter 6.

[7] There have been several psychological studies showing that people think that the most successful generator of forgiveness, by far, is remorse of this sort. See my discussion of this literature in Shoemaker 2021: 35–8.

[8] Again, see Stout 2020: 217.

6 THE ARCHITECTURE OF BLAME AND PRAISE

thought to be something one may well keep to oneself; that is, there is a familiar phenomenon of private blame. We may be motivated to keep it to ourselves for a variety of reasons: we don't want to screw up the relationship, we're worried we might get it wrong, or we don't want to get beaten up. But in any case, there's typically some attitude at blame's core that can be kept to oneself, even if it's difficult. That attitude counts as blame even so.

Praise, on the other hand, seems to be fundamentally expressive: Whatever I'm feeling privately, it doesn't count as praise if I keep it to myself. I don't have to express it to the target, of course, but I do have to express it to *someone*. I may, for instance, praise the chef of our meal last night, but direct it only to my spouse the next morning.[9]

5. *Morality*: Blame is typically thought to be moral in nature, apt paradigmatically for moral failures.[10] If you slice your golf drive, or if you botch a line on your watercolor painting, it would be inapt for anyone, it seems, to *blame* you for these nonmoral failures. Instead, blame seems (typically) reserved for slights, disrespect, or certain kinds of deliberate harm, what we think of as the domain of immorality. This isn't to deny that, say, coaches blame their athletes for screw-ups or that fans blame their musical heroes for selling out, but these aren't the paradigm cases (and a case has been made that these really are moral failings too; see Matheson and Milam 2021).

Praise, however, as a kind of compliment or credit, is typically offered in *nonmoral* domains, for things like good athletic, aesthetic, and culinary performances or outcomes. In the positive versions of the examples just given, it would be perfectly apt for me to praise you for a straight and towering golf drive, or for a delicately executed line in your watercolor. Of course, I don't at all deny that we do praise one another for morally supererogatory actions (e.g., returning a found wallet to its owner), but these are by no means the most familiar cases, and these are also, importantly, not cases in which we could conceivably morally *demand* that people perform such actions.

6. *Excuses*: You can typically get off the hook for blame with a good excuse: "I didn't know!"; "It was an accident!"; or "I was overwhelmed with grief at the time."

---

[9] See Arpaly and Schroeder 2014: 159–60 for more on this point. They prefer "crediting" as the true opposite of blame insofar as crediting *is* an attitude and not necessarily an action. They think "condemning" is the true opposite of "praising," therefore, as they are both actions. I'll say more about their view later. Tim Kwiatek (Cornell Ph.D. dissertation 2023) suggests that Romeo's monologues about Juliet ("Hark, what light in yonder window breaks?") are cases of private praise. The dramatic and aesthetic features of this case muddy it a bit, however, as the dialogue is spoken aloud. If I'm truly just mouthing those words internally about someone, it strikes me more as an example of admiration than praise. A tougher counterexample would be one in which Romeo simply writes those things about Juliet in his diary.

[10] See Nelkin 2011; Clarke 2016; Matheson and Milam 2021.

Praise, however, is typically immune to excuses. There is considerable empirical evidence for this claim. For example, survey subjects tend to reduce their blame for someone who, overcome with angry rage, smashes the window of a car parked too close to his versus someone who does so calmly and deliberately, whereas they don't alter their degree of praise for someone overwhelmed by sympathy who helps a homeless man versus someone who does so with calm deliberation (see Pizarro et al. 2003).[11] Subjects do the same for moral ignorance: Where someone has grown up in morally deprived circumstances and is ignorant about some features of right and wrong, that person tends to be viewed as less blameworthy than a morally aware counterpart, yet people who do good things out of moral ignorance (e.g., Huck Finn) are thought to be just as praiseworthy—and sometimes *more* praiseworthy—as those who are morally aware (see, e.g., Faraci and Shoemaker 2014 and 2019).

7. *Quality of Will*: Relatedly, what a successful excuse in the blame domain tends to do, as Strawson taught us, is make clear that, while we might have injured someone, there wasn't any ill will behind it (Strawson 1962; see also Sliwa 2019). What we tend to blame people for are injuries manifesting a poor quality of will toward us, often found in a wrongdoer's motives or practical reasons. Many theorists enamored with blame have thus advanced Strawsonian Quality of Will theories of responsibility built on top of this theory of excuses (see, e.g., Watson 2004: 219–59; McKenna 2012; Shoemaker 2015; Björnsson 2017).

   Yet while we tend to blame people for actions and attitudes primarily in virtue of their quality of will, that typically matters far less for praise than do simply good performances, the skillful execution of some intentions, regardless of motives or reasons. When I praise you for your delicious pie, I really could not care less *why* you made it so delicious (perhaps you wanted to get me to like you or to invest in your fledgling pie-making business); all that matters is that you made it delicious.

8. *Moral Justification*: As noted earlier, blame can hurt and harm, and so it seems to require some sort of moral justification. There are several candidates. Some are forward-looking, for example, direct consequentialist appeals to the good effects of doing so (see, e.g., Smart 1973; Pereboom 2021b). Most appeal to backward-looking moral justifications, however. R. Jay Wallace, for one, appeals to *fairness*, saying that it could only be fair to hold someone responsible with blaming emotions like resentment, indignation, and guilt to the extent that they have the functional capacities to recognize and respond properly to moral reasons (Wallace 1994: 5–6 and

---

[11] See also the work by Doris and Knobe 2010, about which more later.

8   THE ARCHITECTURE OF BLAME AND PRAISE

throughout). Most others, however, prefer appeal to the *justice* (of what we owe to each other, say) found in something like desert: we are morally justified in setting people's interests back by blaming them only to the extent that they deserve it (see, e.g., McKenna 2012: chs. 6–7; Pereboom 2014; Clarke 2016 and 2023; Carlsson 2017; Portmore 2022; and many others).

Praise, though, seems to need no moral justification, insofar as it neither hurts nor harms.[12] It typically feels *good* to be praised, and who needs a moral justification for that (other things being equal)?

9. *Standing*: Many philosophers have been exploring our *standing to blame* in recent years, an issue brought out most clearly by hypocrisy. When I blame you for something I myself am unapologetically guilty of as well, I'm a hypocrite, and you may rightly ask, "Who are *you* to blame me?" This response, many have thought, points out my lack of standing to blame you, even if you are blameworthy (see, e.g., Smith 2007; Wallace 2010; Fritz and Miller 2018 and 2019; Rossi 2018; Todd 2019; and many more).

But there seems to be no analogous worry about praise. There is no such thing as hypocritical praise, at least of the sort in which someone might question the praiser's standing, as in "Who are *you* to praise me?"[13] Anyone has standing, it seems, to praise anyone else.

10. *Danger*! Because of how painful it can be, blame can be very dangerous. When parents won't let up blaming their children, it can wreak psychological havoc. When people on-line pile on in their blame of a purported wrongdoer, it may easily drive the target into depression or worse.

Praise, on the other hand, seems utterly innocuous, delivering only the warm fuzzies, so there seems to be no analogous danger in over-praise to worry about (what, even warmer fuzzies?). Kids soak up their parents' praise, and on-line piling on of praise is just going to be make the target feel better and better (if not also perhaps somewhat sheepish).

These appear to be significant asymmetries. Blame most generally is typically thought to be a serious, demanding, and pain-causing attitude or treatment

---

[12] Some have noted that there are comparative fairness concerns relevant to praise. For example, if I praise Jones for doing something Smith has also done, failing to praise Smith might be unfair. See, e.g., Watson 2004: 282–5; Nelkin 2009; and Telech 2022. What I'm emphasizing here is a noncomparative prima facie immorality present in individual instances of directed blame that are missing in individual instances of praise.

[13] Isserow and Klein 2017 offer some cases of what they call hypocritical praise, but it's not of this variety. They are rather cases in which people praise others for doing great things (suggesting that they themselves are committed to them) that they themselves don't do. They thus don't question the praiser's *standing* to praise. See Jeppsson and Brandenburg 2022: 665 for a more recent attempt to defend the possibility of hypocritical praise, in which the praiser fails to respect the equality of persons, by "inaccurately appraising someone on the basis of irrelevant considerations…" They admit, though, that even on this construal, the "conditions for praise and blame aren't strictly symmetrical…" For recent discussion of the possibility of hypocritical *self*-praise, see Lippert-Rasmussen 2022.

targeting the poor quality of will of a moral wrongdoer, something only certain people have standing to engage in, and requiring serious moral justification; whereas praise is simply thought to be a morally innocuous kind of compliment or credit for a variety of positive characteristics or accomplishments, apt independently of quality of will, something anyone can engage in. Consequently, continuing to so closely associate responsible agency with those who are apt candidates for "blame and praise," as if they were obviously symmetrical counterparts targeting the very same (type of) responsible agency, seems seriously problematic.

Two Strategies for Dealing with the Asymmetries

The first strategy for dealing with the seeming asymmetries between blame and praise is theory-driven: philosophical and revisionary. It's to admit that, yes, there are some asymmetries, but we need not accept them as they are to do the work we need done on responsible agency.

One route to this conclusion is to deny that responsible agency of a certain sort has anything to do with praise at all. This was Wallace's strategy, who took the story of morally responsible agency to be exclusively about only our negative, reactive emotions—resentment, indignation, and guilt—given their connection to failures to live up to interpersonal demands and expectations, the kinds of failures to which we hold people to account (Wallace 1994: 25–33). It doesn't really make sense to say that we are holding anyone to account when praising them, after all.

A second route is to allow that blame does have a symmetrical positive counterpart, but to heavily restrict which of our many positive responses it is. This was T. M. Scanlon's strategy.[14] Indeed, he abandons talk of blame and *praise* in favor of blame and *gratitude*, the latter of which is the response he puts forward as blame's proper (and only) positive counterpart (Scanlon 2008: 151).[15]

---

[14] It's also essentially the strategy of Arpaly and Schroeder (2014: 159–60), who advance *credit* as the true opposite of blame (insofar as blame and credit are both attitudes), and who also advance *condemning* as the true opposite of praising, since both are *expressions* of those underlying attitudes. This strategy, I think, still doesn't adequately capture the whole range of blame, praise, and blaming or praising expressions, missing out on gratitude, for one, as a natural type of positive responsibility response (in its attitudinal and expressive form), and missing out on the type of non-condemnatory blaming expressions I'll discuss later.

[15] There might be a third philosophical option here, suggested by an anonymous referee but inspired by previous work of Gary Watson's and mine. That would be to differentiate between types of responsibility, and then classify blame of the sort I have articulated as a response to *accountability*-responsibility, which is about one's capacity to recognize and respond to certain kinds of demands and expectations, and then to classify praise of the sort I have articulated as a response to *attributability*-responsibility, which is about one's capacity for cares and commitments (character traits). This is all quite complicated machinery, which I will discuss briefly later in the book, but let me simply jump to the conclusion here: This is not the distinction that matters for dissolving the various asymmetries.

Many have found Wallace's exclusion of positive responses from the domain of responsibility to be arbitrary or mistaken (see, for one, Fischer and Ravizza 1998: 5, n. 5). We absolutely do have positive responsibility responses to each other, goes the thought, so why think an adequate account of responsible agency could plausibly ignore them? Perhaps accountability, as such, is exclusively about adhering to interpersonal demands and expectations, but (a) it's unclear why praise couldn't also be cashed out in terms of something akin to demands or expectations (*à la* Telech 2021), and (b) it's unclear why we should take accountability to be the whole of responsible agency. Contempt and admiration, for instance, may not be about the demands and expectations to which we hold others to account, but they are surely responses to exercises of people's practical agency (see, e.g., Watson 2004: 260–88; Shoemaker 2015: ch. 1).

Scanlon, on the other hand, thinks of blame as a kind of relationship modification appropriate to the breach in a relationship that the blameworthy party caused, so were his view of blame correct, then he'd be exactly right to pair it with gratitude, as that too involves a kind of relationship modification in light of the significance of someone's beneficial treatment of the grateful party. In other words, switching to a focus on gratitude as blame's positive counterpart fits well with his particular (and possibly revisionary, as he admits) theoretical aims and commitments (see Scanlon 2008: 211–14). But this move still leaves a large swath of what seem to be our responsibility responses behind, as a ton of (merely) praising practices do seem to respond to responsible agency without being instances of gratitude, for example, complimenting someone for making a tasty meal or for swishing a beautiful basketball shot. Both philosophers' theoretically driven revisionary responses ignore, reject, or revise too many of our actual responsibility responses to provide us with the full story about responsible agency.

The second strategy is the (moral) psychologists' response-driven route: Take seriously our actual praising and blaming responses, they say, and then revel in their asymmetry. This is what John Doris, Joshua Knobe, George Newman, Paul Bloom, and David Pizarro, with various colleagues, have done in several influential articles. One way to do so is to show that people tend to attribute only (what they view as) good qualities to people's true selves, downgrading or dismissing (what they view as) bad qualities in others as not truly "theirs." If people judge others in this way, then we can safely predict that they will have asymmetrical blame and praise responses—as they in fact do—for example, attributing the bad actions of the morally ignorant less to those agents than they do their good actions, or by attributing beliefs and desires they see as good to various agents more than the beliefs and desires they assess as bad (see, e.g., Pizarro et al. 2003; Doris and Knobe 2010; Newman, De Freitas, and Knobe 2015; Faraci and Shoemaker 2014 and 2019).

The first problem with this approach, though, is that, by simply taking all of our responses as they are at face value, the psychologists overlook the very real possibility that some of those responses are just *inapt*. But surely some are. If my spouse blames me for an infidelity I purportedly committed in her dream, then she's just wrong. If I praise you for pushing me out of the way of an oncoming car, but it was actually the woman next to you who did so, or if it turns out that you were actually trying to push me *into* that car's path, then I'm wrong to praise you. Or, to consider the examples actually used in surveys, we might be wrong to praise Huck Finn, and other morally ignorant right-doers, for their behavior, just as we might be wrong to attribute actions, desires, and beliefs to people asymmetrically based on our antecedent normative commitments. We need an account of *apt* blame and praise before we can make any judgments about their (a)symmetry.

The second problem with the pure response-driven approach is that the psychologists who employ it don't provide us any real insight into *responsible agency* at the end of the day. If there are such asymmetries between blame and praise, what does this mean for the nature of responsibility? Are we responsible only for the blameworthy *or* the praiseworthy things we do, but not both? Does responsible agency require different *capacities* for blame and praise, given the asymmetry? Or perhaps what has been deployed is a debunking strategy: Maybe we ought not to be drawing from our actual practices at all when investigating the nature of responsibility, as those responses are just an asymmetrical mess? Perhaps the asymmetry renders all such responses illegitimate?[16] As usual (and this isn't a complaint, just a description), we get no normative conclusions from the empirical psychological approach, whereas an investigation into responsible agency cries out for it.

My aim in this book is to develop and defend a third strategy, one that co-opts the best features of both the philosophical and psychological treatments: Examine *all* of our blaming and praising responses (as the psychologists do), lay out their normative conditions (as the philosophers do), and in so doing reveal several previously unrecognized types of blame and praise, whose places in the architecture fill in crucial gaps that will help to dissolve all of the apparent asymmetries. There is in fact a general symmetrical structure to blame and praise, and their deployments do have normative grounds capable of revealing many important things about the nature of responsible agency.

To get started on this adventure, I first need to discuss the nature of blame and praise, so that we have a clear story about what it is we're even talking about.

The Architecture of Blame and Praise: An Interdisciplinary Investigation. David Shoemaker, Oxford University Press.
© David Shoemaker 2024. DOI: 10.1093/9780198915867.003.0001

---

[16] See Faraci and Shoemaker 2019 for a query along these lines.

2

Functions

Every year during the trade winds season, on the Ifaluk coral atoll in Micronesia, several tribesmen spend a couple of exhausting weeks gathering, drying, and weaving coconut fronds into elaborate torches and hand nets. They then use those torches and nets at night to catch flying fish, which they then use as bait to catch dogtooth tuna in deeper waters. This ritual takes them well beyond their ordinary fishing regimen. The entire process is grueling, leaving them sleep-deprived and spent, and it ultimately involves a net caloric loss for those fishermen: the fish they catch aren't enough to replace the calories they've expended in catching them. So what's going on here? Why do it?

These torch fishermen are engaging in what's known as *costly signaling*. While all of their efforts may seem irrational in the short term, they actually pay off in the long term, as their participation in the ritual conveys valuable information to their tribemates, information about their excellent work ethic, about how reliable and productive they'd be as providers. The signaling of this otherwise hard-to-glean information ultimately tends to pay off in terms of their getting beneficial mates and achieving high community status (Sosis 2001).

The information signaled is valuable because it is, crucially, taken to be *honest*, that is, there's a strong correlation between those who engage in the torch fishing and their having the desired mate and social traits. The honesty of the signal stems directly from its cost. This is such a costly enterprise that, for those without the positive traits it signals, impersonating or trying to fake the signal would itself be more costly than it would ever be worth. Yes, those without the productivity and provider traits would certainly benefit if they could get people to believe they'd make for good mates without having to go through the elaborate torch fishing ritual, but it would just be too hard and expensive to pull off. So participating in the ritual sends a hard-to-fake signal, which enables them to get valuable prudential benefits (Sosis 2001).

The same general story is true of blame, or so Manuel Vargas and I argued in our 2021 paper, "Moral Torch Fishing: A Signaling Theory of Blame." I now think that the theory is both too limited in some respects and too promiscuous in others, and the explanatory story it told wasn't quite on target. But the core of the theory is still, I believe, true, its identification of an essential but overlooked social phenomenon valuable and significant. I will thus articulate and develop that core, provide the proper explanatory target, show where I now think we took our theory too far and where we didn't take it far enough, and then defend the revised theory from three challengers. I start, though, by motivating the new method that generates the theory in light of previous and more familiar philosophical theories of blame.

Theories of Blame

Philosophers exploring the nature of blame have typically tried to identify its core unifying feature, some particular attitude, expression, action, or practice that all and only instances of blame have in common. What follows is a brief history of those attempts (in roughly chronological order), some of which are put in the constitutive terms I'm going to focus on later.

- *Influence*: Classic utilitarians held that blame is an *influencing expression of disapproval* of people's acts or traits, an expression predictably generating certain good effects, such as improving the offender's character or deterring others from performing similar actions or having such traits (see, e.g., Smart 1973: 49–50, who actually preferred the label "dispraise"; Nowell-Smith 1954: 306; see also Schlick 1966; and Smart 1970). Blame, on this account, is a kind of "punishment light" (Sher 2006b: 73).
- *Accounting*: On this view, blame is constituted by a *judgment* that there's now a stain or blemish on the blamed offender's life ledger, that the offender's "'record' has been 'tarnished'; that his 'moral standing' has been 'diminished'" (quoting from Zimmerman 1988: 38).
- *Affective*: Even if he didn't explicitly advance a "theory" of blame, P. F. Strawson is at least the inspiration for this popular view, according to which blame is constituted by one of the Holy Trinity of reactive attitudes: resentment, indignation, or guilt (see, e.g., Strawson 1962; Wallace 1994; Wertheimer 1998).
- *Relationship*: In light of what he took to be the inadequacy of a Strawsonian affective theory, T. M. Scanlon advanced a view of blame that had it consisting in two parts: (a) a judgment that the offender had impaired one's relationship, and (b) a modification of one's relationship with the offender "in a way that this judgment of impaired relations holds to be appropriate" (Scanlon 2008: 128–9; see Chislenko 2020 for helpful discussion of what precisely Scanlon meant). This characterization was intended to widen considerably the set of responses that could constitute blame, so it could include not only the Strawsonian reactive emotions but also (a) a greater range of emotions (e.g., disappointment); (b) non-emotional criticism; (c) alteration of interactions; and (d) mere withdrawal of warm feelings.
- *Communicative*: This might also be called the *expressive* theory (Watson 2004: 226). It too is often traced to Strawson. On this view, blame is

14 THE ARCHITECTURE OF BLAME AND PRAISE

constituted by the expression or communication of a "demand for reasonable regard" (Watson 2004: 229), a demand typically made by the Holy Trinity. The Strawsonian reactive attitudes aren't simply vexed or pouty emotions; they instead "are incipient forms of communication," and like all attempts at communication, they lose their point as such if the addressed agent can't understand it (thus making sense of the exemption of psychopaths, say, from the domain of blameworthy agents) (Watson 2004: 230; for other versions of communicative theories, see Darwall 2005; Shoemaker 2007; McKenna 2012 and 2013;[1] Fricker 2016).

- *Protest*: This theory is quite popular in the philosophical literature right now. It has roots in Pamela Hieronymi's groundbreaking work (2004) on the "force and fairness" of blame. I take its articulation here from Angela Smith (2013). In addition to its including a judgment of blameworthiness, à *la* Scanlon, blame on this view consists in a modification of "one's own attitudes, intentions, and expectations toward [the offender] as a way of *protesting* (i.e., registering and challenging) the moral claim implicit in her conduct, where such protest implicitly seeks some kind of moral acknowledgment on the part of the blameworthy agent and/or on the part of others in the moral community" (Smith 2013: 43; emphasis in original; see also Talbert 2012).

- *Minimal*: In light of what he took to be failures of some of the theories of blame above, George Sher (2006b) offered a theory according to which blame is constituted, quite minimally, by a simple belief-desire pair: (a) a belief that the offender has performed a bad act or is a bad person, and (b) a desire that the offender not have performed that bad act or have been a bad person (Sher 2006b: 112). Sher took this to be a natural phenomenon, a theory of "what blame amounts to," not an analysis of a concept or word. More recently, though, a few people have offered just such an analysis, of what they take to be blame's universal *conceptual core*, purportedly shared by every instance of blame, even if many forms go well beyond it. Brink and

---

[1] While Michael McKenna explicitly categorized his original conversational theory of blame as a "communication-based theory" (in McKenna 2013: 139), there are some important differences. First, his is explicitly *not* a constitutivist account of blame; instead, it aims to develop a paradigmatic, family resemblance-style view, one that is nevertheless meant to be a member of the Strawsonian family (see McKenna 2013: 139–40). Second, for McKenna, blame is, at least in its ostensibly prototypical *directed* (offended to offender) form, a stage in a responsibility conversation; specifically, it is the (morally) angry second stage he labels *Moral Address* (McKenna 2012: 89). Agents' actions have meaning, manifesting their quality of will, and when an agent wrongs me in a blameworthy way with an insufficiently good quality of will, that's the first contribution in a back-and-forth responsibility conversation we can have. The details of these contributions—what counts as what kind of contribution—are seriously contextual, though, and so one might take it to render the theory more of a functionalist approach to blame and/or responsibility than a constitutivist one. Nonetheless, it has enough in common with the communicative theory as given in the text (which is what it was originally meant to be, as indicated in McKenna's [2013] own writing), that I include reference to it in this category.

Nelkin argue that this core "is an aversive attitude toward the [offender] that is predicated on the belief or judgment that the target is blameworthy," which "involves wrongdoing for which the agent was responsible" (Brink and Nelkin 2022: 185). They take this analysis to be immune to counterexample. They also take it to have great explanatory value, explaining, for instance, what's attractive about various alternative approaches (such as functionalist and prototype theories). Likewise, Douglas Portmore analyzes someone's blame of an offender as constituted by her representing the offender as having violated a legitimate demand without yet having suffered as much guilt, remorse, or regret as the offender deserves for it, coincident with the blamer feeling, "as a result of these representations, disapproval of or disappointment in" the offender (Portmore 2022: 50).

Now thatsa lotta blame!

In our original paper, Vargas and I discussed only four of these theories: *Affective*, *Relationship*, *Protest*, and *Communicative*. We argued that all of them were vulnerable to various prima facie counterexamples, cases which forced them to engage in what we puckishly called "fancy dancing" to deal with adequately. All that we meant was just that the cases didn't fit very easily—on their face—with the motivating contours of the theories. So, for example, cases of private blame or blaming the dead are, on their face, non-*Communicative*. Cases of self-blame are, on their face, neither about *Relationship*-modification nor a matter of *Protest*. (How could I alter a relationship with myself? Wouldn't I be both protester and protestee? Indeed, who am *I* to protest me?) Cases of emotionless blame are, explicitly, non-*Affective*. These are all cases of prima facie false negatives. Each theory was also vulnerable to prima facie false positives, cases of angry affect, relationship-modification, protest, and moral-demand-communication that weren't very obviously cases of blame at all (Shoemaker and Vargas 2021: 583–5).[2]

We knew full well the brilliance and sophistication of the theorists behind these theories, and we knew full well that they had all attempted to deal with these prima facie counterexamples before, sometimes in exceedingly clever fashion. Our point was thus *not* that they couldn't do so, nor was it that the counterexamples falsified their theories. It instead was that the fixes to which they typically had to appeal were often ungainly, and, more importantly, their fixes didn't seem within the spirit of what motivated the original theory. There was a *reason* they were forced to dance fancy to deal with the outliers, a reason which motivated our move to a very different sort of approach. None of them could very

---

[2] Resenting the infirmities of old age = anger without blame. A mother modifying her relationship with her blameworthy son by loving him more = relationship modification without blame (Smith 2013). Sister Helen Prejean standing in front of a prison holding a lit candle during an execution = protest without blame. Quietly but firmly making clear that you won't stand to be treated so disrespectfully = moral-demand-communication without blame.

16 THE ARCHITECTURE OF BLAME AND PRAISE

easily wrangle and unify the vast array of blame-types and -tokens that are part and parcel of our interpersonal lives.[3]

And even though Vargas and I didn't discuss them, the first two theories— *Influence* and *Accounting*—run into similar problems. In brief, *Influence* has several prima facie counterexamples, including cases of private blame, blaming the dead, third-party blame (blaming an offender only to a third party), self-blame, and stranger blame (e.g., blame of evil foreign leaders that you'll never interact with). None of these blamed parties are going to be influenced by your blame. In addition, as Sher argues, the unpleasant (and motivating) effects blame purportedly creates are generated only if it is actually taken to be a sincere expression of the blamer's more fundamental attitude of disapproval. But then blame wouldn't be about an expression; it would really have to be about the underlying attitude (Sher 2006b: 74).

Accounting also has several problems. For one thing, many who blame don't view the blamed as having been "soiled" by their wrongdoing, or that we are all running "moral tabs" (Sher 2006b: 76). The view also fails to sufficiently capture the emotional element blame very often contains in our lives. Insofar as blame is typically tinged with anger, say, that's the reason it has the kind of effect on the blamed person that it very often does. A mere judgment (especially coming from a stranger) isn't unpleasant and likely won't deter me in the least. But surely blame itself often *stings* (see Hieronymi 2004 for this accurate metaphor, one I will return to and lean heavily on in a later section). We tend to be quite averse to it. We want to avoid it. *Accounting* lacks any clear means to explain why (Sher 2006b: 76–7).

What all of this seems to drive us toward is *Minimal*, a theory which aims to articulate the minimum core component(s) necessary to all forms of blame, with the aim of unifying the concept or phenomenon while also allowing for numerous variations built on top of that core. These theories have been created precisely to deal with the cases that have forced others to dance fancy: private blame, blaming the dead, self-blame, stranger blame, third-party blame, and more. But they too founder on other cases, depending on their details.

Roughly, for all three versions (Sher's, Brink/Nelkin's, and Portmore's), blame consists in a belief, judgment, or representation that an offender culpably did something bad, wrong, or blameworthy, in combination with some aversive (and

---

[3] Consider just two examples. First, a communicative theory might try to explain cases of private blame by presenting a theory of emotions such that the relevant "communicative" emotions are what they are in virtue of their having characteristic public expressions. We can thus understand private resentment as being what it is in virtue of its characteristically being expressed to the offender. This takes a lot of new theoretical machinery to pull off, however, machinery that cuts against many extant theories of emotions. It also seems like an ad hoc patch. Second, a protest theory might explain private blame or blaming the dead by insisting that, even though protest is also incipiently communicative, sometimes the party to which protest (incipiently) communicates is oneself. Besides being obscure (aren't I also the communicator, so don't I already know the message?), this too seems rather ad hoc.

non-instrumental) attitude in response to that thing (e.g., for Sher, the desire that they not have done that thing; for the others some general attitude like disapproval or disappointment). Yet there seem to be prima facie false positives even to this minimalist approach. Many cultures consider purity to be a moral value, and so see various impurities as morally wrong. They may thus have an aversive attitude—*disgust*—to "dirty" people for activities or ways of living that they view as culpably wrongful (they also likely have the desire that they not have done that thing). But disgust doesn't seem to be blame. After all, we get disgusted at all sorts of foul smells and moldy food, and our disgust isn't blame in those cases. Adding in the thought that the object of our disgust is also *culpable* for the disgusting state he's now in doesn't seem enough to edge that aversive attitude itself into the blame zone; the disgust response in and of itself feels (phenomenologically) identical in all cases.

Indeed, we have all sorts of aversive attitudes to people that may be paired with, or even spurred by, beliefs or representations about blameworthiness in the targets of those attitudes, where the attitudes themselves don't seem to count as blame. These include horror, dismay, and frustration. Now Brink and Nelkin, to their credit, note these responses as well, but they *include* them as blaming attitudes, contrary to my (and I'd think, many other people's) conceptual intuitions. Nevertheless, they do worry that they might be overly inclusive after all, as it may seem that *fear* and *dread* could also count as blame on their view (where presumably they are not?). Countering their own worry, though, they say that fear and dread are actually responses to the various disvalues present and "not responses to culpable wrongdoing as such." Fear or dread respond (aptly) to the fearsome or the dreadful, not to "wrongdoing qua culpable" (Brink and Nelkin 2022: 186, n. 13).

But often it's precisely culpable wrongdoing *as such* that inspires fear or dread in people (and certainly in me). That people culpably do horrible (immoral) things to each other is (or can be) terrifying. But terror just isn't blame, even on the stretchiest definitions thereof.

Turn now to prima facie false negatives. All versions of *Minimal* have difficulty with cases I'll refer to as *counterfactual* blame. *Minimal* theorists all take blame to be a response to perceived actual wrongdoing, that is, to desired-otherwise, blameworthy, or demand-violating past behavior (or attitudes, or character). But sometimes we blame people *for things they have not done* and perhaps will not ever do. Here's a great example. In the excellent film *Force Majeure*, a husband abandons his wife and two young kids on a ski resort terrace as a controlled avalanche heads their way. When the avalanche stops before it reaches the terrace, through the cloudy air we see his wife still on the terrace, her body blanketing her frightened children. As the scene clears, the husband strolls back in as if nothing had happened. As his wife realizes who he really is in a moment of crisis, their marriage begins to crumble. Now here's the relevant bit: A younger couple, friends of the family, come to join them for a few nights. After the wife recounts

18   THE ARCHITECTURE OF BLAME AND PRAISE

the tale to them in increasing frustration and irritation (while the husband insists that he doesn't recall things as happening in that way), their friends go back to their own room, where the younger woman whacks her partner on the shoulder and says, with evident anger, "That's something *you* would do!" She is, I think it's fairly clear, blaming him, albeit for *something he has not done* and will likely never be in a position to do. She is not blaming him for his bad character or bad attitudes, I hasten to add, although they would be the causal sources of his doing the blameworthy thing, were he ever in a position to act on them. She is, quite simply, blaming him for what he *would* do.[4]

Anyone who is or has been in a close relationship (most often of the romantic sort) has very likely experienced such a response. If it's admitted to be blame (and it's hard to construe it otherwise), then none of our *Minimal* theorists—nor any of the others (except, oddly, the otherwise least plausible *Influence* theory)—can account for cases like this, at least without fancy dancing.[5] The fanciness of the dancing is required given their emphasis on blame as being exclusively an appraisal of what people have already done (or attitudes they've formed).

One way to "account" for counterfactual blame, of course, is simply to deny that it's "real" blame after all. Perhaps it's a way of *holding responsible*, but without blame.[6] This seems a kind of unmotivated and all-too-convenient conceptual regimentation, however. The anger is quite real, and it feels perfectly akin to the anger of "ordinary" blame. Perhaps these examples of blame aren't *apt*? That's irrelevant to these theories, which are supposed to be about the nature of blame *period*, apt or not.

---

[4] Some may think this a too-quick rejection of the possibility that her blame targets his character (I'm grateful to several discussants at a workshop in Lund, Sweden for pushback on this point). There is some theoretical machinery in the background, to be sure. I agree that there may be apt blame responses targeting poor quality of character, but they are (to be apt) *aretaic*, basically by definition, and they include responses such as contempt and disdain. This is the rubric of what I've elsewhere called attributability-responsibility (Shoemaker 2015: ch. 1). The anger expressed by the woman in this case is quite clearly meant to be a form of blame that is about *accountability*-responsibility, and that is blaming anger's proper domain (Shoemaker 2015: ch. 3). In my technical machinery, to be explicated more in Chapter 5, blaming anger responds to actions or attitudes flowing from insufficient empathic regard, which may include those who simply fail to see certain facts about others in a reasonish light (as putative reasons). What's going on in this case, I think, is that she is blaming him for what he would do given his insufficient empathic regard, and so not for his character as such. But given that he hasn't done anything or even formed any bad attitudes based on his poor empathic regard, there's nothing yet that constitutes the proper target of blame for any of the *Minimal* theorists.

[5] In Part Two of this book, I will defend a fittingness-based account of apt blame. It, like desert, is (typically) backward-looking, but it's about accurate representation. One might then wonder, as did an anonymous referee, how *my* view could account for counterfactual blame. While a desert-based view of blame only makes sense for things people have in fact done, a fittingness-based view is, I think, flexible enough to account for what people *would have done* as well, which gives it another leg-up on desert-associated views of blame, such as the ones under discussion here. My blame of you for what you would have done may still fit, whereas a desert-based theory could never aptly apply.

[6] Coleen Macnamara (2013b: 160) seems to be making such a move when she says, "We demand that another do as she ought not in response to actual moral violations—this is the domain of blame—but rather in response to threatened infractions. Sometimes we anticipate that someone might flout a moral requirement, and when we do, we might hold her responsible before wrongdoing commences."

There is another, perhaps more compelling, concern about *Minimal*: Sometimes we blame others for things we deem neither morally wrongful nor violations of legitimate demands.[7] As your chess coach, I may blame you for a blundering move that cost you a game; I may blame you, my friend, for throwing out a painting I'd created as a gift for you; or my partner may even blame me for buying her a cheap anniversary present from the supermarket. I don't think of the offending agents in any of these cases as being "blameworthy violators of legitimate demands," though; rather, they have simply done things that, respectively, were disappointing, hurt my feelings, or didn't live up to my ideals or hopes for the relationship. But these responses often sure seem like blame nonetheless.

So here's where we are. Each of the discussed theories aims to understand and explicate blame's nature mostly by appeal to some kind of agential response as its unifying constitutive feature, e.g., a bad grade, a kind of anger, a communique, a relationship-modification, a protest, or a minimal combination of aversive attitude and belief or representation. Each proposal on its own is indeed often associated in some way with obvious cases of blame. But there are also obvious cases of blame that aren't associated—at least on their face—with each individual item, and sometimes the ostensibly constitutive responses put forward aren't on their own enough to amount to blame either (or aren't paradigmatically cases of blame).

There are surely responses and amendments available for each theory. I have not eliminated any of them from contention (nor have I meant to). Indeed, I have merely aimed to highlight that each has prima facie gaps they have to fill, gaps created precisely by the overly narrow motivating spirit of their original proposals (which also tends to make their proposed fixes ungainly).

A natural solution thus immediately presents itself: be more inclusive. Perhaps, then, a *disjunctive* theory of some sort is true, according to which blame is constituted by at least one of such agential responses as these: a bad grade, a kind of anger, a communique, a relationship-modification, a protest, or a minimal combination of aversive attitude and belief or representation.[8]

I think something like this disjunctive constitutive "theory" may be true. But now it's not at all interesting, and it's hardly even a theory; instead, it's just a long

---

[7] This claim may seem in tension with the first asymmetry I discussed in the previous chapter, on the demands of a kind of angry blame, but recall that those were meant to be familiar aspects of our paradigmatic conceptions of praise and blame. They all admit of exceptions.

[8] Manuel Vargas (2013: 116–21) is the only one I know who does offer a distinctly pluralistic theory of blame, although the "plural" is only two. The first part is a "judgment-like attitude" and the second is a blaming reaction (e.g., reactive attitudes and their expressions). These are independent of one another, and so count as blame when occurring on their own. The first, though, is really just a judgment of blameworthiness, which I've always had difficulty thinking of as blame itself (as does Sher [2006b: 6], who writes that actual blame has to add something to the bare belief that someone has acted wrongly). And as should already be clear (and will be even clearer momentarily), I think that blaming reactions range far more widely than the ones that Vargas favors.

20   THE ARCHITECTURE OF BLAME AND PRAISE

list of responses without any unifying explanation. Why are *these* responses on the list, one now wants to know, and not some others?

For the answer to that question, we need to take up a fundamentally different approach.

Let's Get Functional, Functional!

We are looking for a theory of blame. At this point, we've basically got just a data set to work with, a long list of familiar agential responses. In *some* contexts, and in response to *some* things, these responses are *sometimes* bad grades (or more general accounting practices), emotions, relationship-modifications, communiques, protests, or minimal attitude-belief pairs. *But not always*. And this may not seem like much to go on.

But there's one more relevant data point that puts us on the right track: our set of agential blame responses is an organized, recognizable, longstanding, and thoroughgoing part of our interpersonal lives. It is, in other words, a *stable social system*.[9] There is thus a new move available to us, one familiar from the philosophy of science and the philosophy of social science: To understand the nature of various organized systems (in biology, psychology, and society) we need to switch our focus from what makes various responses members of that system—which seems to call for a unified constitutivist theory—to what such responses are doing in and for that system in the first place—which calls for a *teleological functionalist* theory (Wright 1976; Boorse 1976; cf. Cummins 1983; Couch 2017). That is, we cannot understand what makes something a member of a stable and organized social system until we first understand what that system's function is, where the right question for us to ask is what is all this blame *for*?[10]

But—and this is a key amendment to the original Shoemaker/Vargas theory—we cannot restrict the target of our investigation to blame alone. That's because the actual stably organized system here is instead the far more inclusive system of blame *and praise*. There are several reasons. First, not only do we respond to agents negatively for their actions or attitudes, we also respond positively to them, in a huge variety of ways that are, like blame, nevertheless often

---

[9] It's the general system of blame and praise I'm talking about. This is compatible with there being lots of variation of specific deployments across different contexts.

[10] I'm glossing over some controversy in the functionalist literature, between a pure "Wright function" and a more explicit "teleological function." Wright functional statements emphasize etiology, completing this schema: "Trait T exists because it did Y." Teleological functional statements emphasize that the functions of traits (for example) are explained in terms of their causal contribution to the goal of some system (see Boorse 1976). I actually think both interpretations of functional statements apply to blame and praise: these agential responses are parts of this particular social system because they did—and do—contribute causally to a goal of that system. I'll specify all of these features in the text. (I'm also grateful for very helpful discussions on these matters with Coleen Macnamara, Shaun Nichols, and Manuel Vargas.)

easily recognizable and perfectly continuous with our negative responses. There are praising attitudes, expressions, and actions. Their instances also range from influencing expressions (e.g., positive feedback to children), to accounting (e.g., adding a mental checkmark on the positive side of someone's life ledger), to affective (e.g., gratitude or warm feelings), to relationship-modifying (e.g., getting closer to a benefactor), to communicative (e.g., complimenting), to touting or honoring (the positive analogue of protesting?), to minimal-attituding (e.g., thinking positively of someone you deem to have done something praiseworthy). These positive responses too are all part of our stable social system of agential appraisals.

Further support for including praise in the system comes from the fact that we sometimes disagree, both with each other *and ourselves* over the sorts of responses—blame or praise—that are appropriate for someone. Consider an athletic case. Suppose you and I are fans of a basketball team whose best player fouls out by committing a hard foul on an opposing player in the final minutes of a crucial game. You blame him for doing so; he's going to cost our team his skills when we most need him! But I praise him for doing so, as he prevented a flashy dunk that would have given the other team momentum. We both agree on the facts about his behavior, let's say. We are genuinely disagreeing over whether blame or praise is appropriate in this circumstance, where this is a domain in which we also agree *that either might be appropriate.* That's because blame and praise are both ways of appraising agents, so no matter which evaluative stance on them we think is right, both are drawn from the same general appraisal response pool. We might, after all, merely disagree over how much *blame* is appropriate. In such a case, we're obviously disagreeing over the right responses within the very same organized system of agential appraisals. So too our disagreement over whether blame *or praise* is appropriate is of the same sort. We could, for instance, easily imagine the coach having the same back-and-forth uncertainty with herself, unsure whether to praise or blame the player, depending on which agential properties of the player she focuses on.

Perhaps sports blame isn't "real" blame (this suggestion is false, but for now I'll tolerate it). Even so, we have such disagreements in the moral domain too, where the negative and positive agential appraisals we're trying to sort through and fix upon all come from within the very same organized system. For example, suppose I decide to deter cheaters in my classroom by requiring one cheater to stand in the front of the class every day for two weeks wearing a scarlet "C." I also do this for the good of the student and the good of all the other students (if they can internalize the badness of getting caught in this way, they'll avoid cheating and do better for themselves in the future). Some might praise me for this creative lesson, some might blame me for its "toxic rigor," and both might be torn about it. But in every case, they are wrestling with a variety of possible responses within the very same recognizable and organized social system.

22 THE ARCHITECTURE OF BLAME AND PRAISE

A third general reason to think that these appraisals are all part of the same stable system is that, in order to be a good blamer, one must regularly and competently engage in praise, and vice versa. Were one *only* to blame, and never praise, one would be a curmudgeon, and, in an important sense, unjust, *even if every single instance of one's blame were apt.* If all you do as my coach is blame me (aptly) for my mistakes, and you never praise me for my successes, you're just a bad coach, as you're preventing me from the warm (and incentivizing) feelings I'd get from your praise, especially if it's hard-earned. So too, were one *only* to praise, and never to blame, one's praise would lose *its* power, and it too could be viewed as unjust. I once sat in on a grad seminar by an excellent philosopher who assigned discussion questions to his graduate students for each week's meeting. They varied widely in quality, but each was met by the professor with "Excellent! That's a really great question!" What that did was to discourage the better students, those who were sharper or who had worked harder on their questions, and had them thinking (as they reported to me), "If he's just going to praise us all equally, then what's the point in trying so hard?" This was an excellent philosopher who nevertheless wasn't a fully competent praiser, as he didn't seem to know when to withhold or dampen it (or even, perhaps, when to blame for poor questions).

I thus think that both blame and praise are agential responses which are part of the same recognizably stable system. What, then, counts as a blame or praise response? I don't want to beg any questions against any of the constitutivist theorists I've discussed, so I'm simply going to provide a long list of agential responses that at least some people in some circumstances have claimed to sometimes count as instances of blame or praise. You may disagree over whether some truly belong on this list or not, but for now, I want to be as welcoming as possible. They include the following attitudes, expressions, actions, and practices (which move gradually from the "blamey" to the "praisey"):[11]

- Punishment (institutional, parental, and informal)
- Sanctions (formal or informal)
- Disincentives of various sorts
- Demerits noted on a life "ledger"
- Anger/rage/resentment/indignation
- Disappointment
- Yelling
- Decreasing respect for

---

[11] Some of the listed responses are obviously from the philosophical literature. Others were gathered more informally, from many friends and acquaintances, some of whom are philosophers, others of whom are psychologists, and some of whom are not academics at all. These helpful people include Samantha Berthelette, David Brink, Brad Cokelet, August Gorman, Bob Hartman, Jesse Hill, Ron Mallon, Per Milam, Adam Patterson, Neal Sinhababu, David Sobel, and Ninni Suni.

- Contempt/disdain
- Guilting
- Shaming
- Feeling guilt/shame/regret (in self-directed cases)
- Protest
- Distrust
- Avoidance
- Ostracism/shunning
- Complaining about
- Indifference/disengagement (e.g., pointedly refusing to laugh at someone's jokes)
- Directed (threatening) demands ("Apologize to your sister!")
- Finger-wagging, head-shaking, eye-rolling
- Assigning more responsibilities/taking away some responsibilities
- Demotions
- Sharp criticism
- Burning in effigy
- Thinking poorly of
- Giving the cold shoulder/silent treatment to
- Withdrawing warm or friendly feelings
- Modifying a relationship (more generally)
- Having warmer feelings toward
- Thinking well of/admiring
- Putting positive marks down on a life "ledger"
- Compliments/saying nice things about
- Applauding
- Remembering/memorializing/honoring
- Increasing respect for
- Crediting
- Freeing up from some responsibilities/giving more responsibilities to (e.g., more administrative things to do because one is good at it)
- Rewarding/promoting
- Gratitude
- Increased trust

Most of us engage in various items on this list from time to time, in all sorts of normative domains, in response to all sorts of agential activities. This *system* of responses is stable and readily recognizable. So let's return to the question we need to ask, now about the entire system of blame and praise: What's it all for?

Robust functional explanations in the philosophy of science typically aim to identify the causal contribution of some trait of an organism to some goal of the organism itself, where this is connected with its etiology and so is often put in terms of evolutionary fitness. For example, zebras have stripes today because stripes deterred flies, and that also contributes to the zebra's survival and flourishing today. Or the function of the human heart—what our hearts are for—is to pump blood, as that's what enables us survive and reproduce, and as that's what enabled our forebears to survive and reproduce. In social science, by comparison, functional explanations often articulate some causal contribution of a social system to the survival and thriving of society itself (sometimes referred to as a kind of organism), where the system also has a connected etiology (see Kincaid 1990 for insightful discussion).[12] And that's the approach we can take here.

In the most general terms, the responses above are all appraisals of performances relative to standards, and so make sense only as responses to agents who are capable of *violating* certain standards, as well as *ignoring*, *adhering* to, or *superseding* them. The standards against which they are appraised are normative for them, or *norms*, for short.

These norm-recognizing agents must also be capable of *responding* to blame or praise, in a huge variety of ways. Blame and praise, to them, can be educative, informative, resented, gratifying, rejected, embraced, and, of course, action-guiding.

Some may think my use of "norms" is too inclusive.[13] They may think such talk should be restricted exclusively to *social* norms, i.e., to people's expectations about what one should do in particular circumstances, expectations which regulate and coordinate interpersonal behavior and are backed up by sanctions. People's preferences in following such norms are conditional on what others' normative expectations actually are. Typically, people no longer adhere to social norms if others no longer have those normative expectations (see, e.g., Bicchieri 2017).

I agree that social norms are absolutely an essential subset—perhaps *the* essential subset—of the regulatory targets of the blame/praise system. But that system governs much more than social norms in this technical sense. Several of the listed items above are also deployed in response to violations or supersessions of unshared or unconditional prudential and moral norms, despite what social norms theorists have explicitly insisted. Bicchieri, for instance, remarks that we can differentiate prudential and moral norms from social norms by noting that violations of the former trigger no negative responses from others ("punishment" or "condemnation") (Bicchieri 2017: 72). This is false, though. Those who overeat

---

[12] Manuel Vargas has impressed upon me the possibility of what he calls "found functions" of some social systems, which may have only the teleological component without the etiological component. The blame/praise system could well be illustrative. As I remarked in an earlier footnote, however, I'm going to proceed on the assumption that both components obtain for the blame/praise system, but I'm certainly open to the proper functional story here ultimately winding up being a found function story.

[13] Thanks to Shaun Nichols for raising this worry as well as for extremely helpful discussion about functionalism generally.

or smoke are often viewed with tut-tuts and shaking heads, sometimes wagging fingers and voiced criticism. These responses are solely directed at those who are failing *themselves*, regardless of whether the imprudent people think others will respond that way. And those who violate purely personal moral norms may also face some of these blame/praise responses, as when an omnivore praises someone who sticks to their vegetarianism in the face of severe bacon-ey temptation.

Furthermore, it's not just failures relative to expectations about what one *should* do that trigger some of these blaming responses. Sometimes, dashing what someone *hopes* you'll do is enough to trigger responses such as disappointment or the silent treatment. If you give your partner a slapdash or cheap supermarket gift for a big anniversary, you're very likely to be blamed in some way, despite having performed a kindness (you gave a gift!); the disappointed partner certainly has no right to *demand* a better gift. Your partner's dashed hopes or expectations may be enough on their own to trigger a kind of blame.

We also blame or praise one another in non-social/-moral/-prudential domains, relative to performance standards. Our favorite band's new album may be great or suck, and so be the object of our praise or blame, as may an artist's new painting, a chef's new dish, a chess mentee's moves, or a star athlete's final game.

Finally, and this is very important, we deploy some of these forms of blame and praise to *ourselves*. These may be for failures or successes relative to various social demands or performance standards, where others also have standing to criticize or praise us. But they may also be for failures or successes relative to our own ideals, where no one else has any standing or right to make a peep. Think here of elite athletes who, when they fail to live up to their ridiculously high standards of success, beat themselves up, angrily yelling at themselves, breaking their tennis rackets or golf clubs. Surely, we must include these responses as (self-) blame, even though they aren't at all responses to violations of social, moral, prudential, or ordinary performance norms.

Given all of these features, then, I propose that the function of our stably organized system of blame and praise is what I will label *norm maintenance*, where the "norms" are regulative interpersonal or intrapersonal demands, expectations, hopes, or ideals. These may be internalized or conditional (on one's expectations of how others will respond to their violations). This is meant to be a substantive description of the system's function that is also capacious enough to include all of the items, in some contexts or other, on our list. In the right contexts, these are blame/praise responses to agents only insofar as they appraise a perceived or anticipated failure, violation, adherence, or supersession with respect to demands, expectations, hopes, or ideals contained within some norm or other, in any normative domain. Let me now explain and defend this idea.

First, the norms against which targets are appraised via blame and praise are those to which the appraiser is *committed*, in some sense. I have a very wide

26 THE ARCHITECTURE OF BLAME AND PRAISE

understanding of "commitment," intending for it simply to run the entire gamut of practical or deliberative import: To be committed to a norm is simply for it to provide *some reason or motivational pull* within the framework of one's deliberations, attitudes, ends, or actions. And I want to be as ecumenical as possible about *why* it may have the import it does. It may do so for intrinsic or instrumental reasons. Regarding the former, and as I've already noted, some norms are completely internalized, so that they directly counsel or motivate our adherence to them for the sake of the norm or the values implicated therein. For instance, I might think it morally wrong to wear white after Labor Day, so the fact that it's after Labor Day gives me a moral reason, a reason I heartily embrace, not to wear my snazzy white pants to a Hanukkah bash. Alternatively, perhaps I haven't internalized this norm (I actually think it's stupid), but nevertheless it's a stringently enforced norm in my neck of the woods: I know that there will be fashion police at the Hanukkah bash who will sharply criticize or ostracize me if they see me wearing those snazzy white pants. In this case, I'll avoid wearing white, but I will prefer to do so only so as to avoid being called out by the fashion police; I would not have any such preference, though, were that norm not to be policed. In both cases, I am *committed* to the norm, given the regulatory role it plays in my deliberations and motivation, either because of my internalization of it as the morally right counsel or because I wish to avoid others' negative responses to my flouting it. Either way, adhering to the norm matters to me.

Our commitment to norms is manifested in our dispositions to have and express attitudes or engage in behavior that tends to promote, uphold, highlight, and/or police those norms—that is, to *maintain* them. This is what our system of blame and praise is for. Call this the Norm Maintenance Theory (NMT).

But how does it do so? This is the second part of the functionalist story.

Stings and Buzzes

There are other social activities and systems whose function is to maintain norms as well. The most obvious one is education. We teach children from early on what the norms are, for many normative domains. We also take adult education classes to learn what the norms are for domains we aren't familiar with, for example, by taking creative writing or painting classes. Or we may become an apprentice at an auto body repair shop. In such educative cases, we learn both the norms and (typically) the value of those norms, and we often become committed to them as well, as they come to regulate our deliberations.

The fact that there are multiple social systems serving the same function isn't a problem, though. In the (entirely function-explained) world of artifacts, forks and chopsticks both have the function of delivering food to mouths. Nevertheless, we can differentiate the two by pointing out their distinctive features and just how those distinctive features serve the same function distinctly. In the case of forks versus chopsticks, we can appeal to the puncturing power of tines versus the pressure-point power of chopsticks.

What NMT thus needs next is a story of what's distinctive about the blame/praise system relative to its function. There are actually two importantly distinctive features.

The first draws from and expands on what Pamela Hieronymi calls blame's *characteristic force* (Hieronymi 2004). This special "feel" is what she thinks distinguishes blame from mere judgments of someone's wrongdoing, blameworthiness, or performance error (judgments which are all compatible with nudging, teaching, or merely incentivizing them). Philosophers have characterized the nature of this force in a wide variety of ways. Hieronymi talks about the *sting* it delivers, and this is such a beautifully descriptive (and sufficiently neutral) term that I'm going to steal it. Hieronymi is focused exclusively on moral blame, of course, which she claims delivers its sting via a resentful judgment of someone's disregard or ill will (Hieronymi 2004: 125–6). Others in this vein appeal to the sanctioning nature of angry moral blame (Pereboom 2014). Still others widen the domains of application by appealing to the painful guilt, regret, or remorse at which they think blame (in all those domains) properly aims (Clarke 2016; Carlsson 2017; Portmore 2022). All of this should be perfectly familiar. There is a categorical difference in feel between being publicly called out or yelled at, say, and being privately and gently taught or corrected. Blame stings.

None of this is to say that *every* instance of blame stings, or that every time you're stinged it comes from blame! Some people are callous or uncaring, so that when you blame them they are completely unruffled (see Carlsson 2017 for discussion of this contingency). Others are overly sensitive, taking any instance of gentle nudging or critique to heart in a painful way. But there's a recognizable—*characteristic*—kind of sting attached to blame—*characteristically*. This is undeniable. We must thus incorporate that characteristic sting into the functional account of blame, so as to differentiate it from other kinds of norm-maintaining social systems.

The way that stinging expressions (which may take a wide variety of forms) contribute to norm maintenance should be rather obvious. They are startling and sometimes scary, and they serve to draw our attention to how we've failed.[14] Sometimes they draw our attention toward seeing what we've done through the eyes of the stinger, and that different perspective triggers feelings we'd like to avoid. We can best avoid these unpleasant feelings in the future by adhering to the norms. They dramatically remind us, in ways no mere lesson or sermon can,

---

[14] Sam Reis-Dennis (2018) makes the case that angry blame is scary, and that's certainly one way in which it could achieve its norm-maintaining aims: our fear of incurring it keeps us on the straight and narrow.

what is supposed to matter, what norms we should take more seriously, and how we should be striving to uphold them. Stings deliver a *jolt*, voltage which serves both as a reminder of how we deviated from the norms and an incentive not to do it again. Stings get us to toe the normative line, and that's how blame contributes to norm maintenance.

But blame isn't the only jolting norm-maintenance device. The other is praise. What praise delivers, of course, isn't a sting; it instead characteristically delivers what I'll call a *buzz*, a pleasant, warm feeling. It includes the familiar feelings of being tickled or a little high, of the warm fuzzies, of gratification, or of the swell of pride.

The buzz of praise also contributes to norm maintenance in rather obvious ways. If you cause me to feel these pleasant feelings in response to something I've done, I'm clearly going to be incentivized to do it again, so to the extent that you are causing me these feelings in response to my adhering to some norm (and this is clear to me), then I'm going to keep adhering to—directly maintaining—that norm. If you cause me these warm feelings in response to my supercession of some norm, say, then I'll typically be motivated to improve even more, which serves to highlight (and so maintain) various norms pertaining to *goodness*, in skills and character. For example, if you praise my meal, and I'm a fledgling home chef, I'll have my attention drawn to what I did right, and I'll be motivated to keep it up, to get even better, as your praise delightfully incentivizes me to do. To the extent that I do get better, then, I'm now adhering to—and so maintaining—norms of *excellence* in chef-ery.

As with blame, not all instances of praise deliver the warm fuzzies, and sometimes people get the warm fuzzies from responses other than praise. Some people are callous or psychologically resistant to praise, or they may not think they're worth it, and so they may not feel its warmth. Others may take mere kindness or even neutral comments ("That was okay, I guess") as delivering the warm fuzzies when they aren't really meant to. Nonetheless, praise *characteristically* delivers this buzz.

What is distinctive about the way the blame/praise system contributes to norm maintenance, therefore—what differentiates it from other social systems that also have this function—is its characteristic delivery of a recognizable set of *feelings*, of stings and buzzes.

But there's another distinctive way in which the blame/praise system contributes to norm maintenance. Indeed, it's the feature that kicked off this chapter.

Costly Signaling Theory

Male peacocks have a ridiculously showy—and beautiful—tail, or train. It serves a valuable function, namely, to attract mates. And the showiest, most ornate trains attract the best mates, peahens who select mates based on the size and shape of their train. But trains are heavy and tough to drag around and maintain. And the biggest, most ornate, trains are the heaviest and most difficult to deal with. They are, in a word, *costly*. So what's going on?

As it turns out, the train's cost contributes directly to its function. That's because the train is what *signals* the fitness of its bearer. The train conveys valuable information to peahens who need it, information that would otherwise be very hard to fake, namely, that this male is strong and healthy and so would help generate strong and healthy offspring.

This explanation is a classic in what is known as Costly Signaling Theory (CST), which was actually developed first by economists in the early twentieth century, and then quickly adopted in the biological (and other) sciences. CST was originally brought in to explain the existence, stability, and sensibility of certain systems of information exchange in markets, where the distribution of valuable information is asymmetrical: some parties need accurate information about the qualities of other people, information it's hard to perceive directly but that can nevertheless be signaled, and information that, if its signal could be faked, would generate huge payoffs to the faker at great cost to those they deceive. The classic example given in economics pertains to employers and job applicants. Employers need to know if applicants have certain valuable cognitive and non-cognitive traits: intelligence, social skills, creativity, emotional stability, and more. Applicants thus provide resumes or CVs to their potential employers. These documents include items that signal that the applicant has the desired traits. Listing the top-notch school the applicant graduated from, as well as the applicant's GPA, signals their level of intelligence and/or work ethic. Listing the volunteering work they've done or team sports they've played signals their social skills. Listing displayed art projects can signal their creativity level. Listing references allows employers to investigate as to the applicants' level of maturity and emotional stability—do they work well with others? If these signals are accurate, then employers can hire these applicants with the knowledge that they'll have what they need to get the job done well. If, however, an applicant can get the employer to believe a fake signal—through a deceptive resume or CV—then the applicant would gain at the expense of the employer (see Piopiunik et al. 2020).

What's needed in such cases is a *costly* signal, one that's too costly for a deceiver to try and fake. In this case, the cost comes from the actual hard work the applicant put in, which is reflected on their resume or CV: They studied and sacrificed for several years at the top-notch school, they worked hard at the prior jobs, they curried good relationships with their prior employers, etc. To the extent that resumes and CVs have schools and references listed, all of these items can easily be checked. The costs that convey the relevant information accurately thus pay off for the applicant when they are hired, and these costs—actually going to the top school and engaging in all that work—are just *too* costly for a would-be deceiver even to attempt to fake (imagine having to arrange all the confederates you'd need to pull this off).

This document is thus a costly signal. While in the throes of paying all these costs in the short term, it may seem quite irrational for the would-be applicant to do what they are doing. But it nevertheless makes rational sense in the long run, given the ultimate payoff of all that hard work: a dream job at a top corporation, say. This is occupational torch fishing.

CST was adopted in a wide variety of other disciplines, including anthropology, religion, organizational management, social psychology, decision theory, and more. But, as I noted, it eventually became all the rage in evolutionary biology (and associated game theory), as the go-to explanation for seemingly expensive, arbitrary, or wasteful traits found in many species, such as the peacock and his train. Lower-quality signalers either receive smaller benefits than higher-quality signalers, or they pay greater costs to signal. "[O]nly those cocks who are vigorous, disease-resistant, and excellent foragers can afford the cost of producing, maintaining, and dragging around a heavy and showy tail" (Bird and Smith 2005a). This valuable information about their rigor and qualities can't be perceived directly. The costliness of their display signal is very hard, if not impossible, to fake: male peacocks can't just muster up colorful and long tail feathers at will. But this significant cost actually benefits these peacocks in the long run, in terms of mating and reproductive fitness.

Generally, then, within evolutionary biology and game theory, a costly signal can arise and become part of an evolutionarily stable system when the following four conditions are in place:

1. Some members of a group have a quality that is difficult to perceive directly but to which a reliable signal could attach.
2. There are some members (observers) who would stand to gain from gleaning accurate information about that quality.
3. Signalers and observers have a conflict of interest, so that signalers who could successfully deceive observers about the quality would be benefited at the observers' expense.
4. The cost of the signal must have some benefit to the signaler (Bird and Smith 2005b: 224; quoting here from Shoemaker and Vargas 2021: 586).

It's worth noting here a crucial point about costs. The costs focused on by economists (and some other non-biological adherents of CST, such as consumer behavior researchers) are subtly different than those on which evolutionary biologists focus. For the latter, the relevant costs are attached to having or sending the signal. It's the costliness of the actual *signaling*, in other words, that makes the information it conveys honest (so call this the *signaling cost*). It's a huge burden for the peacock to have to drag around that heavy signal all the time, but it's the fact that it can and does bear that costly burden that makes the information its tail signals so hard to fake.

For the former (economic) theorists, though, the costliness is located earlier, attached to what it takes to *acquire* the signal, found in the all work and effort involved in coming to be a competent signaler, an honest information-conveyer (so call these *competence costs*). The job applicant, for instance, has worked tremendously hard for a long period of time so as to be able to have her CV convey all of those valuable qualities. But the signaling itself isn't at all costly at the time of the signaling (she just hands over her CV); instead, it had already cost a lot for her to acquire it, for her to have become a competent signaler.

Of course, sometimes—perhaps often—these different types of costs will *both* be borne by a signaler. "Automatic" altruistic behavior, for instance, which signals valuable cooperative traits, may be both costly at the time (it involves a sacrifice of resources) and the result of costly past sacrifices, those that were necessary to cultivate the dispositions for unhesitatingly producing the right altruistic responses in the right place and time. So such altruists bear costs both in acquiring and emitting their signals. These points will matter a great deal for my project here, which now applies this machinery to the blame/praise system.

Costly Signaling in Blame

Thus far I have argued both that the blame/praise system's function is norm maintenance and that one distinctive way in which these responses contribute to that function is by what they characteristically deliver, namely, a sting or buzz. In this section, I aim to argue that the second distinctive way in which these responses contribute to their function is by what they characteristically *signal*. I will begin to make the case by considering blame, before moving to what might seem to be the tougher case of praise.

Delivering blame's sting can obviously be costly. Wagging your finger at a stranger who won't wear a mask in a crowded store during a pandemic might get you a broken finger, or worse. Getting angry at people, sanctioning them, revealing your contempt for them, yelling at them, or even just criticizing them can be dangerous. Especially when it comes to moral criticism, people get defensive and often fight back. Blame's sting can generate backlash, in the form of physical or psychological harm.[15] It can corrode, damage, or destroy relationships. It can be emotionally exhausting (the energy anger sometimes takes can leave us breathless and shaking). Blamers also risk getting blamed themselves if they blame mistakenly, disproportionately, or dishonestly (through, e.g., mere virtue signaling).

---

[15] See Pereboom 2021a for the "backfire effect" of anger.

32 THE ARCHITECTURE OF BLAME AND PRAISE

And even seemingly "safe" third-party blame is dangerous. After all, if I blame someone else to you, I risk you squealing on me to the blamed party or turning on me as a gossip or moralizer.

And sometimes our blame, with all its attendant risks, is just ignored, all for naught.

These are serious costs attached to our participation in the blame game. There also seem to be no clear short-term benefits. Blame is typically a response to people's irreversible past attitudes or actions. If those attitudes or actions were wrongful or hurtful, there's no changing that fact.[16] So what could possibly be the point? How can we make sense of such practices? And why would supposedly rational people participate in them?

As with the peacocks and the torch fishermen, there are significant long-term benefits attached to what they're doing. In our case, competent blamers are conveying valuable and hard-to-glean information about themselves by blaming (whether they know it or not, and whether they do so deliberately or not); that is, they are emitting an honest *signal* about what norms they are committed to, what practical reasons they take seriously, and, crucially, what steps they are willing to take to patrol and enforce them (Shoemaker and Vargas 2021: 587). If a construction worker on his lunch break were to verbally harass women as they walk down the street, and someone were to take him to task for it, yelling at him or angrily pointing out how disrespectful he's being, that blamer sends a clear signal not only to him but also to the harassed women and other passersby: The norms of respect matter to the blamer, given that she's so willing to risk real costs in enforcing them, so she is, we can easily infer, very likely to be a respectful person herself, worth trusting, working with, or being in a relationship with.

The information signaled by norm-maintenance-via-blame is incredibly valuable (and otherwise very difficult) for others to garner, as it reveals the blamer's commitment to enforcing norms those others may also deem important. I'll come back to this point momentarily. But the signal also conveys information about the blamer's own trustworthiness, cooperative tendencies, excellence-valuing, and many other virtues. It's normally impossible to glean such information directly. To the extent that blamers signal these commitments, those who pick up on the signal need a way to know that it's reliable, that it's hard to fake, that it's *honest*. Otherwise, they could easily be exploited. Putting your trust in someone, for example, is a big and scary step. Those who might fake such signals could thus exploit the trust of others and gain huge benefits on the cheap.

For this signaling system to work, then—for it to be a stable system of information exchange benefiting both parties (and avoiding exploitation by the

---

[16] This is Martha Nussbaum's complaint, about the irrationality of a kind of "payback" blaming anger (Nussbaum 2015).

nefarious)—what's needed are *costs* attached to the signal, costs significant enough that it becomes very hard to fake if one lacks the valuable traits in question. We've already seen some of these costs incurred in the act of blaming itself: emotional exhaustion, time and effort, risks of backlash, and more. We can also see now why these sorts of costs actually make sense to risk incurring: they can be outweighed by the long-term benefits one may get for being correctly recognized *as a good, normatively committed, and trustworthy person.* These benefits come in the form of friends, mates, business partners, and more.[17]

It thus makes rational sense for people to risk incurring the costs of blame. But how precisely does blame's signal contribute to the purported function of the system, norm maintenance? It does so by signaling the blamer's *willingness to patrol and enforce the norms.* Yelling at the harasser, in front of others, and at the risk of backlash, obviously signals that the blamer has no compunction about policing norms of respect, and this willingness puts those who pick up that signal on notice: Watch it, *toe the line,* or I'll deliver blame's sting to you as well. It's that information that contributes most directly to norm maintenance.

There might seem to be an obvious counterexample: What about the many cases of blame without any costs at all? When I snippily chide my best friend for being late for the third time this week, there's no real risk of backlash or violence, and I don't get emotionally riled up or exhausted in the least. When I don't offer my friendly "hello!" to my neighbor one morning because he ran his lawnmower at 5 a.m., there aren't any costs attached to that "relationship-modifying" blame (Scanlon 2008: 143–5). If I criticize a celebrity on-line from my anonymous account, there is zero risk. When people blame outsiders or the downtrodden from the comfortable or lofty heights alongside their privileged and likeminded fellows, they risk nothing either (McKenna 2018). Perhaps, then, the costly signaling theory applies to some paradigmatic cases of blame, but surely it's not true for all.

These are, it's quite true, cases of blame in which there are emitted signals with no costs attached to the signaling itself. There are two replies, though. First, as Adam Piovarchy rightly notes, one key aspect of CST generally is that "beings with the quality [being signaled] need not actually incur any costs; it is sufficient that enough beings without the quality *would* incur a cost."[18] That is, what

---

[17] I've adapted here the incisive and persuasive story told by Robert Frank (1988) about many of our emotions generally, as being commitment devices generating long-term benefits like trust and cooperation.

[18] This is from a key footnote in Piovarchy's unpublished paper, "Signalling, Sanctioning and Sensitising: How to Uphold Norms with Blame." Piovarchy's is an excellent exploration of what he takes to be the *plural* functions of blame. My own view is that these plural features are all indeed *sometimes* features of the general system of blame and praise (sanctioning, as we'll see, isn't as much of a feature as he thinks), but that they are subsidiary to its overarching function: norm maintenance. Regardless, we are close allies in this cause.

matters to establish the existence of signaling costs is that it would be very burdensome for those without the quality in question to successfully fake the signal that those who *do* signal in these cases emit with such ease.

Second, even if there are no signaling costs in such cases, there remain plenty of competence costs, the costs in coming to acquire such a signal. Coming to be an honest blamer—someone who is disposed to blame in a way that honestly signals their relevant commitments, *even in uncostly cases*—is itself incredibly costly, akin to having to work hard at a top-notch university and getting valuable occupational experience and strong references, so that one can put it down on a CV that one then simply emails to a hiring committee. It requires investing significant social and psychological resources. One must pay attention to and begin learning the norm system one is to maintain from a very early age, learning what the relevant norms are, coming to internalize them, recognizing what their violations look like, and so forth. And, crucially, what must also be learned are the norms for patrolling and enforcing the norms, that is, for how to be a competent blamer. This includes learning and internalizing what kinds of blame are appropriate for what violations, how much blame is appropriate for what violations, as well as how to respond to being blamed oneself. And after all of this learning, one must then keep up with the evolutions and subtle alterations that all of these norms inevitably go through. It's thus not just one's commitment to patrolling the violated norms that one signals in honest blaming; it's one's commitment and competence with respect to *all* of these related sets of norms—the norms attached to the entire blame system—that one is signaling in blame. And this information can occasionally be signaled without there being any occurrent signaling costs whatsoever; rather, the signaling itself is hard to fake to the extent that one has actually borne significant antecedent costs *already* just to have it.

Costly Signaling in Praise

The two replies just given to the worry about costless signaling in cases of blame enable us to see just how the theory also applies to *praise*, an activity which may strike many readers as entirely costless. It is, however, not; indeed, praise risks many costs similar to those risked by blame. I'll here articulate three.

First, praise, especially praise delivering its characteristic buzz of warm fuzzies, often involves an expenditure of emotional energy. Expressions of emotion, even positive ones, can leave one spent (think, for example, about the exhaustion that often accompanies a come-down from the exuberant joy one felt in response to a favorite sports team's big win). Enthusiastic praise of another may enervate.

Second, praise, like blame, risks backfire. Here, the risk comes, not from the target of praise (as it most typically does for blame), but from others, in response to perceived unfairness in the interpersonal distribution of praise, disproportionate deployment, or dishonesty. Regarding unfairness, if I stand in a similar relation to two people who have done the same praiseworthy thing, and yet I praise only one of them, then, other things being equal, the unpraised party may well have a complaint against me: "Why not praise me too?" After all, praise delivers the warm fuzzies, so the complaint is that one is unfairly being deprived of a good, however trivial. And one also risks such complaints and blowback from bystanders, on behalf of the unfairly unpraised target. Regarding disproportional praise, one may also praise someone too much or too little, in which case the target (or those speaking on the target's behalf) may also aptly complain. If you work your ass off for your coach, and he merely mutters one day a begrudging, "Good job," you may well be pissed off at him for the mismatch between the amount of work you put in and how much you were praised for it. Finally, one might be the target of blame or other blowback for one's dishonest or insincere praise. One can engage in (mere) virtue signaling via both blame and praise, and one can be called out for both.

A third general cost risked by praise is something I will detail in full in the next chapter. For now, I'll just say this: Praise of children, of a certain sort, risks creating little monsters. This is a just a teaser of coming attractions, but trust me, it's a significant cost being risked.

Perhaps surprisingly, then, there are plenty of signaling costs attached to praise, many of them similar to those attached to blame. (There is a reason for this, one I'm going to detail shortly.) But there are also plenty of the same sorts of *competence* costs attached to praise as there are to blame. When I praise your excellent basketball shot, your tasty meal, your commitment to social justice, your punctuality, your academic presentation, your gardening prowess, your driving skills—or anything else—I'm signaling my commitment to, and *willingness to patrol, highlight, and reinforce*, whatever set of standards or norms you've met well or superseded. This is valuable information about me that's hard for others to perceive directly. In order to convey this information honestly, though, in a hard-to-fake fashion, I have to have undergone the very same rigorous and costly training that I underwent with respect to blame. I have to have learned and internalized the relevant norms that praise highlights and reinforces. But I also have to have learned and internalized the norms of proper praise, including how to distribute it fairly, proportionately, and honestly.

I believe that one can have a fully competent grip on the norms of blame only if one has a fully competent grip on the norms of praise. The costs of coming to have the knowledge and skill necessary to send the honest signal of one's normative competence and willingness to patrol those norms in both stinging and buzzing ways are essentially identical. Given that the overall function of the system of blame and praise is norm maintenance, individual practitioners of blame and praise must bear significant costs in order to be signalers in good standing in that system.

Responding to Constitutivist Critics

We are now in a position to respond to some complaints that might be lodged by constitutivist critics of NMT (the Norm Maintenance Theory). First, as we've already seen, there may indeed be tokens of expressed blame and praise that are signals without any attached costs, but this fact doesn't count against the costly signaling feature, as they are the predictable upshot of significant competence costs, and what ultimately matters is that it would be costly for those without the quality being signaled to successfully fake the signal.

Second, though, what are we to say about cases of blame and praise with *no signaling*? We can blame people entirely in our heads, after all, without any visible signs.[19] I may stand at my dad's gravesite and rehearse in my head all the wrongs he did to me, angrily thinking about how much I hate him, where all anyone else sees is me just standing there grieving.

But there is no trouble at all here for the signaling theory (nor is any fancy dancing required). First, don't be so sure that there aren't any signals being emitted in these sorts of cases. When I'm golfing by myself and get angry for missing an easy putt, I may slump or shake my head or yell at myself. These are all easy-to-detect signals, were anyone around to pick up on them. This makes clear a point that I'll revisit in more detail later: signaling is crucially different from *communicating*. The latter seeks uptake; the former does not. So I may in fact be signaling all sorts of things without communicating any of those signals to anyone when I blame myself privately. If self-blame goes down in a forest with no one else around, it can still emit a signal.

But there may also be various reasons why my signals in other-directed cases of blame or praise are *blocked*. At the funeral for my domineering father, I may control my anger, so as not to make the others in attendance uncomfortable. Or when I'm at my daughter's soccer game, I may swallow my joy and pride when she scores her eighth goal of the game, as it would be too "in your face" for the parent of a girl on the other team who's sitting next to me. What I'm nevertheless experiencing counts as blame in the first case and praise in the second, even though I've emitted no signal, and that's because what I'm engaged in in both cases *is what it is* in virtue of the signals it typically emits, as well as its relationship to the practice that gives it its psychological shape and meaning (Shoemaker and Vargas 2021: 594). That my anger at my dad urgently urges me to reveal it in certain ways—to yell, shake my head, or howl with rage—along with the fact that I have to work so hard to squelch it, is precisely what makes my private response blame,

---

[19] Nomy Arpaly, in a response to our original presentation of the CST theory of blame at an APA conference in Seattle in 2016, claimed that 95 percent of the blame she has for others is exclusively in her head.

as these are just the kinds of signals ordinarily emitted in response to norm violations. So too, squelching the expression of praise of my daughter is really tough, and what I'm thinking or feeling privately counts as praise in virtue of *its* relationship to the practice of signaling it. Consequently, the fact that some blame and praise is utterly private, emitting no signals, is no challenge to the costly signaling feature of blame and praise.

There is also no trouble at all here in dealing with the other kinds of cases that cause many of the constitutivist theories to dance fancy, namely, cases of self-blame, emotionless blame, or counterfactual blame. Start with the first. As already noted, we typically emit all sorts of signals in blaming ourselves, which is again a predictable upshot of our having internalized various norms and performance standards. Breaking putters, smashing tennis rackets, muttering "You idiot!" when making stupid mistakes—these are all easy-to-read signals of self-blame, regardless of whether anyone else is around to pick up on them.[20] So too with praise: the pumped fist, the joyous smile, the "*Yes!!!*"—these are all easy-to-read signals of self-praise.

As for emotionless blame, well, emotions aren't the only things that send signals of normative commitment. Seeing your parent glance at you with a quiet headshake and downcast eyes can devastate in a way that few other blaming responses can. Perhaps people avert their eyes from those they blame: when I walk down the hall and notice my enemy in my peripheral vision, my steely forward gaze sends a clear blame signal, even if I'm without any more rage. Perhaps a sneer sends the signal, or cutting sarcasm, or a flushed face. On the positive side, a subtle smile, or a quick affirmative nod or fist pump from your beloved coach in response to your sporting success can raise you to heights that few other praising responses can.

Finally, insofar as the function of the blame/praise system is norm *maintenance*, then it sometimes won't matter whether the person being appraised has actually violated any norms. To give one obvious reason, the system includes praise, which of course just isn't a response to normative violations; it's rather a response (typically) to norms being well met or superseded. But appraisals relative to maintenance of a normative system don't always have to be in response to past violations. It also (predictably) will involve ensuring that people toe the proper line in the future, that they *don't* violate the relevant norms. And this may best be achieved sometimes through counterfactual blame, a preemptive blame of the sort illustrated in *Force Majeure*. Here blame's sting serves purely as a deterrent. And an analogous incentive is sometimes delivered with praise: In praising the players who do well, a coach encourages the others on the team to do well too,

---

[20] I'll say much more about these features of self-blame and -praise in Chapter 8.

which may sometimes be achieved through counterfactual praise. Perhaps the coach, while watching a competing player make a spectacular game-winning shot, may nudge one of her own players and say, in delight, "That's something *you* would do!" This remark delivers a buzz to the player in a way that may incentivize her to take her game to the next level.

* * * * *

So that's the NMT. Blame and praise are for norm maintenance, which they achieve both through their delivery of stings and buzzes and through the valuable information they reveal about signalers, that, if they have paid the costs required to be a competent signaler, and if they risk the costs of actual signaling in blaming and praising, then their blame and praise convey honest and valuable information about their commitments to patrolling (and so maintaining) the pertinent norms. The costs they pay to patrol are rendered rational, in the long run, by a variety of possible benefits, doled out by those who recognize, act on, and trust in the accurate information their signal conveys. Being a competent blamer and praiser makes one's overall life better, the theory predicts, than it would otherwise be. This is why it makes sense to participate in the system, and this is why the system itself is so stably persistent.

One final note, before I defend the view against possible competitors. Nothing about NMT is, or is meant to be, *normative*. It is certainly not a justification for that system, nor is it a justification for any particular deployments of blame or praise within that system. The normative account of blame and praise—of the blame- and praise*worthy*—is a topic that I don't take up until Part Two. What this means is that the story told thus far—a theoretical explanation of the function, structure, and characteristics of the blame/praise system—is perfectly compatible with our trying to get rid of it, trying to alter it, or trying to find justificatory grounds for it that have nothing to do with its function. It also means that participants in the system may not even be aware of the function of some of its features (e.g., the signal), nor may they care about it. Indeed, the system works most efficiently when people *don't* think about these things. My angry blame of you emits a signal that's hard to fake most often precisely because I don't think about it as a signal or its possible contribution to norm maintenance.

Of course, we're not blind to our blame's signals. Fighting couples are conscious about trying to hide their anger at each other from their kids, and some people aim to manipulate the signal, by, for example, pretending to be outraged about some social injustice just to get brownie morality points from their friends. In those cases, though, the fakery is often seen through. Most kids can tell when their parents are angrily fighting, even if they try to hide it, and virtue signalers are rather easily sussed out. But again, this is the beauty of the costly signaling feature: honest blame and praise are really hard to fake, and *that makes sense*.

Defending against Competitors

None of the constitutivist theories of blame surveyed at the beginning are straightforward competitors of NMT. While they each have some intuitive force, they are also vulnerable to prima facie counterexamples, examples which I just noted can easily be handled by NMT, a theory which also diagnoses why the traditional views have to dance fancy in the first place: They all correctly identify *some* content that does count as blame *sometimes*, but when we gather all of the various proposed bits of content, we wind up with just a long disjunctive list, one without an explanation of why such things count as blame when they do (as well as why some don't count as blame when they don't). They also don't have straightforward stories for praise, responses which have to be included as well in any adequate theory.

These explanatory gaps motivate making the functionalist turn. Instead of asking, "What responses constitute blame or praise?" we should ask, "What is all this blame and praise for?" The prediction, then, is that the proposed bits of constitutive content are blame/praise responses, when they are, insofar as they are the types of responses that contribute to the function of norm maintenance, typically through the delivery of a sting/buzz and by the emission of a signal of the blamer's commitment to norm patrol.

The only true competitors to this theory, then, are going to be other functionalist theories. Their challenge is to provide an alternative account of the blame/praise system's function(s) and specific characteristics, where they can explain all the relevant data points in a better (simpler or more encompassing) way than can I. There are three contenders: protest, affective, and communicative theories. In the literature, they have all been put entirely and exclusively in terms of *blame*. As we'll see, though, that's part of the problem. (Although I should stress at the outset that at least these theories are playing the same functionalist game that I think we ought to be playing, and so to that extent, I'm a total fanboy.)

1. Protest: On the first competitor, the aim—the function—of blame is *protest* (see Boxill 1976; Hieronymi 2001; Talbert 2012; and Smith 2013). When various agential responses count as blame, it's because they are "a way of *protesting* (i.e., registering and challenging) the moral claim implicit in [the blameworthy agent's] conduct, where such protest implicitly seeks some kind of moral acknowledgment on the part of the blameworthy agent and/or on the part of others in the moral community" (Smith 2013: 43; emphasis in original). The protest theory thus explains why a wide variety of attitudes and actions are a part of the blame system, when they are, as well as why they aren't when they aren't.

There's a lot to like about this theory, which was certainly one of the first—if not the first—explicitly functionalist theory in the philosophical literature on blame (see, e.g., Coates and Tognazzini's [2013: 15–17] framing of Smith's protest view in functionalist terms). However, I've come not to praise protest but to bury it. I have several worries.

First, it's very hard to see how this functional story can be coherently applied to the entire system of blame and praise.[21] Perhaps blame is protest, but what is praise? What's the opposite of protest? It would seem to be something like *touting* or *honoring*. But these activities are a relatively small subset of our praising attitudes and practices. It's what goes on, I suppose, in a Hall of Fame induction ceremony, but that's pretty rare and leaves a big swath of praise behind.

In addition, extant protest theories typically say that the proper target of blame is a wrongdoer's nasty quality of will, and angry blame protests that person's ongoing status as a threat. Once the protest is heard and taken up by the target and he acknowledges his wrongdoing and apologizes, then the reasons for protesting blame are undermined and blame should be withdrawn (in an "uncompromising forgiveness," as Hieronymi 2001 puts it). What could be the positive analogue of this functional account, though? My reasons to admire you, say, aren't withdrawn once you "accept" my praise for your kindness. And what is it about your quality of will that poses the positive analogue to a *threat*? Perhaps you offer a cozy and safe space for me? That again might well be true of a small portion of the praise domain (perhaps that for which some expressions of gratitude are apt?), but it isn't true with regard to something like my praise of my teammate's sweet three-point nothing-but-net shot to beat the buzzer, or my praise of my mentee's clever chess move in a tight match.

Further, and pertinent to the examples just given, the protest theory has been explicitly built, it seems, just for *moral* blame, a response to ill will, where the persisting ill will constitutes a kind of (moral) threat. But that's not what a lot of the blame we dish out consists in. For example, there is no protest of moral threats in any cases of athletic blame ("Why did you try to steal second base with such a short lead off the bag?"), culinary blame ("Oh my god, there's too much salt in this dish!"), or aesthetic blame ("Their new album is way too commercial"). But all of these instances are certainly about norm maintenance.

There are other gaps in the protest accounts as given. Counterfactual blame isn't blame, on the protest view, given that there just hasn't been any *conduct* performed by the target, so there's no moral threat for someone to protest against. On the other hand, when we gently protest our children's mistaken homework methods—"No, you have to solve that problem differently"—we aren't blaming them. And when I blame my partner for not washing my favorite spoon after using it, I'm certainly not protesting an ongoing *threat*.

---

[21] Importantly, this is not what it was meant to do. But as I've tried to argue, we have to include praise in the system as data to be explained, so it's fair to make the point that it would be rather tough to see how this theory might be expanded in a way that could adequately explain all that data.

Now it's of course true that a lot of blame has a protest-ey feel to it. That makes perfect sense, as one very powerful way of maintaining norms is to publicly speak out in response to their violation. But protest sometimes just registers dislike or serves as a (mere) corrective, and maintaining norms is sometimes not at all a matter of protest (as in most cases of praise, and in many cases of purely private blame). When protest *is* a form of blame, I think, it's instead because it's the sort of thing that contributes to a system of norm maintenance by delivering stings/buzzes and emitting certain sorts of signals. When protest is not blame (as when we protest our children's homework mistakes), the reason is that it's not the sort of thing that contributes to norm maintenance in the specified ways. NMT has greater explanatory power than does the protest view.

2. Affective: The second competitor to NMT is one that appeals primarily to a functional affective state, *moral anger*, a state that is "apt for being caused by perceived wrongdoing and apt for producing certain behavioral effects" (McGeer 2013: 169; see Nichols 2007: 413 for the phrase "moral anger"). More precisely, the function of moral anger is likely to secure "social norms including conventions of cooperation.… [M]oral anger and its punitive expressions work to discourage cheating, defection, and violations of reciprocity," and they "solve problems in the social domain" (Nichols 2007: 419).

Both McGeer and Nichols are at pains to say that the primitive angry response isn't the whole story of human blame, as it's too involuntary and cognitively unmediated. Indeed, we've evolved in ways that allow us to step back from that emotional state and resist or direct it in various ways, that is, to widen it (Nichols 2007: 415–16) or to mentalize it (McGeer 2013: 173–5). But in any event, it retains its backward-looking (appraisal, retributive) aspects and its forward-looking (regulative, incentivizing) aspects, and it either can't or shouldn't be "sanitized" out of our lives (Nichols 2007: 420–4; McGeer 2013: 175–83). While we can "civilize" it, by rethinking the expressions and practices built on top of it, that affective functional core has valuable benefits, both individually and societally, which we don't want to lose (Frank 1988; McGeer 2013: 183–8; Nichols 2007: 417–18).

This is a naturalistic, psycho-biological functionalist story, and it has many elements in common with NMT, especially in its connection to norm maintenance. Moral anger surely contributes in the specified ways to the maintenance of cooperative norms. It also has the explicit benefit of not being unsettled by certain sorts of purported counterexamples. As McGeer explains:

> Now on a functionalist approach, the fact that blamers characteristically experience a range of core emotions that color their blaming acts and attitudes (anger, indignation, resentment, outrage) strongly suggests two things. First, the state that typically plays the causal role of blame in human beings is an affective state, though perhaps not invariably so; there may be various deviating background conditions in place…Second, the emotional character of the state is not

42 THE ARCHITECTURE OF BLAME AND PRAISE

> incidental to the causal role it typically plays; on the contrary, emotions are motivational drivers in human beings, reliably and involuntarily priming certain action tendencies. (McGeer 2013: 169)

Indeed, the emotional aspects of blame are what McGeer calls *criterial*, in the sense that "they account for our interest in identifying a kind as such, even though things belonging to the kind do not invariably manifest the feature in question" (McGeer 2013: 168, following Jackson and Pettit 1995). Consequently, the fact that there are plenty of cases of blame without anger doesn't dent the theory in the least. Just as a heart can malfunction and cease to pump blood without ceasing to be a heart, so too can someone's blame be dispassionate and still count as blame. The "exceptional cases are besides the point": "blame would not be blame absent the characteristic presence (and effect) of certain core emotions" (McGeer 2013: 170).

I like this theory quite a lot. It has been underappreciated in the philosophical literature. It has much in common with NMT, of course. Indeed, sometimes McGeer, following Robert Frank (1988), explicitly appeals to anger's "signaling function" (McGeer 2013: 172). But as will be familiar by now, this affective view, like the protest view, doesn't do as well as NMT in accounting for the entire system of blame and praise. To do so, it would have to provide the affective core of praise, an emotional syndrome analogous to moral blame's anger. But it's not clear what that would be, or if there would be just one. Lots of praise is a kind of compliment and encouragement, neither of which seem to have a characteristic emotional tone. Admiration? Sometimes, but not really in the domain of child rearing, where praise is very often deployed purely as a learning incentive. Admiration also seems too rich an emotion to accompany most non-moral praise (for a good meal, good speech, good basketball shot...). Gratitude? Again, sometimes, but that's not at all what we feel in praising people's displays of skill. Moral approval (as suggested by Macnamara 2015: 546)? This doesn't strike me as a genuine emotion, or at least the kind of basic or core (evolved) emotion needed by the affective theorists.[22] But even if it is, it isn't characteristic of praise as such, which applies quite widely in the *non*moral domain.

Indeed, this affective view, as it stands, has trouble explaining the very wide world of nonmoral *blame*. Moral anger isn't at all the characteristic emotional tone of culinary, prudential, or aesthetic blame, where disappointment, disdain, tut-tuts, or sharp criticism play much more of a role. These nonmoral blame responses are also typically made relative to certain performance standards, and so they aren't really aimed at securing social cooperation (e.g., blaming a bad chess move or poor philosophy paper) (cf. Dorsey 2020). But these responses *are*

---

[22] As will become clear in Chapter 5, I think plausible stories about our core emotional syndromes need to provide detailed accounts of their various components, including their action-tendencies, appraisals, and affect. I don't know how the story of moral approval could clearly be told in those terms.

all still aimed at norm maintenance in the ways I've detailed. So while there is definitely a *subset* of blame that is angry in the way proposed by the affective view, it just doesn't deliver (again, at least as it stands) nearly as complete and satisfying a functionalist explanation of the blame and praise system as NMT.

3. Communicative: The final competitor to NMT is a communicative functionalist theory, a view explicitly advanced as such by Coleen Macnamara (2015) and Miranda Fricker (2016) (one might also try to read McKenna's [2012, 2013] conversational theory of responsibility and blame through this functional lens as well). Macnamara is primarily moved to understand the nature of private blame in light of the overwhelming number of responsibility theorists who have insisted on its communicative nature. How can something we keep private be communicative? She takes the relevant forms of responses here to be affective: Strawsonian reactive attitudes like resentment in the case of blame, moral approval in the case of praise.[23] I've already worried about the latter as an emotion, but at least Macnamara is explicitly concerned to make sense of the blame *and praise* system in fundamentally communicative terms, so that forestalls my most familiar complaint about the competitors thus far. At any rate, she argues that we have to view these reactive attitudes as having a communicative function, and when we do so, we can solve her motivating problem. Paradigmatic cases of communication involve sending a message, and they "are *for* eliciting a response in a recipient, where that response amounts to uptake of the message sent" (Macnamara 2015: 553; emphasis in original). That was the effect of past communicative instances, and it explains why current instances of that general type exist. And just as the function of sperm is egg fertilization, the fact that lots of sperm don't achieve it doesn't at all undercut that it's still their function. Reactive attitudes are communicative entities. They seek uptake in their recipients. But that this is their function doesn't mean that they are always *communicated*. Just as one can write a letter one never sends, where the letter still has a communicative function, so too can one experience reactive attitudes (purely) privately, without undercutting the fact that they have a communicative function as well.

I take it that the reactive attitudes themselves are less important to the account than their communicative function. And the fact that many of our (non-blaming/praising) activities and attitudes have a communicative function as well doesn't yield a false positive to this account, as functions can be multiply realizable: as I've already noted, both forks and chopsticks are for delivering food to one's mouth. So too emails, letters, and conversations can also be for communicating messages to others, without undermining the fact that the reactive attitudes have a communicative function too.

---

[23] Strawson himself explicitly notes that "approval" is *not* a reactive attitude, as it permits, like moral condemnation and punishment, "a certain detachment from the actions or agents which are their objects" (Strawson 1962/2003: 75). It's thus surprising that Macnamara appeals to it as a positive paradigm of a Strawsonian reactive attitude.

44 THE ARCHITECTURE OF BLAME AND PRAISE

A worry arises, though, if we are really meant to take this account as providing the whole story of the blame and praise system.[24] As we've seen, there are plenty of ways to blame and praise dispassionately. What, then, are we to say of such cases? Are eye-rolling (behind someone's back), thinking poorly of, reducing respect, withdrawing trust, or noting demerits on someone's life ledger meant to communicate some message to offenders? Quite often not. Many participants in economic games, like the ultimatum game, prefer to sanction (over not sanctioning) those they take to be playing unfairly, even when the sanctioned parties don't know they're being sanctioned (and the sanctioners know this). Sanctioning blame, for these people, is not meant to send a message (see Nichols 2015: 125–6 for discussion).[25] What matters is simply that the wrongdoers not get away with it, that they be sanctioned (retributively). And the same goes for the positive analogues of blame. Perhaps there's a pluralist story of the blame/praise system's functions, where the function of the reactive attitudes version of blame/praise is communicative, and the function of the non-reactive attitudes version of blame/ praise is something else, but this will be less satisfactory than a theory, like NMT, that can account for them all under a single, simple, and straightforward functionalist tent.

Fricker's version of the communicative functionalist story might avoid this worry. Her aim is to articulate the point of the core of blame, its paradigm function. She agrees that the practice of blame is incredibly diverse and disunified. What she thus hopes to do is identify "a basic second-personal interaction of X blaming Y for an action, motive, or attitude (or lack thereof) from which other variant practices can be seen as derivative" (Fricker 2016: 167). Its core is communicative, having the "illocutionary point" of "inspiring remorse in the wrongdoer," which is "a pained moral perception of the wrong one has done" (Fricker 2016: 167). This exchange is meant to align the moral understanding of the wrongdoer and the wronged. Where forms of blame lack this particular point (e.g., private blame), it may be for a variety of reasons that outweigh its expression all-things-considered. For example, perhaps one wants to take a more relaxed, less judgmental, perspective on others (Fricker 2016: 179–80).

Again, I like this story a lot, and I think it's spot on with respect to a leading form of emotional blame, namely, *anger* (see Shoemaker 2015: ch. 3; 2018b; 2021, and Chapter 5 of this book for such stories). It may also be the right approach for capturing the wide array of ways we morally blame others for wrongdoing, so

---

[24] It's unclear whether Macnamara thinks this is indeed the right takeaway. She cites many authors who seem to suggest this connection between the reactive attitudes and blame/praise (or at least blame), but she doesn't say whether she agrees. She's instead explicitly and exclusively concerned simply to explain how reactive attitudes are communicative entities, regardless of whether they capture the whole of blame and praise.

[25] One of the main aims of Chapter 9 is to investigate exactly what's going on in these games and to see to what extent it may apply to our interpersonal lives.

that we can understand non-paradigmatic forms of moral blame in ways that nevertheless make sense relative to the paradigm. But what it doesn't do well is account for (a) the wide variety of ways that we blame each other for nonmoral things, and (b) the wide variety of ways we praise one another, in both moral and nonmoral ways. I shouldn't need to say much about these features anymore, as I've hammered them both home earlier. But it's quite hard to see how we could connect up Fricker's story about painful moral remorse with the blame we often engage in with respect to others' athletic, culinary, epistemic, prudential, or philosophical failures. And what is the relevant analogue to remorse supposed to be in the positive cases? How am I aiming at moral realignment when I praise you for an excellent basketball shot? Again, we may have a good explanation here for a *subset* of the blame/praise system, but the communicative story falls well short of the explanatory power that NMT has for the whole system.

Conclusion

NMT has greater and more accurate explanatory power than its functionalist competitors. It explains the existence, function, and characteristics of the entirety of our blame/praise system, from the moral to the nonmoral, from the private to the public, from other-directed to self-directed, from the communicative to the reticent, from the retributive to the educative, from the actual to the counterfactual. It is a thoroughly naturalistic story, one that's compatible and continuous with other functionalist accounts in disciplines ranging from evolutionary biology to social science. And it has the benefit of being pretty obvious once pointed out: blame and praise are surely for the maintenance of norms. What else would they be for?

I thus assume NMT in what follows. Those agential responses that fall under the rubric of blame or praise do so because they are the sorts of responses that contribute to norm maintenance, typically through the delivery of a sting/buzz and the emission of a signal of the responder's commitment to norm patrol. This view may seem unremarkable, but it will have surprising and far-reaching results as I go about dissolving the many seeming asymmetries between blame and praise laid out in the previous chapter. The key to resolving them starts with the revelation of a type of blame over the next two chapters that has heretofore been unrecognized as such.

The Architecture of Blame and Praise: An Interdisciplinary Investigation. David Shoemaker, Oxford University Press.
© David Shoemaker 2024. DOI: 10.1093/9780198915867.003.0002

3

Hazards

In Chapter 1, I enumerated ten seeming asymmetries between our ordinary conceptions of blame and praise. In order to determine whether to embrace or dissolve them, I first had to delve into the nature of blame and praise, which turned out to be an investigation into the function of the blame and praise system. Agential responses that are members of that system are there insofar as they are the kinds of responses that contribute to norm maintenance via their stings, buzzes, and signals.

In this chapter, I'm going to focus on those stings and buzzes, as a way of beginning to address some of the seeming asymmetries. It was blame's sting, after all, that motivated the final asymmetry articulated in the first chapter: Blame can be dangerous, precisely insofar as it stings, as the pain of its sting might sometimes actually harm.[1] Praise, on the other hand, doesn't sting, instead delivering merely a pleasant buzz. It thus seems as if praise lacks any risk of harm, and so, when it comes to the possibility of dangerous deployments, blame and praise aren't symmetrical.

This thought, however, is false. Praise is dangerous too, perhaps even *more* dangerous, at times, than blame. It is my aim in this chapter to develop and defend this idea. If blame and praise are in fact both dangerous, and more or less equally so, then this fact will provide the first step toward dissolving the purported asymmetries between the two. I will begin by laying out the hazards of blame, before turning to explicate the hazards of praise.

Hazardous Blame

Robert Alton Harris is well known in the philosophical literature on responsibility, made famous by Gary Watson's detailed and sensitive discussion of the case, as part of his rich expressivist interpretation of Strawson's view of responsibility (Watson 2004: 229–59). Harris was an awful man who brutally killed two teenagers, calmly ate their fast-food order, and then joked about dressing up as a policeman to inform their parents. He was sentenced to death for his crimes. The other

---

[1] And its connection to harm, as we'll see in Part Two, is what most often motivates the rush to appeal to desert to justify it.

criminals on death row despised him. If anyone has ever deserved the death penalty, it was Harris.

What Watson reveals, though, is just how horrifying Harris's childhood was. He was beaten regularly by an alcoholic father, who also beat and tortured his mother, who then in turn took it out on Harris. As his sister recalled of their mother, "She began to blame all of her problems on Robert, and she grew to hate the child...She ended up blaming Robbie for all the hurt, all the things like that. She felt helpless and he was someone to vent her anger on" (quoted in Watson 2004: 240). All Harris wanted was love, as a child, "just one pat or word of kindness" (quoted in Watson 2004: 242), but he was continually pushed away and beaten by both parents, regularly abused. He hardened as he grew older, and he was sent to youth detention centers for minor thefts, where he was serially raped and beaten. His crimes became more and more serious, he lost his "feeling for life, [and had] no sense of remorse. He reached the point where there wasn't that much left of him" (quoted in Watson 2004: 241). Harris was executed in California on April 21, 1992.

This is a devastating narrative. It raises all sorts of hard questions, both about the nature of responsibility and our own "there but for the grace of god" realizations about the fragility of our moral selves. Many have written insightfully about these issues. What I want to focus on, however, is the *blame* that was rife in Harris's early life, as well as the thoroughgoing lack of love and praise. He was a sensitive child, desperate for some kind of attention and kindness, for a simple pat on the back or compliment, and all he got was blame: trumped up, brutal, and misapplied. And while there may be no simple causal, deterministic, inevitability story to be told about how he got from that sensitive child to his murderous adult self, there is, at the very least, an obvious reaction that surely very many of us have to Harris, once we know this background, a reaction Watson puts accurately and succinctly as, "No wonder!" (Watson 2004: 243). It is, indeed, no wonder that someone from this horrifying background would turn out the way he did. There were beatings, there was repeated abuse, and there was neglect that shaped him. But as his sister repeatedly notes, there was also blame, blame all the time, blame for things that weren't his fault, blame for who he was. And it's this sort of blame that is, quite obviously, very dangerous.

The Harris case illustrates the most extreme hazards of *characterological* blame, whose far less dangerous (and perhaps even healthy) contrary is *behavioral* blame. The latter aims at actions and implicates both agential control over them as well as the ability to avoid such behavior in the future. When you steal the cookies from the cookie jar, I may blame you behaviorally by saying, angrily, "Hey, I saw that! Those were for the kids! How could you do that?" Characterological blame, however, aims at the agent's character, not (just) at what the agent did, so it aims at something that is seemingly unmodifiable, and it also implicates personal desert, as the agent may come to think that she ought to

48 THE ARCHITECTURE OF BLAME AND PRAISE

be blamed like this, as it's what she deserves *for being a bad person* (see, e.g., Janoff-Bulman 1979).

It's relatively easy for parents to slide into characterological blame of their children, moving from "You shouldn't have done that!" to "You're a very bad boy (for doing that)!" When children hear this latter sort of blame, it lingers, worming its way deep into their psyche. After all, you can't discharge a characterological complaint simply by altering your behavior in the future, or by realizing that you could have done something else to have avoided the blame. If the complaint is about *who you are*, then it's inescapable, at least for a very long while (character changes take place at a glacial pace, if at all). And to the extent that you can't do anything about this sort of complaint, it's likely to eat away at you.

This sort of corrosive effect is most clear in cases of characterological *self*-blame. There's plenty of empirical evidence here. Start with the strong correlations between those who blame themselves for things characterologically (as opposed to behaviorally) and depression (Janoff-Bulman 1979; Peterson, Schwartz, and Seligman 1981). This comes out quite concretely in smokers who have developed COPD. When they perceive their family members as blaming them characterologically, as opposed to behaviorally, for the COPD, it is strongly associated with their greater depression (Plaufcan, Wamboldt, and Holm 2012). This is also the type of self-blame that those with low self-esteem engage in (Janoff-Bulman 1982), whereas behavioral self-blame is more "adaptive" in enabling people to take control over their circumstances.[2] And in young adolescents, characterological self-blame is a distinct risk factor for new and ongoing peer victimization (Schacter et al. 2014; see also Tilghman-Osborne et al. 2008). Internalized characterological blame is also associated, in those who are shame-prone, with fear of intimacy (Lutwak, Panish, and Ferrari 2003). And characterological blame attributions actually increase the recovery time of victims of serious illness, trauma, rape, and other assaults, as well as decreasing the effectiveness of people's immune systems (Segerstrom et al., 1996; discussed in Stratton 2003: 137). It is strongly associated with PTSD, self-harm, maladaptive coping, and worse (Pagel, Becker, and Coppel 1985; Swannell et al. 2012; Bryant and Guthrie 2007; Ullman 1996; Baumeister 1990).

These are nasty correlations, and they are very likely causal. But even if not, it's surely a risky sort of blame best avoided, if possible. Being made to think that you are a bad person, without any way of avoiding it, can be the beginning of a downward spiral, sometimes even a death spiral, as illustrated by the tragic case of Donnie Moore. Leading three games to one in the 1986 American League

---

[2] Interestingly, rape victims tend rather overwhelmingly to engage in *behavioral* self-blame, and while one might think *any* self-blame is inappropriate in such cases, this form of self-blame—as opposed to characterological self-blame—seems to be a valuable coping strategy, given its connection to modifiability, and so it enables victims to exercise a crucial control over their lives (Janoff-Bulman 1979).

Championship Series, and with one strike to go to seal a fourth victory and get his team to the World Series, Moore, a solid relief pitcher for the California Angels, gave up a go-ahead home run to Dave Henderson of the Boston Red Sox. The Red Sox won that game, and they went on to blow out the shell-shocked Angels over the next two games to make it to the World Series. After the game, Moore admitted he had made a bad pitch to Henderson. He said, "I was horse-shit....Somebody's got to take the blame, so I'll take it...I threw that pitch. I lost that game." He was never the same. He struggled with injuries for two more years before he was finally released. Two months later, in July 1989, he killed himself. His agent said, "I think insanity set in. He could not live with himself after Henderson hit the home run. He kept blaming himself. That home run killed him."[3]

I've been surveying the dangers of a certain kind of over-blame. When the blame keeps on coming, it can easily be internalized as characterological, and when blame from the start is characterological, it feels unavoidable and unmodi-fiable, and so predictably may lead to all sorts of depression-related psychological problems. But it's also important to point to the hazards of *under*-blame, which are themselves underappreciated, especially by some blame skeptics. When kids aren't blamed (or aren't blamed enough) for their misbehavior, when parents engage only in what's called "positive parenting," the kids may take this indul-gence to give them free rein to trample on the rules. They think of themselves as exceptions, as entitled to do whatever they want, and bad results follow. We see this most often in some talented athletes who commit rapes and break other rules "because they can," given that their previous bad behavior was always overlooked or covered up. In Scandinavia, there is some evidence to suggest a causal relation between "positive parenting" practices (generated in part by state bans on some forms of anger-related discipline) and increases in minor-on-minor assaults (Larzelere et al. 2017, although see Holden et al. 2017 for a critique).

Blame is dangerous, without a doubt. In its over-use, it can harm the blamed person by becoming internalized in a way that can ruin their life, sometimes even leading to self-harm and suicide. But in its under-use, the insufficiently blamed person can ruin the lives of *others*, given their sense of entitlement.

These facts about blame's dangers seem on their face to render blame quite disanalogous with praise: Praise has no sting, we think, and it would seem to have no correlation whatsoever with bad psychological and physical effects in either its over- or under-deployment. Indeed, how could something that feels so good be bad, right? *Right*?

Wrong.

---

[3] Taken from Baker 2011. During that 1986 World Series there was another series-losing mistake, this time by the Red Sox's own Bill Buckner. Buckner did not kill himself, though, and he seemed to move past the error, even parodying himself on an episode of *Curb Your Enthusiasm*. I discuss this case in Shoemaker 2022b.

Hazardous Praise

As it turns out, there are numerous dangers associated with praise. Some of its dangers are moral. Emily Bingeman (Forthcoming) and others have recently been discussing these moral dangers.[4] They have to do with the ways in which praise can reinforce bad social norms, especially norms about gender. For instance, men are praised far more for their childcare than are women. This pattern reflects the morally problematic view that women are expected to engage in childcare, whereas for men, it's supererogatory. And there are morally problematic ways in which people may praise trans men and women, as in, for example, "Oh my, you look so much like a real woman!" or "I would never have guessed that you used to be a man!" These are deeply insulting forms of praise, reflecting and reinforcing as they do morally problematic gender norms about what "real" men and women should look like (Bingeman Forthcoming).

This is problematic praise, for sure, but the problem lies more in the sexist and transphobic *norms* being maintained by praise than in the praise in and of itself. What I want to focus on, therefore, are the ways in which praise itself, in its over- and under-deployment, risks damage in analogous ways to that of over- and under-blame. The main way it does so is by creating *narcissists*. This is a bad condition to be in, both for narcissists and for those around them.

Narcissism is most generally defined as a personality disorder in which the person has a constant need for admiration, is dependent on others for self-esteem, and tends to be emotionally dysfunctional (for an overview, see Ronningstam 2010). In the most up-to-date psychological literature, there are two forms. *Grandiose narcissists* have a massive sense of entitlement and superiority, they disregard and exploit others, they have a desire for dominance and an inflated sense of self-worth, and they tend to be immune to guilt and shame. *Vulnerable narcissists*, on the other hand, have a high but fragile sense of self-worth that is contingent on environmental feedback, they are prone to depression, anxiety, and grievance, they devalue the need to be close to others, and they are immune to guilt but can experience "withdrawal shame," wherein they hide behavior that has been publicly shamed by others (Jauk et al. 2017).

Both conditions are, it turns out, mostly a function of improper praise by their parents when they were kids. Grandiose narcissism, on the one hand, has its etiology in parental over-praise and reward. When children are praised abundantly for every little thing they do, they start to think they are worthy of such praise all the time. This is a characterological internalization. It's embodied by the thought, "*I* am this good, I am worthy of this praise for *who I am*." The same occurs when parents explicitly praise them characterologically, as in, "You are so good, so

---

[4] See also Jeppsson and Brandenburg 2022.

much better than those other kids!" Consequently, when these children are praised in what they deem to be an insufficient fashion, they get angry, as they feel they are worth more than that.

Vulnerable narcissism, on the other hand, has its etiology in inconsistent discipline and *under*-praise. These children like the feeling of the praise they do get when it's doled out in stingy fashion, and when they fail to get even that (or get it too inconsistently to predict with any accuracy), they tend to feel worthless, so they need praise to overcome these feelings of depression and anxiety about their worth (see, e.g., Mechanic and Barry 2015).

Narcissism can be bad for both narcissists and the people around them. All narcissists used to be universally thought to be quite unhappy and dissatisfied with their lives, but this evidence was primarily drawn from clinicians who were only seeing troubled patients from the get-go (Rose and Campbell 2004). The verdicts now are more mixed, but they buttress the distinctions between the two types of narcissism. Grandiose narcissists actually tend to be relatively happy with their lives, reporting high levels of subjective well-being and satisfaction. They set goals and think of themselves as attaining them (Rose and Campbell 2004). But vulnerable narcissists tend much more toward unhappiness: their sense of self is much more fragile, and they tend toward uncontrollable rage and aggression (Czarna, Zejsnkowski, and Dufner 2018). They also seem to have much lower self-esteem and generally lower satisfaction with their lives (Rohmann, Hanke, and Bierhoff 2019).

When it comes to the effects of their narcissism on *other* people, though, the evidence is uniformly grim: narcissists tend to make other people miserable. They are often studied as part of the Dark Triad, a gruesome threesome that also includes Machiavellians and subclinical psychopaths, studied together for their shared callousness and manipulativeness. The common cause is that all three types of people are quite low in empathy (see, e.g., Jonason and Krause 2013; Jonason et al. 2013; Wai and Tiliopoulos 2012). Insofar as empathy, emotional engagement, and non-manipulation are crucial cornerstones of cooperative interpersonal life, narcissists who lack these features aren't going to be pleasant to be around. And, by god, they aren't. This is particularly true of grandiose narcissists, who engage in internet trolling (March 2019), social disruption, deceit, manipulation, and unprovoked aggression (Schoenleber, Sadeh, and Verona 2011). Vulnerable narcissists, alternately, tend toward cyberstalking (March et al. 2020), negative emotionality, and interpersonal distrust (Miller and Maples 2011). If narcissists become business managers, they often do significant damage to their organizations (Lubit 2002).

Both types of narcissists are interpersonally antagonistic, and they are hardest on those with whom they are in intimate relationships. They are aggressive, manipulative, vindictive, and downright cruel to their partners. They often aim to humiliate them, to grind down their self-esteem (Green and Charles 2019).

52   THE ARCHITECTURE OF BLAME AND PRAISE

Being in a relationship with a narcissist is, for many, a living hell. It may start off with a deep attraction, as some narcissists can be quite charming, always drawing attention to themselves. But day-to-day life with them takes a deep toll, leaving partners with feelings of loneliness, being a mere accessory, having one's wants and needs totally ignored, and being manipulated or cruelly taunted (Firestone 2013).

Recall that over-blame correlates pretty strongly with harm to the over-blamed party, whereas inconsistent or under-blame correlates with harm to those around the under-blamed party. A roughly mirrored image seems true of praise: over-praise correlates pretty strongly with misery and harm to those around the over-praised grandiose narcissist, and inconsistent or under-praise correlates pretty strongly with misery and harm to the under-praised vulnerable narcissist (as well as significant harms to those around them too).

Praise, therefore, in both its over- and under-deployment, risks serious hazards, tending to generate psychological pathologies, disorders, misery, and harm. Indeed, the hazards it risks may be just as bad as those risked by over- and under-deployments of blame. If this is right, we have now eliminated the tenth asymmetry I listed in Chapter 1 between praise and blame: They may both be just as dangerous in their extreme or improper deployment.

Nevertheless, by introducing narcissists into the mix, it turns out that we might well have introduced a *new* asymmetry between blame and praise, perhaps forcing us to play Whack-a-Mole in our attempts to build a symmetrical architecture. Narcissists, I'll now show, may in fact be asymmetrical *people*, which, if true, might mean that there's a different asymmetry we have to deal with now between blame and praise in terms of the different *capacities* their targets require.

Asymmetrical People?

Narcissists of both stripes have significant impairments in empathy, which predicts a poor sense of responsiveness to a certain kind of angry blame. I will develop what I'm about to say in much more detail in Chapter 5, but for now I hope the idea will be intuitive enough to allow me to sketch the asymmetry I will go on to address in subsequent chapters. Suppose you wrong me, in a fairly significant way. Perhaps you laughingly reveal to my colleagues a humiliation I'd told you in confidence. My blame of you will tend to be *angry*.[5] This particular sort of anger is confrontational: It motivates me to get in your face about it, not just for the sake of the yelling itself; rather, my anger *demands* something from you, namely, that you feel and acknowledge what it was that you put me through. You

---

[5] I will disambiguate what are actually two types of angry blame in Chapter 5 and especially Chapter 8. For now, I'll use the term "angry blame" in a rough and ready sense.

need to appreciate just how you made me feel with this betrayal. You need to experience guilt or remorse. Only then can the reasons for my angry blame be withdrawn so that we can (perhaps) move on and repair our relationship.

But if ordinary angry blame of others demands their pained emotional acknowledgment, and the person who is angrily blamed simply cannot respond in the demanded way because they have an empathic impairment, then that agent is likely to reject any angry blame that comes their way as inapplicable, as *inapt*. And indeed, this is precisely what narcissists do.

Narcissists love and crave praise, accepting and bathing in it in all its forms, but boy, do they ever deflect blame, simply refusing to accept it in *any* form. Try blaming a narcissist for wronging you and all you'll hear are deflections: "You made me do it!" "Everybody does that!" "You shouldn't have done what *you* did!" "There was so much traffic!" "You should be glad I showed up at all!" "I don't need this shit." "You think that's bad? You should see what that other guy did!" "Well, if I did it, you deserved it." And so on, and on, and on.[6] Angry blame just can't *stick* to them, it seems.

This pattern might well thus give us reason to believe that narcissists are asymmetrical *people*. They seem to have the capacities to accept praise but not blame. This fact in turn may then suggest that there are different *capacities* required for being intelligibly and aptly praised versus blamed. Narcissists seem to have only the capacity for the former and not the latter. But if apt praise and blame each presuppose different agential capacities in their targets, then they couldn't, it seems, be symmetrical contraries with respect to responsible agency, *period*, which would be the most important asymmetry of all.

While narcissists have gotten us out of the seeming asymmetry regarding the dangers of blame versus praise, their actual responses to blame and praise may have revealed a deeper and more irrevocable asymmetry between the two responses, a capacity-based asymmetry. In the next chapter, I aim to dissolve at least this purported asymmetry by introducing a heretofore unrecognized kind of blame to which narcissists are indeed quite vulnerable, and this will be the key to dissolving all of the other purported asymmetries as well.

The Architecture of Blame and Praise: An Interdisciplinary Investigation. David Shoemaker, Oxford University Press.
© David Shoemaker 2024. DOI: 10.1093/9780198915867.003.0003

---

[6] This is precisely the sort of exchange that played out between Anderson Cooper and the USA's former Narcissist-in-Chief when he was running for president in 2016. In asking about his retweet of a picture of Ted Cruz's wife Heidi standing next to Melania (where there was supposed to be an evident difference in terms of the beauty of each), Trump said, in faux innocence, "I thought it was nice picture of Heidi." Cooper responded, "Come on, you're running for president of the United States." Trump replied, "Look, I didn't start it," to which Cooper said, "Sir, with all due respect, that's the argument of a five-year-old." Trump, predictably, replied, "No it isn't." See the story here: https://variety.com/2016/tv/news/anderson-cooper-donald-trump-5-year-old-1201741634/.

4
Forms

Over the past twenty years, psychologists have been studying people's *humor styles* (Martin et al. 2003). These are the types of humor to which people tend to be attracted and in which they tend to participate most. There are four humor styles, the first two correlating positively with well-being, the last two correlating negatively. First, an *affiliative* humor style consists in the typically friendly banter, teasing, joshing, taking the piss, and so forth that occurs between friends, family, and colleagues, assumes a shared normative background, and often serves to bond people together. A *self-enhancing* humor style is the (misleading) label for the type of humor people engage in to cope with the vicissitudes of life, making light of morbid or painful events, sometimes in a self-deprecating way. This humor style has a very positive effect on well-being. By contrast, *self-defeating* humor involves serving oneself up as the butt of *other* people's jokes and put-downs. This is associated with reduced levels of well-being, as being a punching bag hurts. And the *aggressive* humor style leans into sarcasm, ridicule, and cruelty (Martin et al. 2003). This style is associated with reduced levels of well-being too, insofar as one who engages in it tends to alienate others (that is, potential mates, friends, business partners, and so on).

Psychologists study these humor styles in those with various psychological and personality disorders, among whom are members of the Dark Triad. The core features of those in the Dark Triad—and the reason they are studied together—are their manipulativeness and callousness, which have, as I noted in the last chapter, a common cause in their empathic impairments (Wai and Tiliopoulos 2012; Jonason et al. 2013; Jonason and Krause 2013). As a result, their overwhelming, and almost exclusive, humor style is, quite predictably, *aggressive* (Veselka et al. 2010; Martin et al. 2012). They engage in, and are amused by, mostly just mean humor, humor where the butts of their jokes are made to feel low (and to whom those in the Dark Triad get to feel superior). Indeed, members of the Dark Triad score higher than any other group of humans in the experience of *schaden-freude*: the misfortunes of others cause them endless amusement (James et al. 2014; Porter et al. 2014; Erzi 2020).

To have this sort of one-eyed focus on aggressive humor—on cruel jokes, sarcasm, and ridicule—is to have a poor sense of humor. The poorness comes from two directions. First, people attracted only to aggressive humor fail to see any value in the less caustic affiliative forms of humor, where there is a clear give and take, a *mutuality* to the bantering that is inclusive and bonding. They also fail to see the value of self-deprecating (i.e., self-enhancing) humor, making fun of yourself as a way of coping with the vicissitudes of life. They'd much rather make fun of others for their failures, not reveal their own! It's thus no wonder that their well-being tends to be lower relative to those who do engage in these forms of humor. Second, they fail to see reasons *against* participating in the meanest forms of humor. Yes, some forms of humor are funny only in virtue of the meanness contained within them (as in a stingingly hilarious impersonation of a hypocritical politician), but that doesn't imply that there are no reasons to be morally *worried* about such humor! (See Shoemaker 2018a and 2024 for detailed discussion of these points.)

In the world of humor, just as in the world of blame, therefore, narcissists (and other members of the Dark Triad) seem to be asymmetrical *people*, capable of appreciating and participating in only some forms of humor but not others. This point comes out most clearly when we consider the nature and deployment of *mockery*.

Mockery

In the world of affiliative humor—the sort typically exchanged between friends, family, teammates, and colleagues—mockery occurs all the time. It consists in making fun of someone for a failure relative to some standard, drawing public attention to the failure in a way that typically causes some embarrassment or shame. For example, after your terrible basketball shot misses the rim by 10 feet, a teammate may sarcastically remark, "Ooooh, you wuz robbed." If you brag about your familiarity with Japanese food but in your first actual visit to a sushi restaurant you eat a heaping spoonful of unadorned wasabi (as my rather pompous dad once did), prepare to have that moment relived at every sushi restaurant you visit for years to come (as we did with my rather pompous dad). Mockery can be really effective in bringing people down to size. Making fun of an accomplished but now full-of-herself sibling for a foolish failure of some sort serves to remind her that she's not "all that," that she's still one of us. Mockery restores normative equality. And self-deprecating humor is full of self-mockery as well, as when Jon Stewart once said, "I'm 145 pounds of asthma."[1]

The sort of mockery I've just been touting is either *affiliative* or *self-enhancing*, and it can be valuable in several ways. First, it can create and/or maintain special familial, friendship, and social bonds. It is often quite affectionate.[2] Its

---

[1] I argue for this and many other points about mockery in Shoemaker 2024: ch. 4.

[2] It can also, of course, be deeply painful and serve to maintain oppression in some families, especially those in which dominant family members are enforcing sexist norms. I'm clearly highlighting mockery's positive values, but I certainly acknowledge its potential disvalues as well. As it turns out, the same is true of blame generally, which will turn out to buttress my overall point.

importance in family relationships and friendships cannot be overstated, especially for family members who have a hard time expressing their love in other ways (Norrick 1993: 80). Second, it can define common enemies and so rally one's in-group against them. For example, the bullied can unite and gain power by mocking their bullies. On this general point, Cicero noted mockery's power in the political context, as a way of downgrading or embarrassing political rivals (see Morreall 1987: 17–18). Third, *self*-mockery increases one's attractiveness to others, and it serves as a powerful preemptive defense against attack by others (when you make fun of yourself before others do, it takes all the wind out of their sails). Fourth, and most importantly, mockery can be a valuable corrective, as Frances Hutcheson insightfully noted. When you mock people for their faults, he said, they "are apt to be made sensible of their folly, more than by a bare grave admonition. Men have been laughed out of faults that a sermon could not reform…" (in Morreall 1987: 39–40).

But of course mockery isn't exclusively affiliative or self-enhancing. Sometimes it's quite aggressive. Indeed, narcissists dish it out all the time, as a way of expressing their "superiority" over others. For them, crucially, it is most definitely *not* mutual, though. Narcissists (of both the grandiose and vulnerable type) hate being mocked, and they don't engage in self-mockery, that is, in self-deprecating humor, either (Zeigler-Hill and Besser 2013). They hate it because they full well understand what it can be, namely, a method of bringing people down to size, reminding them of their equal status relative to others. To someone who thinks he is *better* than others, who thinks he deserves to be made an exception of, this sort of reminder will of course be maddening. And so they find it to be.

So it seems as if there might be yet another asymmetry generated by thinking about narcissists: Not only can they accept praise but not blame, but also they mock others but can't accept being mocked themselves. What, then, shall we make of these seeming asymmetries? As it turns out, the "asymmetries" of mockery for narcissists correspond precisely to their "asymmetries" when it comes to praise and blame, so dissolving the former "asymmetry" will reveal how to begin dissolving the latter.

Mockery and Blame

We start with the fact that mockery characteristically *stings*. People successfully mocked may feel embarrassment, shame, or humiliation, and these tend to be unpleasant emotions. Of course, as we know, blame also characteristically stings. This, as we'll soon see, is not a coincidence.

Now, as it turns out, the fact that narcissists can't "accept" either blame or mockery is ambiguous. On the one hand, it might mean that they simply can't feel or respond properly to their stings. On the other hand, it might mean that, while they *can* feel their stings, *they don't want to*, and so they seek like mad to avoid them.

I mentioned at the end of Chapter 3 why I think that the former understanding applies to narcissists when it comes to a kind of angry blame, one that demands empathic acknowledgment: To the extent that narcissists are impaired for empathy, they are impaired for being an apt target, for feeling the sting, of this sort of anger. It simply makes no sense to them as a form of communication. Instead, the demands of angry blame to them sound like Charlie Brown's teacher: "Mwah, mwah, mwah, mwah, mwah."

However, they can absolutely feel the sting of *mockery*. It's just that they hate it and want like hell to avoid it. Obama's mockery of a narcissistic Trump at the 2015 Correspondents' Dinner in Washington D.C. has been cited by many as the likely source of Trump's motivation to run for president.[3] That narcissists can't "accept" mockery's sting simply means that they want to avoid it. Why? Because it actually *stings* them: If other people are laughing at them for failing at something—at being inferior in some way—then that perception is in stark contrast with the narcissists' own heightened perception of themselves and how others *ought* to think of them. It's seriously deflating. It chips away at the protective illusion that's at the center of their lives, and that *hurts*.

Now return to the positive values of affiliative and self-enhancing mockery that I laid out earlier: It bonds, rallies, increases one's attractiveness, offers a preemptive defense technique, and can be a valuable corrective. These all come at a cost, however, for mockery, as we all know, risks real retaliation (perhaps even more so than finger-wagging blame), and if people aren't ready for it or don't understand it, it risks serious corrosion of relationships. It risks these costs because of its sting. But then note what we now have on our hands: Mockery is a costly stinging signal of the mocker's commitment to, and willingness to patrol and enforce, some norm or other. Mockers have not only signaling costs but also competence costs. It takes a lot to learn and internalize both the behavioral norms being policed as well as the *humor* norms deployed in properly policing them. Indeed, the fact that mockery is a costly signal of norm commitment is what enables excellent mockers to get the long-term prudential benefits just noted (Zeigler-Hill et al. 2013). People want to affiliate with those whose normative commitments they share, and to the extent that mockers signal their willingness to enforce those commitments through humor, creating enjoyable amusement in their wake, it provides others with even more powerful reasons to associate with them—they are funny!—at least when their mockery is affiliative or self-enhancing (and so is something to which all participants are mutually vulnerable). Finally, the very best mockers toe a Goldilocks empathic line: While their

---

[3] See one story about it here: https://www.chicagotribune.com/nation-world/ct-white-house-correspondents-dinner-trump-20170226-story.html.

58　THE ARCHITECTURE OF BLAME AND PRAISE

mocks have to have some sting in them, they can't contain *too* much sting, else the funny become swamped by the pain.[4]

All of these features make mockery a valuable but previously unrecognized kind of *blame*. Mockery is a way of enforcing some norms by highlighting others' normative failures via stinging (embarrassing, humiliating) amusement, which can in fact be enjoyable: It's *fun* to make fun. But making fun of people can also be really effective at getting them in line, often far more effective than a sermon, as Hutcheson rightly notes. Narcissists thus don't want to "accept" mockery, but they can nevertheless feel its sting, precisely because they can recognize and direct that sting when they mock others. They just don't want to have that sting directed at *them*, precisely because it pricks a hole in their own balloons, in their fragile conceptions of themselves as better than everyone else (Zeigler-Hill and Besser 2013). It brings them back down to size in the eyes of others, and they hate that. It enables them to recognize that others don't think they are as great as they themselves think they are (and desperately need others to think they are).

If mockery is indeed a kind of blame, then the purported asymmetry about agential capacities broached at the end of the preceding chapter can immediately be dissolved. To be vulnerable to the reach of mocking-blame—to have the capacity for being its apt target—is simply to have a sense of self that's vulnerable to being affected by the stingingly funny appraisals of others, a sense of self that can be deflated. Narcissists have precisely this vulnerable sense of self, just like they have a sense of self that can be inflated by a certain type of praise, a type that I will now label *complimenting-praise*.[5] Indeed, as I'll now show, mocking-blame is what's actually analogous to—symmetrical with—complimenting-praise. While mockery delivers blame's sting, compliments deliver praise's *buzz*. And even though narcissists do have an impaired capacity to be reached or affected by paradigmatically *angry* blame, insofar as it demands emotional empathic acknowledgment, they're fully capacitated to be reached, affected, and corrected by mocking-blame.

The Symmetry between Mocking-Blame and Complimenting-Praise

Mocking-blame is, I propose, the actual negative counterpart of our ordinary conception of complimenting-praise. We can see all of their detailed symmetries by revisiting the list of purported asymmetries from Chapter 1. As it turns out,

---

[4] Here I want to stay completely neutral on the relation between these two sets of reasons, the comic and the moral. My use of the term "swamped" is deliberately ambiguous, then, between "eliminated" and "heavily outweighed."

[5] There's a sense in which what Arpaly and Schroeder (2014: 160) refer to as *crediting* is akin to this conception of praising.

the praise we were talking about there was just *complimenting*-praise, and it fits perfectly now with its actual negative counterpart, mocking-blame:

1. *Demands*: Complimenting-praise demands nothing of its target, recall, and there's not much of a response even expected from it, other than "Thanks!" But mocking-blame is also undemanding. When you mock someone for a screw-up, you're certainly not demanding anything like guilt, remorse, apology, relationship repair, or compensation from them. Perhaps the most appropriate response to such mockery is just sheepish amusement, an embarrassed acceptance of having been brought down to size: "Yup, you got me." But not even that response is *demanded* by mocking-blame (just like a "Thanks!" can't be demanded by a compliment); it's at most an expectation or hope of good-humored teasing that the butts of the teasing will "take it" with good grace (and learn from it, perhaps).

2. *Desert*: Desert seems to be unnecessary for both complimenting-praise and mocking-blame. Although you'll have to wait for the full story of this claim until Chapter 6, suffice to say that we sometimes mock or compliment people for accidents, or cases in which they lacked the sort of knowledge that seems necessary for desert. Now very often, of course, we do engage in both complimenting-praise and mocking-blame for deliberate or voluntary agential exercises (e.g., culinary or athletic performances), but not always, and even when we do, thoughts of desert may play little role in what we deem their apt deployment. A wobbly performance coming down the stretch of a marathon may well be made fun of by a runner's friends and family, despite her dehydration *or the fact that she'd just run 26 miles*!

3. *Emotions*: No particular emotional content is required or expected for either complimenting-praise or mocking-blame. Just as my praise can be dry and uplifting, so too can my mockery be dry and cutting. Indeed, mockery is often funnier the dryer it is.

4. *Attitudes*: Just as one can't, in any ordinary sense, praise someone without expressing it (either to that person or to someone else), so too one can't really mock someone without expressing it (either to that person or to someone else). Neither complimenting-praise nor mocking-blame is purely attitudinal, then, so no private version of either seems to count as such.[6]

---

[6] Must there be some blame or praise *attitude* of which these are expressions, though? This, I take it, is the view of Arpaly and Schroeder 2014: 159–62. Yes, if these expressions are to count as signals of one's *commitment* to some set of norms. But the attitudes grounding these expressions are different from those of what I'll call the *demanding* forms of blame and praise, which are fundamentally emotions (anger and gratitude) with action-tendencies that incline those who feel them to express them to the people who triggered them. Given the different attitudinal grounds of these different forms of blame and praise, I'm once again inclined to think that Arpaly and Schroeder are missing part of the story (namely, the *demanding* part) of blame and praise. Thanks to Tim Schroeder for valuable discussion, though.

60 THE ARCHITECTURE OF BLAME AND PRAISE

5. *Morality*: *Most* tokens of both complimenting-praise and mocking-blame are responses to nonmoral activities, I think. This is a pretty speculative claim, I admit, but I'm hard-pressed to see many counterexamples. Just as compliments are mostly responses to good performances in nonmoral domains, so too mockery mostly responds to poor performances in non-moral domains. We typically don't say "Good job!" to those who are honest or who keep their promises, or even to those who go above and beyond the demands of morality. So too, we typically make fun of one another mainly for athletic, aesthetic, academic, etiquettal, prudential, philosophical, and/or epistemic blunders. Perhaps we think morality is too serious a domain for "mere" mockery-blame? I'm not sure. I suppose I can sarcastically mock you for being a serial promise-breaker ("Yeah, yeah, *sure* you'll be there on Sunday, just like always"). But these will likely be for trivial moral viola-tions. (For example, no one would really mock someone for being a serial rapist except perhaps other members of a perverse community of assault-favoring men who don't think it's all that bad.)

6. *Excuses*: Complimenting-praise is typically immune to excuses, but so is mocking-blame. If you save someone from an attack because you think he's your uncle and it turns out that he's the president (and perhaps you actually hate the president and want him to be attacked), then saying, "I didn't know!" may not get you off the hook for praise for saving the president. The same, however, is true of mocking-blame: If you continually miss your crucial free throws in the final minutes of a big game, you're liable to be mocked no matter how long and hard you've practiced.[7]

7. *Quality of Will*: Complimenting-praise doesn't necessarily target quality of will, and neither does mocking-blame. We often make fun of people's fail-ures regardless of their motives or aims in doing what they did. My first goodwilled attempt at making a pie might yield a ridiculous and hilarious disaster of a dessert, something for which mockery from my family may flow till the cows come home.

8. *Moral Justification*: None is needed for complimenting-praise, it seems, as pain or unfairness seem to play no role. But there *is* a sting delivered by mockery: It typically exposes one's flaws to the world, and so it is *meant* to be at least a little embarrassing, shameful, or humiliating, and experiencing any of these emotions involves at least a pinprick of pain. Typically causing pain requires moral justification. I will discuss this point at length in Chapter 6. But for now, I will simply point out that there may be a justification available for and applicable to mocking-blame, but it's not a moral justification; it is, rather, a justification

---

[7] As a longtime Lakers fan, I'm looking at you, Shaquille O'Neal.

appealing to its *funniness*. If a stinging bit of mockery is funny enough, generating enjoyable amusement to all the parties involved (including even the mocked), then that *may* be enough to dampen, eliminate, or outweigh any moral reasons there might be against engaging in it.[8] Mockery in and of itself may or may not be funny, though, so mockery-blame that is unfunny likely *does* need a moral justification (which, again, will be discussed in Chapter 6). One might think here of acid mockery of a corrupt and craven politician: not funny, perhaps, but quite merited, so all-things-considered permissible.

9. *Standing*: Anyone has standing to engage in complimenting-praise, so there's no hypocritical praise that undermines it of the form "Who are you to praise me?!" The same, though, is true of mocking-blame: Anyone has standing to make fun of other people's failures, even if they themselves are guilty of the very same failures they are mocking. For example, suppose you, my basketball teammate, make fun of me with a well-timed "Nice" every time I completely miss the rim on a free throw. I then repeat the sarcastic mock to you when you miss the rim. There's no hypocrisy here, nor do I lack standing to mock you in a way that can permit you to ignore my mock (as is true of hypocritical angry blame of others). You may well get upset at me for mocking you for what I'm also a failure at, but that's because it's grating to have your flaws pointed out by people just as flawed as you, and this feeling has nothing to do with lack of standing or hypocrisy.

10. *Danger*! Because of its sting, mocking-blame (like angry blame of others) can be dangerous. We academics are probably quite familiar with having been mockingly bullied in our youth, an experience neither fun nor funny. Over-the-top mocking-blame can really hurt, and if it's internalized as characterological, as thought to target who one really is, then it may well have familiar pathological results. But this aspect of it is perfectly symmetrical with complimenting-praise, as I detailed in the previous chapter: Over-the-top complimenting-praise that's characterological can be dangerous too, creating narcissists who tend to have lower well-being and cause lots of unhappiness in others, given their poor senses of both humor and morality.

Mocking-blame is thus the symmetrical positive counterpart of our ordinary conception of complimenting-praise. But what now about all the rest?

---

[8] Again, I'm trying to be neutral between various views of the relation between these types of reasons. See Shoemaker 2024: ch. 4 for detailed discussion.

Next Up

By introducing mockery into the architecture of blame, I've dissolved one set of purported asymmetries: Complimenting-praise has, as its actual negative counterpart, mocking-blame. But what about all the rest? What about the kind of blame that yielded all the original asymmetries with what we now know is complimenting-praise? Indeed, it's *that* sort of blame that may look like an ungainly outlier to a symmetrical architecture now, even though it's by far the more familiar kind of blame.

As it turns out, it is representative of an *acknowledgment-seeking* type of blame, acknowledgment which neither mocking-blame nor complimenting-praise seek (see the first asymmetry). What would be ideal, then, is a positive counterpart to the acknowledgment-seeking form of blame, one that would complete a symmetrical design.

It is my aim in the next chapter to explore what that is, along with the nature of the acknowledgment being sought. I will then be ready to begin in Part Two a discussion of the normative grounding of the various parts of the architecture that I've revealed, as well as how the wide variety of our blame/praise responses connect up to the question of responsible agency with which we began.

The Architecture of Blame and Praise: An Interdisciplinary Investigation. David Shoemaker, Oxford University Press.
© David Shoemaker 2024. DOI: 10.1093/9780198915867.003.0004

5
Emotions

The standard expression of the most familiar type of praise—complimenting—is "Good job!" It can be entirely unemotional, and it demands nothing from its target. The standard expression of the most familiar type of blame, however, is, as Coleen Macnamara puts it in the title of a famous paper: "*Screw you*!!" (Macnamara 2013a).[1] Often this is put in even more colorful language. But what that "screw you!" and most of its variants embodies is the expression of an emotion, namely, *anger*. In this chapter, I'll explore the nature of that emotion, as well as the sort of acknowledgment it seeks from others. I will then investigate this emotion's actual positive counterpart, *gratitude*, and in so doing I'll show why some recent discussions of its nature miss the mark.[2]

After discussing these paradigmatic acknowledgment-seeking emotions, I will turn to investigate some lesser-explored blame/praise emotions, including contempt, disappointment, admiration, and pride. These emotions are, I think, lesser explored in this literature because they don't fit well into what's known as the *accountability* type of responsible agency, and most responsibility theorists are mostly obsessed just with accountability (for problematic reasons that I'll discuss at the end of Chapter 9). But these blame/praise emotions respond to manifestations of different agential capacities than those of anger and gratitude, so we can learn something important about responsible agency from them, namely, that it admits of multiple *types*.

By the end of this chapter, I will have put in place most of the overall descriptive architecture of blame and praise, one that aims to capture all of our various forms of blame and praise under an overarching symmetrical structure. But some of its forms will raise serious questions about the connection to responsible agency which motivated this project, questions which spur the normative spadework I undertake in Part Two of the book.

---

[1] Interestingly, the "screw you!" of the title is contrasted with its purportedly positive counterpart, "thank you," which, I've been arguing and will continue to argue in this chapter, is not accurate.

[2] While my full-on discussion of the normative grounds of blame and praise doesn't officially come until the next chapter and beyond, I should warn that I will be discussing some normative issues in this chapter, in particular the fittingness conditions of some emotions (e.g., anger and gratitude). This is necessary as part of my discussion of what these emotions target.

Anger

Anger is a pancultural emotion that has several features in common with other pancultural emotions: It is irruptive, impulsive, urgent, flexible, and involves involuntary bodily changes (see, e.g., Frijda 1986; D'Arms 2013: 3; D'Arms and Jacobson 2023; Scarantino 2014: 157–9).[3] As with other "basic" or "natural" emotional syndromes, anger consists in (a) an affective component, (b) an appraisal, and (c) an action-tendency (see Szigeti 2015 for a nice overview and discussion). This last feature urges us toward a goal pertaining to what the emotional syndrome as a whole can best be interpreted as evaluating (its "core relational theme," in the words of Lazarus 1991). The most straightforward illustration of an emotional syndrome comes from *fear*: its feelings involve trembling, dry mouth, heart-pounding, and so forth. Its appraisal is of some perceived event's being a danger or threat. And its action-tendency—prototypically one of the famous three of fight, flight, or freeze—aims its bearer toward safety.

Disputes among emotion theorists are primarily over which of these three features of emotional syndromes serves to define and differentiate them. To that end, there have been *feeling theorists*, who prioritize the emotion's affective component (e.g., James 1894; Prinz 2005); *appraisal theorists*, who prioritize the emotion's evaluative component (e.g., Lazarus 1982; Solomon 1988; Roberts 1988; Greenspan 1988; Nussbaum 2004); and *motivational theorists*, according to whom "the identity of an emotion is essentially tied to a prioritized tendency to action (or inaction) with the function of being elicited by a core relational theme," a theory which "replaces the primacy of the appraisal and feeling aspects of emotions with the primacy of their motivational dimension" (Scarantino 2014: 168; Frijda 1986 is a forerunner; see also D'Arms and Jacobson 2022 and 2023).[4]

I favor the motivational theory, which implies that various natural emotions are identified and differentiated from other natural emotions in terms of their "action-readiness," what the emotions urgently urge us to *do*. I cannot here give a full explication and defense of this theory, but I will at least offer a few considerations in its favor. The strongest argument for it, I think, comes from considering emotion's role in both natural and cultural selection. We can best understand why we have the emotion of fear, for example, by considering what it's *for*, and that answer must surely make reference to how it enabled our ancestors to survive and reproduce (and thus pass the trait along), namely, by better enabling their safety in the presence of danger via its irruptive and urgent action-tendencies. Fear was selected for as a result of its effects in achieving fear's goal (safety) in the presence

---

[3] I draw much of the material in this section from Shoemaker 2022b: 33–8.

[4] In the philosophy of emotion, there are also *perceptual theorists*, who view emotions on analogy with perceptions (see Tappolet 2016). I set this view aside here, although I think the motivational theory I embrace has distinct advantages over the perceptual view.

of danger (Scarantino 2014: 178). This functionalist view has normative import as well. As Scarantino puts it, "[F]ear will be *defective* in the absence of danger… In…such cases, emotions do not prioritize relational goals in the presence of those core relational themes that explain why prioritizing such goals in the past was selected for" (Scarantino 2014: 178; emphasis in original).

Another argument in favor of the motivational theory is that there seems to be nothing special or necessary about the affect or appraisal aspects of emotions in and of themselves that would mark them as distinctive or as generating the kind of clamoring-for-attention we most associate with them. The affective features of different emotions are quite often indistinguishable. For example, shame and guilt feel phenomenologically similar (and are also close in terms of bodily changes), as do joy and amusement (both have a feeling of "levity"), grief and sadness, and disgust and contempt. And as for appraising thoughts, they too on their own don't necessarily or even typically generate the sustained attention, urgency, or action-readiness distinctive of emotions. Indeed, it is only the action-tendencies that "tend to persist in the face of interruptions; they tend to interrupt other ongoing programs and actions; and they tend to preempt the information-processing facilities" (Frijda 1986: 78). They produce what's called "control precedence" (Frijda 1986: 78; Scarantino 2014: 171).[5] But appraisals alone need not play any such role. Indeed, appraisals can be distinctly *un*emotional, as in a Special Forces soldier trained not to be afraid when he comes across scenarios he nevertheless rightly appraises as dangerous or threatening (Scarantino 2014: 162–3).

So how does this view of the emotions apply to anger? Everyone agrees on its affect: a heated, aggressive feeling, sometimes accompanied by clenched fists, sweating, and shaking. Disagreement arises, however, over anger's appraisal and its associated action-tendency and aim. On one familiar side of the disagreement are those who follow Aristotle, maintaining that anger appraises *slights* and its action-tendency aims at *retaliation* (Aristotle 1954).[6] This would make anger an apt response only to a rather sophisticated kind of agency.[7]

There are some serious problems with this view, though. First, we don't feel anger exclusively toward sophisticated agents; we also feel anger at lots of non-agential things, including the weather, computers, our chronic pain, and our physical disorders, and we do so without necessarily perceiving those objects as

---

[5] There are important qualifications to be made here. Obviously, one can process information in the meantime, emotions may also be cool, and sometimes the tendency is for *in*action. See Scarantino 2014 for the nuances of the view.

[6] For retaliation as anger's aim, see, among philosophers, D'Arms and Jacobson 2003 and 2023: 193–8; Nichols 2007 and 2013; McGeer 2013. Among psychologists, see, e.g., Shaver et al. 1987; Frijda 1994; Izard 1997; Boehm 1999; Haidt 2003.

[7] Normative talk of "aptness" here, as I'll also note in the next chapter, is intended to be neutral between a variety of possible normative groundings. For now, just think of it in a rough-and-ready way, as *whatever* it is that turns out to make an emotion the "right" sort of response in some circumstances or other.

agents (see Trost et al. 2012; Craig and Brown 1984). But none of these things can slight us, clearly, so retaliating against them would just be silly or impossible. Second, babies and some nonhuman animals also seem to feel anger, yet they surely lack the cognitive sophistication to be tracking and responding to agential slights or to be thinking about retaliation (see, e.g., Lewis et al. 1990; Lewis 1993).

As a result of these problems, the other side describes anger's appraisal instead to be of *goal-frustration* and its action-tendency to be towards *eliminating or bypassing the blockage* (see Haidt 2003 for citations and discussion). This view easily accounts for the non-agential and baby cases, and it might also be able to encompass anger at slights, given that when you slight me you may also plausibly be construed as frustrating my goals.

However, the goal-frustration view of anger has its own problem, namely, it seems to lose anger's typical connection to *holding responsible*. If all I am doing in being angry is looking for a way to get around the goal-blockage, even if you (another agent) are its direct source, then it's unclear how this response could or should be an instance of, or connect up to, blaming and holding you responsible for causing the goal-blockage qua agent. On this account, it makes sense to describe me as merely angered *that* there's a goal-blockage, not angry *at* you (qua agent) for causing it, and this seems to lose a great deal of the intuitive force of Aristotle's original account.

I think there are good considerations in favor of both views of anger, though, so good that I have argued in other work that we ought to be *pluralists* about it, admitting two distinct types of anger (Shoemaker 2018b: 72–4). There is what I'll call, on the one hand, *goal-frustrated-anger*, and there is, on the other hand, what I'll call *slighted-anger*. They have very similar phenomenal feels, but they differ dramatically in their action-tendencies, appraisals, and aims.[8]

Start with the action-tendencies. Very often both types of anger co-occur. When you block the doorway out of a malicious desire to prevent me from getting to work on time, I'll be angry, but looking more closely we can see that I'll be motivated in two different directions: (a) to get around you somehow to get to work on time, and (b) to confront or get back at you (likely later) for blocking my path. But there are cases in which we get only one or the other. If I'm driving to work and come across a rockslide preventing my getting there on time, again, I'll be angry, but I'll be motivated *only* to look for a way around the rockslide, not also to confront or retaliate against it later (Shoemaker 2018b: 73). Alternatively,

---

[8] Why not, then, call them two different emotions, namely, frustration and anger? I'm not crazy about that, but I won't fight it kicking and screaming, as I'm concerned fundamentally only with the emotional syndromes and not their labels. Still, I think it worthwhile to maintain some continuity here with the extensive literature in psychology and philosophy that calls both syndromes *anger*. I think it worth keeping in mind as well that the phenomenological feel of both responses is remarkably similar. So I will continue to label both as types of anger. (For pushback and an attempt to preserve a unified account of anger against my pluralist view, see D'Arms and Jacobson 2023: 193–8.)

suppose someone stayed in my Air BnB spare room last weekend, and I find out after he's gone back to Eastern Europe, never to return, that he was secretly spying on me through a hole in the wall when I took showers. I will be angry, and aptly so, it seems, but there is simply no occurrent goal-frustration in such a case to get around.[9] I merely want to confront or retaliate against him (I will, for instance, surely give him zero stars in my guest review and will report him to Air BnB).

There is a crucial difference between these two types of anger in terms of what they are each appraising. When you meant to hurt me, my anger at you appraises what you did as a *slight*. Slighted-anger is anger at psychologically sophisticated agents for exercises of their agency. But I don't actually get (aptly) angry *at* "the weather" for ruining my long-planned July 4 military parade; rather, I get angry *that* it is raining on my parade. If it stops raining, I (should) stop being angry. So in getting angry when it rains, I am in essence appraising that climatological state of affairs as *frustrating* (or, perhaps better, as *maddening*), and to the extent that the rain is indeed actively thwarting a goal of mine, I have appraised the situation correctly, and so in fact I have a reason to feel goal-frustrated-anger (only) so long as that state of affairs obtains. When it stops raining, I no longer have any reason to feel this sort of anger.

The different action-tendencies and appraisals of the different types of anger also differ in their aims. Slighted-anger, on a story I have told and defended in detail elsewhere (Shoemaker 2015: ch. 3; 2018b), is confrontational and demands a response, aiming at, and being (aptly) satisfied by, the slighter's emotional acknowledgment of how he made the slighted person feel, where what the slighter comes to recognize is how poor (or insufficiently good) his quality of will toward the other person had been.[10]

Let's take this a bit more slowly. Going back to Aristotle, many have thought that slighted-anger aims at retaliation. But this isn't always the case. I may quietly shut the door on my partner if they once again come home late and drunk. I may sit down and compose an angry letter to the editor of the local paper or to my senator in response to some idiotic legislation. Or I may yell at the local teenagers who, in speeding down my suburban street, endanger my children. None of these familiar forms of slighted-anger seek retaliation, necessarily. But they all seek *confrontation*, aiming to draw the attention of slighters to their slights. And indeed, some psychological studies reveal, this is the aim most subjects take retaliation to serve, considering it a dramatic way of confronting the slighter to communicate to her what he or she has done to the victim (Gollwitzer and Denzler 2009;

---

[9] Unless it's the trumped-up "goal" that I not have been spied upon while in the shower. I have a hard time thinking about this as an actual goal, though, given that goals are forward-looking, things one aims to achieve, and so things one thinks one *can* achieve. One can't change the past, though.

[10] My view is thus not merely that anger merely seeks to communicate itself to the slighter, as reported by D'Arms and Jacobson 2023: 196.

68   THE ARCHITECTURE OF BLAME AND PRAISE

Gollwitzer, Meder, and Schmitt 2011). Secret retaliation without such confrontational communication in response to a slight feels undischarged, or at least incomplete. Indeed, what's the *point* of the retaliation unless the wrongdoer knows who did it and why?

But to what end? Why does anger seek confrontation? What slights do is upset the normative balance between people. When you slight me, failing to take me or my ends sufficiently seriously, you take yourself to be normatively superior to me, someone whose ends are *worth more* than mine. But this is false; we're all normative equals. Our interests and ends are all worth equal consideration in normative deliberation (assuming, of course, that we ourselves haven't upset the normative balance). Anger, as an appraisal of slights, seeks ultimately to restore that normative balance between us, to restore how we stood relative to each other prior to your slight. What gets us back to normative balance is your sincere acknowledgment of the slight. But why? And what does that acknowledgment consist in?

Consider a classic case of (filmed) slighting. As they were shooting *Midnight Cowboy*, Dustin Hoffman, as Ratso Rizzo, was crossing a busy Manhattan street while chatting up Jon Voigt's new-to-town character Joe Buck. A real-life taxi turns the corner and nearly hits Hoffman, who then immediately slams on the taxi's hood and shouts at the cabbie his most famous—improvised—line: "I'm walkin' heah! I'm *walkin'* heah!" What does his anger seek? There's no retaliatory desire here (he just keeps on walking heah after that), and there's been no harm caused to redress (he wasn't hit or harmed in any way). He also cares nothing about regulating the cabbie's future activities, and they had no prior relationship to be impaired. Instead, Hoffman-qua-Rizzo (or Rizzo-qua-Hoffman) is demanding that the cabbie *notice* him, that the cabbie *take him seriously*. *I'm* walking here indeed. But then what Rizzo/Hoffman demanded from the cabbie—acknowledgment—was exactly the same thing the cabbie should have provided *before* their exchange, namely, he should have already registered the fact of Rizzo's/Hoffman's presence. The driver's offense consisted in a failure of acknowledgment, and as such, it makes perfect sense that Rizzo would, in enforcing his default expectation of acknowledgment, demand it now.

Slighted-anger seeks—demands—acknowledgment; it is, as I'll say, *acknowledgment-seeking*. But what sort acknowledgment does it seek? It requires more than the slighter's mental revisiting of the slight. After all, the slighter who merely remembers slighting me didn't feel bad about it the first time through, so why should he feel it the second time through in memory? He must instead revisit the slight *through my eyes*, as it were. The slighter has to register what my ends were and how he (the slighter) set them back. Further, he has to see all this from my perspective. This is clearly a demand for *empathy*. When you slight me, my slighted-anger demands that you acknowledge how you made me feel, and in order to successfully discharge anger's demands, you must take up my perspective, to feel how it felt to me when you slighted me. Further, being slighted typically *hurts*.

Consequently, if you properly take up my perspective on the incident, seeing what you did from my perspective, it will hurt for you too. This response—painful empathic acknowledgment—is guilt or remorse, and it is what slighted-anger demands (cf. Fricker 2016).[11]

Goal-frustrated-anger, by contrast, does *none* of this. It aims simply to overcome the blockage and get back on track to achieving one's goals, that's it. Consequently, it doesn't demand anything or seek acknowledgment from anyone. This is why genuine apology, guilt, remorse, excuse, and justification—all features of responsible agency—are implicated only in slighted-anger and are irrelevant to goal-frustrated-anger. Perhaps you have parked your car too close to mine for me to open my door and get out in time to make it to an important meeting, but perhaps you did so by accident (my car was camouflaged), you were justified (it was the only place available to park quickly so that you could help someone who'd collapsed in the street), or you did so under duress (at the flash of a carjacker's gun). In none of these cases would my demand for emotional empathic acknowledgment from you be appropriate. But my goal-frustrated-anger neither wants nor needs such a thing—it just wants your goddam car out of the way! Your reasons *why* you did what you did matter to me only insofar as they reveal what your quality of will was, that is, whether you had a slighting attitude toward me. They are irrelevant, however, in determining whether you frustrated my goals. That fact obtains (or not) independently of your quality of will.

The most familiar form of blame is thus slighted-anger, which paradigmatically seeks rather robust empathic and emotional responses from its targets. It is mostly moral, therefore, because it tracks and responds to insufficient acknowledgment—slights—from others, a matter of disregard or disrespect. This is what slighted-anger demands in response to slights: a restoration of the normative balance, via remorseful acknowledgment, which the slighter disturbed by way of the slight.

To understand and appreciate the expression of this type of angry blame as a form of intelligible address, one must be capable of *empathy*, capable of in fact acknowledging others (sufficiently) in the first place.[12] Narcissists (and other members of the Dark Triad) are impaired for empathy (and emotions like guilt and remorse generally), and so they tend to find demands for it unintelligible, or as inapplicable to them insofar as they are incapable of complying. Demanding

---

[11] I've drawn some material in the previous two paragraphs from Shoemaker 2021: 49. For now, I'm glossing together guilt and remorse, but I'll try to draw some distinctions between them later. They are closely related emotions, and they're often felt together, but they have different motivational profiles, I think, as well as different appraisals and aims.

[12] It's essential to point out that this appeal to the capacities necessary for being an apt recipient of intelligible slighted-anger does not imply that the conditions for being *accountable* for slights rests on one's capacity for being an apt target of intelligible slighted-anger. That is to say, being accountable is not a direct function of being capable of understanding and appreciating such angry address. Rather, as I would have it, being accountable is a function of having the capacity for empathy, which *also* serves to enable one to understand the address of slighted-anger.

70 THE ARCHITECTURE OF BLAME AND PRAISE

empathy from narcissists is like demanding an account of the different hues in a Monet painting from the colorblind. Slighted-anger is thus inapt for narcissists.

Gratitude

But narcissists are also impaired, I believe, for the actual positive counterpart of slighted-anger, namely, *gratitude*. In this section, I investigate the nature of this emotion and its symmetrical relation to slighted-anger.

Slighted-anger appraises actions or attitudes as slights. Slights are failures to take others and their interests sufficiently seriously.[13] Call the opposite of slights *heights*, where this refers to taking others and their interests *more* seriously than expected or demanded.[14] Heighting may range anywhere from delivering unexpected benefits, to providing special consideration, to thinking particularly well of, to servicing and aiding in times of need, and to much more. They include the range of activities and attitudes to which we are naturally disposed to respond with gratitude.

As with anger, gratitude admits of two types, indicated by its two different prepositional objects as well as its two different action-tendencies. I may be grateful *that* the weather didn't ruin my parade or grateful *that* the cop on the side of the road was distracted as I sped by (see Card 1988: 117), without there being any agent *to whom* I'm grateful.[15] Gratitude *that* something is the case is a response to the prevention or removal of goal-frustration, a response to goal-*preservation*, as it were. It thus allows and enables one's pursuits.

Gratitude *to* others, though, like slighted-anger *at* others, is a pancultural emotion whose action-tendency is also confrontational. When you are heighted, your inclination is to address your benefactor, to express your gratitude. But as with slighted-anger, the aim of the expression isn't merely to communicate your gratitude. It seeks something more, namely, that the heighter *acknowledge how he or she made you feel in being heighted*. That is, just like slighted-anger, gratitude seeks empathic and emotional acknowledgment. Now because what you were put through in being heighted was pleasurable, delightful, or enjoyable, when the heighter takes up your invitation by taking up your perspective on the ends of

---

[13] I fully appreciate how vague this is, but all I'm doing is providing a rough gloss on the whole range of things people may count as anger-worthy actions or attitudes. These may vary wildly, given different background frameworks and cultural histories. I also want to include slights to "me and mine" that can include some of the moral or value foundations that western liberals sometimes claim to eschew, such as purity or loyalty/authority violations. I also want to include under this rubric the dashing of hopes and (mere) expectations. So it's a wide category.

[14] Fred Berger says that gratitude is a "response to the valuing of oneself presupposed in another's benevolence" (the quote is from Card 1988: 117, in a gloss on Berger 1975).

[15] It would be too jarring linguistically to say that the latter involves gratitude *at* agents, but that's technically the relevant positive prepositional counterpart to being angry *at* someone (versus being angry *that* some goal-frustrating state of affairs occurred).

yours that were served by the heighting, the heighter ought to vicariously feel what you felt at the heighting, namely, pleasure, delight, or enjoyment. This is for your heighter to feel, in a word, *gratification*.

So when you benefit me beyond what I had any right to expect, my gratitude toward you seeks gratification from you, a form of pleasurable empathic acknowledgment. What this means, though, is that gratitude to narcissists for any ostensible "heighting" (if they were ever to do such a thing) is inapt, just like it's inapt for slighting, insofar as gratitude invites an activity for which they are also impaired or downright incapacitated. While they may beam with delight at your expressions of gratitude, I'd suggest that it's merely a result of the buzz they are feeling from the (characterological) compliments they take you to be simultaneously expressing, rather than their engaging in any kind of empathic acknowledgment of your own emotional state. Why (or how) indeed should they care about how *you* felt?

This is an account of slighted-anger's positive counterpart, and so it would seem to place gratitude into the architecture of *praise*. Some deny that it belongs there. Claudia Card, for instance, explicitly insists, "Gratitude…is not praise" (Card 1988: 119). Gratitude is owed (we have a *debt* of gratitude to those who benefit us); praise isn't, as it's simply giving credit for an admirable achievement (Card 1988: 119). And in theological discussions of proper attitudes to God, the same distinction is run (typically between thanksgiving and praise): We should give thanks to God for all His gifts to us, but that's different from praising God for His wonderful qualities (see, e.g., Greggs 2017; Schneller and Swenson 2013).

But in either case, the fact (if it is a fact) that we owe gratitude but not credit to some agents is compatible with their both being kinds of praise, just with different requisites. Indeed, there is some philosophical precedent for counting gratitude as a form of praise. Kant defined gratitude as "honoring a person because of a kindness he has done us," and honoring seems clearly a form of praise (Kant 1964: 123). Dennett too used the terms gratitude and praise interchangeably (see, e.g., Dennett 1984: 554). More recently, Daniel Telech calls gratitude and approbation "the paradigmatic other-directed reactive attitudes of praise" (Telech 2021: 155), and he has developed the first fleshed-out account of moral praise which winds up providing a "confrontational" emotional address story closely akin to the one I've given.[16]

---

[16] Telech puts what gratitude seeks in the language of "invitation," although what he thinks gratitude invites is a kind of pride in the addressee, accepting credit for "reaching some laudatory standard" (Telech 2021: 164), where praiser and praised can come to co-value the action of the addressee. This seems to me to conflate gratitude with complimenting-praise, however. Reaching a laudatory standard grounds the latter, whereas the co-valuing response seems to track the former more plausibly. (Praising me for coming in first at the hot dog eating contest doesn't seem to call for our co-valuing my accomplishment.) But these are in-the-weeds disputes.

72　THE ARCHITECTURE OF BLAME AND PRAISE

There is another reason to include gratitude in the domain of praise, though, beyond its being the positive counterpart of slighted-anger:[17] It is clearly a *responsibility response*. Recall that our aim is to understand the nature of responsible agency through the variety of responses one might have to it, which are paradigmatically filed under the rubric of "blame and praise." Gratitude is explicitly a response to responsible heighting. Were you to accidentally benefit me, gratitude wouldn't be appropriate, nor would it be appropriate if you did so under some "excuse" like duress (e.g., you were coerced into benefiting me at gunpoint) or with some "justification" (e.g., your heighting me was the only way to save a child from drowning). Accidents, excuses, and justifications all get you "off the hook," as it were, for gratitude, in precisely analogous ways to how they get you off the hook for slighted-anger. It is only when you responsibly height me—whatever that means—that gratitude is the proper response.

It should also go without saying that gratitude also clearly meets the conditions of the NMT, insofar as it is the kind of agential response that contributes to norm maintenance by delivering a pleasant buzz to its target while signaling the responder's commitment to patrolling norms pertaining to heighting.

Gratitude thus surely belongs in the pantheon of responsibility responses. I will from here on out refer to it, in order to emphasize this point, as *gratitude-praise*.

Demands, Authority, Hypocrisy, and Symmetry

Pairing slighted-anger-blame with heighted-gratitude-praise is the proper way to start our architecture. Their symmetry is a function of their acknowledgment-seeking aims. But lots of blame and praise seeks no such acknowledgment. So we have to investigate those parts of the blame/praise system too. I laid out some of those elements in the previous chapter. On the negative side, there is mocking-blame, and on the positive side, there is complimenting-praise. The former stings, tending toward deflation of the self, whereas the latter soothes, tending toward inflation of the self. Both can be overdone, though, and when they are, pathologies and disorders may well be generated thereby.

Now as I noted as well in the previous chapter, the ten "asymmetries" I started with were really between slighted-anger-blame and complimenting-praise. These are indeed not symmetrical counterparts, as the former is acknowledgment-seeking and the latter isn't. But to legitimately seek acknowledgment from someone requires a special status that also explains some of the additional "asymmetries," namely, a kind of normative *authority*. As Gary Watson put it:

---

[17] A point that Scanlon, recall, explicitly admits, even though he denies that praise is the opposite of blame (and so implies directly that gratitude isn't praise). See Scanlon 2008: 151.

> To be "on the hook"…is to be liable to certain reactions as a result of failing to do what one is required. To require or demand certain behavior of an agent is to lay it down that unless the agent so behaves she will be liable to certain adverse or unwelcome treatment [called "sanctions"]. Holding accountable thus involves the idea of liability to sanctions. To be entitled to make demands, then, is to be entitled to impose conditions of liability. (Watson 2004: 275)

When a slighter disturbs the normative balance, others (especially the slighted one) now have the standing, the authority, to impose any promised "sanctions" (what I'm thinking of here only as the expression of slighted-anger, which may not sanction at all; in Chapter 9, I explicitly investigate the inclusion of sanctions in the blame/praise system). If we have the authority to impose liability to sanctions via the basic demand for good will, then we have the authority to impose sanctions once that demand has been violated.

Legitimate demands of this sort require, of course, *entitled* authority. A hijacker may demand of one hostage that he hold the others in line, but this isn't a legitimate demand, because the hijacker lacks the entitled authority to make such a demand in the first place (Watson 2004: 276).

Being a hijacker isn't the only way to lack entitled authority to issue such demands. So is being a hypocrite. If you're guilty of precisely what you're blaming me for (and you haven't engaged in any remorseful acknowledgment for it), then you are not entitled to demand that thing from me in return, to hold me accountable via slighted-anger for doing what you did. You are presuming to occupy a moral ground with respect to that action that you in fact do not occupy, so I may correctly (and angrily) ask, "Who are you to blame me?!"[18]

Less explored is the symmetrical idea of "hypocritical" (or better: non-authoritative) *gratitude*: If you are "guilty" of having heighted me far more than I've ever heighted you (and you've not yet been *gratified* for those heights), then your gratitude to me for a benefit of a similar sort to you lacks a certain authority too. "Who are you to be grateful to me?!" I might say when you, my constant and significant benefactor, express gratitude to me for some benefit, "as I haven't come close to responding properly to you for your manifold benefits to me!"

Hypocrisy can undermine both slighted-anger-blame and gratitude-praise in virtue of their acknowledgment-seeking features, which require entitlement—legitimate normative authority—to demand or invite of others. Acknowledgment of this sort is transformative, when successful, and we lack authority to demand or invite such transformation when we don't stand on the right moral ground to make it. Neither mocking-blame nor complimenting-praise admit of hypocrisy, however, and that's precisely because neither seeks acknowledgment, that is,

---

[18] I've benefited here from discussion with Julia Markovits and Kasper Lippert-Rasmussen.

neither has a demanding or inviting requisite. This fact is quite obvious in cases of complimenting-praise. Were LeBron James to stroll through a junior high basketball camp, praising the shots, passes, and moves of various kids, there'd be no hypocrisy in it at all, despite the fact that he's light years ahead of those kids in terms of talent. Anyone can compliment anyone; there are no standing or authority requirements for doing so. Being exceedingly good or bad oneself has no effect whatsoever on the aptness of one's complimenting-praise of others.

So too can anyone aptly mock anyone else, although here I can imagine some pushback. It might be thought, for example, that there could be hypocritical mockery. Perhaps I who am a total klutz make fun of you for tripping over a bump on sidewalk. "Who are you to mock me?!" you might exclaim, continuing "You trip all the time!" This is nothing more than a rhetorical attempt to dull my mockery's sting, though, which, recall, simply aims to publicly highlight some failure of yours in an amusing way. But *anyone* can draw attention to failures in an amusing way, even if they themselves have failed in precisely the same way. That I-the-klutz mock you may make you mad or frustrated, but that's because it's even *more* embarrassing when klutzes like me mock you for your own klutziness! The aptness of mockery-blame isn't about demands or invitations—it seeks nothing from its target—so it doesn't require anyone's special normative authority to dish it out.

Furthermore, slighted-anger-blame is asymmetrical with complimenting-praise insofar as the former is aptly satisfied by a particular sort of empathic response, namely, the emotional acknowledgment it seeks, whereas empathy is irrelevant to the latter's aptness or anyone's response to it. Complimenting-praise doesn't seek empathic emotional acknowledgment from its recipient. And once we include mockery as the negative counterpart of complimenting-praise, their symmetry on this front becomes clear as well, insofar as mockery-blame seeks no such empathic or emotional response from the mocked either.

The ground-level reason that there are two general forms of blame/praise—acknowledgment-seeking and non-acknowledgment-seeking—is that one form is primarily about holding others to account for their failures or successes relative *to us*, whereas the other form is primarily about ways of holding others to account for their failures or successes relative *to various standards* (typically of performance or skill). Normative authority and acknowledgment-seeking are appropriate only for the former, as that's the domain defined by how we view and treat *each other*, the domain of *quality of will*. I'll defend this idea more fully in Chapter 7.

I have been pushing for a clear distinction between {slighted-angry-blame/gratitude-praise}, on the one hand, and {mocking-blame/complimenting-praise} on the other. But I also want to insist that they are all part of the very same system, the blame/praise system. How so? What unifies them as such? They all have the characteristic features of the NMT, contributing to norm maintenance by delivering certain sorts of feelings (stings/buzzes) to their targets in ways that typically signal their own commitment to, and willingness to patrol, various sets of norms. The ways in which those feelings may be caused and their signals broadcast are multiple—sometimes they are expressed in acknowledgment-seeking ways and sometimes not—and so the competence costs for knowing which types to express in which circumstances are high. But each individual type of blame/praise has symmetrical counterparts, and all of the types together share in the unified function of the system.

Other Emotions

Acknowledgment-seeking blame or praise is quite often emotional, consisting paradigmatically in anger or gratitude. Mockery-blame and complimenting-praise aren't typically emotional: "Nice job!" can be said sarcastically or sincerely, but neither needs to be emotionally infused. Yet there are many other emotions to be found in the blame/praise system. These include admiration, disdain, pride, contempt, and disappointment.[19] What kinds of blame or praise are these, and where should we locate them in the overall system?[20]

None of these are acknowledgment-seeking emotions. We can admire, disdain, or contemn from afar, with no responses sought from the admirable, disdainful, or contemptible people to whom we're responding. So too we may swell up with pride at the accomplishments of our kids and friends, or be riddled with disappointment at their lack of accomplishment, without seeking any response from them either. Unlike slighted-anger-blame and gratitude-praise, these emotions may all be fully and successfully discharged without any response from their targets. They are simply appraisals of some qualities of their targets, period.

They thus need to be placed into the non-acknowledgment-seeking camp of blame/praise responses, alongside mockery-blame and complimenting-praise. But there's a distinction that needs making within this camp as well. While mockery and compliments don't seek any response from their targets, they *do* want expression. One cannot, I've claimed, mock or praise privately. While one doesn't have to mock or compliment the mockable or complimentable people to their faces (one can do so quietly just to one's friends, say), one does at least have to express it for it to count as such. But admiration, disdain, pride, contempt, and disappointment need no expression to count as what they are. We can and often do merely admire, disdain, contemn, and feel pride or disappointment privately, and with no urge whatsoever to express it to anyone. Nevertheless, these all seem to be forms of (private) blame and praise.

---

[19] What about sadness or joy? These may be taken by some targets to be instances of, respectively, blame or praise, but as emotions they may be triggered by much too wide a range of qualities (both agential and non-agential) to fall cleanly under our rubric. Rather, I think an emotion like sadness, say, is better described as *accompanying* (some forms of) blame rather than as counting as an instance of it.

[20] I'm thinking here mostly still in terms of *other*-directed blame/praise emotions, so I've deliberately left off the list emotions like shame, regret, and guilt. I deal with these explicitly in Chapter 8, which is about self-blame and -praise, as they raise special problems.

76 THE ARCHITECTURE OF BLAME AND PRAISE

But how can private emotions like these count as members of the blame/praise system if, as I've argued, those members contribute to norm maintenance by delivering stings/buzzes and signaling one's commitment to norm patrol? How could privately felt admiration or disdain, say, contribute to the blame/praise system's function?

Thus far I have focused solely on forms of blame or praise that typically aim to maintain norm adherence or excellence in *others*, so, for example, my slighted-anger of you typically serves to sting you back onto the right normative path, while simultaneously signaling to you and others that I'm committed to patrolling the norms in question. But there are also forms of blame/praise that serve to regulate our *own* behavior, buttressing or altering (for the better) the strength of our own normative commitments. And that's what these non-expressive emotions (mostly) do. So when I see you working at a homeless shelter one beautiful Saturday afternoon, I may admire you. And while admiration of others doesn't necessarily urge any expression, it gives me a feeling of *elevation*, and it urges *emulation* (Haidt 2003; Algoe and Haidt 2009). Your action is inspiring and generates a buzz within me (indeed, it warrants complimenting-praise, for sure). *I should be more like you*, I think, and so may sign up to do the same, or at least donate money to that shelter when I get home. These are the activities that signal (albeit more subtly) my commitment to normative betterment, that there are norms of excellence toward which I myself want to strive.

Contempt and disdain work in an analogous way. They feel ugly, aversive, and so they urge me *away* from contemptible or disdainful behavior, and in striving to avoid being such poor agents myself, I also signal my normative commitments: away from the disdainful and toward the admirable. Doing so buttresses that commitment.

Pride and disappointment can operate in similar ways. When self-directed, the buzz of pride serves to keep us on some excellent normative path, and the sting of disappointment urges me away from the disappointing path. These emotions also emit signals, in our facial expressions, body language, and the actions they motivate. And even when other-directed, these emotions can play these roles, as the signals of our pride in others can deliver buzzes, and the signals of our disappointment in them can deliver stings. We are also attracted to the prideworthy and averse to the disappointing, so our expressions and activities in response to these (private) emotional appraisals can emit the relevant signals as well.[21]

Conclusion

We now have in place a significant portion of the architecture of the blame/praise system. There are, first, acknowledgment-seeking and non-acknowledgment-seeking

---

[21] And of course recall one of the points made in the discussion of functions in Chapter 2: it's consistent with NMR that some tokens of blame/praise may not actually signal anything or deliver any stings/buzzes at all, either through dysfunction or being actively squelched.

EMOTIONS 77

Table 5.1 The partial architecture of blame and praise*

	Blame	Praise
Acknowledgment-Seeking *(whose paradigmatic forms are symmetrical with each other)*	Paradigmatic Emotional Form: *Slighted-Anger*	Paradigmatic Emotional Form: *Gratitude*
Non-Acknowledgment-Seeking *(whose paradigmatic forms are symmetrical with each other)*	Paradigmatic **Expressive** Form: Mockery Paradigmatic **Non-Expressive** Emotional Forms: *Disdain, Contempt, Disappointment*	Paradigmatic **Expressive** Form: Complimenting Paradigmatic **Non-Expressive** Emotional Forms: *Admiration, Pride*

* To be filled in by the end of Part Two: non-emotional forms and expressions of blame/praise (including sanctions and rewards), self-directed forms, and general normative underpinnings, where illuminating.

types of each. The former consists paradigmatically in the slighted-anger/gratitude pair. The latter admits of two types as well: expressive and non-expressive. Expressive types are mockery and compliments. The non-expressive types, in their emotional guises, include admiration, contempt, disdain, pride, and disappointment. This last group needs neither expression to, nor response from, their targets.[22] All of these members of the blame/praise system are united, however, in being (characteristically) signaling and sting/buzz-delivering contributions to norm maintenance. Sometimes the targets of our norm patrols are other people; sometimes they are ourselves.

We've now come to the conclusion of the descriptive part of the project, which yields the partially completed architectural design of the blame/praise system seen in Table 5.1. The full design will be completed by the end of the book.

But so what? That we can categorize blame and praise in ways that dissolve our original asymmetries is an accomplishment, of sorts, as this seemed quite a stretch at the beginning. But our ultimate aim is to learn something about responsible agency thereby, and that's a normative enterprise. The fact that we respond in such a wide (but ultimately symmetrical) variety of ways to other agents is one thing; whether it's *appropriate* for us to do so is another. It's thus time to turn to that normative project.

The Architecture of Blame and Praise: An Interdisciplinary Investigation. David Shoemaker, Oxford University Press.
© David Shoemaker 2024. DOI: 10.1093/9780198915867.003.0005

---

[22] While people may of course—and often do—express their admiration or contempt for people to their faces, all I'm saying by calling these "non-expressive" emotions is that expression (to anyone) isn't a necessary part of their motivational profile (i.e., it's not an action-readiness or goal).

PART TWO
NORMATIVITY

6

Grounds

The first part of the book was about blame and praise, what they are and what they are for. The second part is about blame*worthiness* and praise*worthiness*. It is this second topic that has most interested philosophers, especially those who study it with the metaphysics of free will ready to hand. It is a normative topic, of course, not about what blame is but about what renders it apt.[1]

As we saw detailed in the first part of the book, there are actually many different types of blame and praise. And it is fairly obvious, I think, that this pluralism carries over to their aptness conditions. My slighted-anger of you can be apt for something (e.g., an assault) for which my mockery-blame of you may not, and vice versa (e.g., a chess blunder). Analogously, gratitude for a benefit may be apt for something (rescuing me from a burning building) for which complimenting-praise is not, and vice versa (a chess success). Further, contempt but not disappointment may be apt for some things (cruelty to animals), and pride but not admiration may be apt for some things (a mud wrestling victory). What the pluralism of Part One reveals is that there really isn't such a thing as blameworthiness or praiseworthiness, *full stop*. Rather, the question of the worthiness of blame and praise—their aptness conditions—must be asked and answered with respect to each of their individual types.

And this is what I aim to do. There are several important questions to discuss: What renders particular types of blame or praise apt? Within those types, what renders particular tokens apt? Blame characteristically stings its target, I've urged, so don't we need some moral justification for engaging in it? If so, what is it? Does praise need any moral justification? If so, what is it? What, if anything, justifies a *system* of blame and praise? Indeed, could there be good reason to revise or even eliminate it altogether?

These are all good and difficult questions, and I hope to have addressed them all by the end of the book. I begin, though, by getting clear on which direction we should look to find our normative answers.

---

[1] Once again, I'm going to use the term "apt" in order to remain neutral for now between various possible normative grounding terms, including "fitting," "warranted," "justified," "fair," "just," and "deserved." As we go, I'll narrow in on the ones that I think are relevant.

82 THE ARCHITECTURE OF BLAME AND PRAISE

Backward- vs. Forward-Looking Justifications

There is a vigorous contemporary debate over whether holding people responsible is (or ought to be) rendered apt most fundamentally by appeal to backward-looking or to forward-looking considerations, that is, whether the proper normative grounds for blame or praise are to be found, at bottom, in what the agent did or in the future effects that might be generated by deploying them. On the former approach, if you stole the cookies in the cookie jar, then my blaming you is rendered apt wholly and exclusively by the fact *that you stole the cookies.* Fundamentally forward-looking theories, in their purest form, have been simple act-utilitarian theories, justifying praise or blame entirely in virtue of the utility it will generate (see, e.g., Smart 1970). Of course, this "pure" version is seriously problematic, as it could in theory require us to blame innocent people were doing so to have net positive effects (this is known as the *scapegoating objection*). More sophisticated versions of forward-looking views, then, say that the most fundamental grounding of blame consists in its success at getting blamed people to change their ways, or to increase the intelligence of their capacities, or to learn to recognize and respond to reasons they'd previously overlooked or ignored, while nonetheless requiring accurate attributability of blamed/praised actions to their agents as essential to achieving these effects.[2]

The most plausible theories of blame, of course, are likely to include both forward- and backward-looking elements, but they typically do hold that one or the other direction is more important or fundamental for determining the aptness of blame. For example, many backward-looking theorists will allow that blame typically has *some* forward-looking features—e.g., the blamed agent should, many think, come to acknowledge and repent her wrongdoing—but that is not what fundamentally renders it apt, as the blame could still be apt entirely in virtue of what the wrongdoer did, regardless of whether it achieved that forward-looking aim in any individual case. Similarly, a forward-looking theorist will likely want to target blame exclusively to those who actually committed the blamed wrongs (so as to avoid scapegoating worries), but only given the fact (so they think) that blaming innocents would moot the positive forward-looking effects that actually justify blame in the first place.

I am not going to take a stand on which direction is the right one. I believe, minimally, that most of our blame and praise responses are in fact not forward-looking, that they are fundamentally rendered apt by facts about what agents did or what attitudes they had.[3] But I also don't want to rule out the possibility that

---

[2] See, in various incarnations, Calhoun 1989; McGeer 2019; Pereboom 2021a: ch. 2 and 2022; Williams 1995. Vargas 2013 offers a forward-looking theory of responsibility too, but at the higher level of *system* justification.

[3] Some of our responses, like contempt and admiration, may properly target simply how agents are currently constituted, not how they came to be that way. But these facts too, if not strictly backward-looking, are also definitely not forward-looking.

some of our agential blame/praise responses are (or ought to be) rendered apt wholly and exclusively by forward-looking considerations. It may be that my child's drawing is objectively terrible, but because I want to encourage her to keep nurturing her artistic side, my "Good job!" in response to her dreadful drawing counts as apt praise thereby. It may also be that my angry reproach of an utterly clueless and ·faultless sexist—someone raised in a sexist environment without having been provided access to any non-sexist reasons—is rendered apt entirely in virtue of the fact that it may cause him to come to have access to the right reasons to refrain from his sexism in the future (see, e.g., Calhoun 1989). So I'm going to remain officially agnostic here and allow for the possible pertinence of both directions of apt-makers.

However, forward-looking apt-makers aren't of much interest to the metaphysics-minded.[4] To the extent that blame/praise is most fundamentally rendered apt by appeal to good future effects, say, then it doesn't really matter whether the targeted agents had some sort of robust free will when they did what they did. All that matters is whether the blame/praise can achieve those good effects. True, this may sometimes require that agents have certain capacities, typically those enabling them to adjust their future behavior in light of blame's sting or praise's buzz, but hardly anyone doubts that those abilities are perfectly compatible with—and some think they actually require—determinism (see, e.g., Stace 1952).

It is only with regard to backward-looking blame/praise apt-makers that there arise such metaphysical worries, the classic concerns driving investigation into free will lo these many years. Insofar, then, as my primary aim in Part Two is to drive away those worries, I will simply assume in what follows that what would be necessary to render apt the blame/praise attitudes and practices that I will discuss are, indeed, facts about the past (or at least not facts about future effects). What they seek are normative grounds drawn fundamentally from facts about what their targeted agents did or the attitudes they had.

Fittingness ... and Something More?

There are several respects in which many of our blame/praise emotions are just like all of our other "basic" or "natural" emotions. They have an affective feel, they have recognizable action-tendencies and aims, and, importantly, they include *appraisals*.[5] In blame and praise, such emotions appraise actions and attitudes.

---

[4] I should stress that they are of interest to some philosophers who are metaphysics-minded, but these are skeptics and revisionists who make the case for exclusively forward-looking justifications of some of our attitudes and practices as replacements for their metaphysically implausible backward-looking justifications (e.g., Pereboom 2022).

[5] On emotions as, or as closely associated with, appraisals, there is a vast literature. See, among many others, Lazarus 1991; Frijda 1993; Roseman and Smith 2001; Scarantino 2014; Tappolet 2016; D'Arms and Jacobson 2023.

84   THE ARCHITECTURE OF BLAME AND PRAISE

Consider slighted-anger. As I urged in the previous chapter, when you disrespect me, my slighted-anger appraises what you did as a slight. Appraisals generally are rendered apt simply as a function of their being *correct* or *accurate*. The aptness of my slighted-anger is, then, at the very least, a matter of its correctness. If you slighted me, my anger's appraisal is correct; if you didn't, it's not. Correctness of appraisal, then, obviously has nothing whatsoever to do with any positive effects that that appraisal might have; indeed, reasons that appeal to such effects are called "wrong kinds of reasons." And if an emotional appraisal is correct, it is what's known in the literature as *fitting*.[6]

My focus in the last chapter was primarily on anger and gratitude. Nearly everyone believes that at least part of what makes these emotions apt is their fit with (their correct or accurate appraisal of) their evaluative objects. I believe something much stronger, however, namely, that these emotions' aptness-makers are *entirely and exclusively* a function of their fit. To vindicate this more controversial belief, I will need to defend it against those who think that there is something in addition to fittingness necessary to render these emotional responses fully apt, namely, whether or not they are *deserved*. Desert too is of course backward-looking: agents could deserve such responses only in virtue of what they've done. But desert ostensibly provides a crucial moral justification, something mere fittingness does not do. And desert seems to require the robust metaphysical conditions or capacities associated with free will, in a way that fittingness does not. There are thus significant differences here that warrant careful and detailed exploration.

I start with a quick little argument that might be taken to put the burden of proof on those thinking blame/praise emotions require desert. Suppose you slight me and I respond with slighted-anger. My anger fits your slight. Slighted-anger is, in this respect, just like other familiar natural emotions. Fear fits danger. Grief fits great losses (the grievous). Amusement fits the funny (the amusing). And in each case, the fittingness generates a *reason*, of the *pro tanto* variety. If you're faced with danger, you have a *pro tanto* reason of fit to feel (that is, to appraise it with) fear. If your partner dies, you have a reason of fit to feel grief. If you hear a funny joke or wisecrack, you have a reason of fit to feel amusement. So too, if you slight me, I have a *pro tanto* reason of fit to be slighted-angry at you. And so it goes for the remainder of our blame/praise emotions: gratitude-praise fits heights, disdain fits the disdainable, admiration fits the admirable, regret fits the regrettable, and contempt fits the contemptible.

---

[6] There is now a pretty big literature on fittingness, especially as it pertains to value and reasons, where there is lots of disagreement. Where there is not much disagreement, though, is with respect to the gloss I just gave, that fittingness, at least as it pertains to emotions, is essentially just about correct or accurate appraisal. For all sorts of excellent discussions on this topic, see D'Arms and Jacobson 2023 and the essays in Howard and Rowland 2022.

Now when it comes to fear, grief, and amusement, we don't ask for any normative grounds for feeling them other than fit. But when it comes to blaming emotions, and to our blame responses more generally, many theorists have indeed thought we need something more. There are two significant reasons.

First, while the story of fitting appraisal I've just told may in fact provide some normative grounding for many of our blame/praise *emotions*, perhaps even all of them, it's just not the case that all of our blame/praise *responses* are simple emotions, and so it's unclear how my story about fittingness might generalize to them. Sometimes, for instance, our blame sanctions people, and it may do so dispassionately. (Rewards can be doled out in emotionless fashion as well.) Further, we often *express* our anger to each other, but it's unclear how the fittingness story applies to expressions of emotions. Indeed, it's unclear whether such expressions and treatments are properly construed as *appraisals*, so it's unclear whether fittingness even applies to them. Perhaps sanctions are like traffic camera fines, triggered simply by norm violations, without any evaluative appraisal attached, and so without any standards of accuracy in appraisal being implicated.[7] And punishment and reward may be better construed as *responses* to appraisals, not necessarily as appraisals themselves. But then if there are non-emotional or non-appraising forms of blame/praise like these, and fittingness fits (only?) appraisals, then these forms of blame/praise don't seem like they could be grounded by appeal to fittingness alone.

I'm sympathetic with this first concern. It's a matter of contention whether fittingness is applicable to non-emotional or non-appraising responses.[8] For my part, I think that fittingness does apply to non-emotional appraisals but doesn't apply to non-appraisals. I will eventually illustrate this view. For now, though, I will set this first concern aside to focus on a second concern, one which is much more sweeping and urgent anyway: Regardless of how many sorts of (backward-looking) blame/praise responses to which it might apply, fittingness is, it has seemed to most, insufficient to provide the full and necessary normative grounding for *any* of them.

The source of this concern comes from a data point which is cited as the primary motivation for the longstanding metaphysical investigation into free will: Blame *harms*. It may do so in several ways. First, it can just plain hurt: Being the target of anger or guilting is often emotionally painful. Blame may also alienate people from each other, severing interpersonal connections. It may demand answers, which can be burdensome to provide. It can generate the withdrawal of trust, or friendly feelings generally. It may generate shame. It can challenge one's social and moral standing, and so deny one of a voice in important interpersonal

---

[7] I explore this possibility, favorably, in Chapter 9.

[8] Again, see the many excellent essays in Howard and Rowland 2022 for state-of-the-art discussion of the fine points of fittingness.

86 THE ARCHITECTURE OF BLAME AND PRAISE

affairs.[9] These are all genuine and occasionally very serious setbacks to people's interests.

Inflicting harms on people requires moral justification. Fear, grief, and amusement don't, so they don't. That, in a nutshell, is the crucial difference between our blame emotions and these other natural emotions. Consequently, if we want to preserve them, then we need a moral justification for them. Moral grounding is different, and much deeper, than fittingness. What might it consist in?

The most familiar appeals are to *fairness* or *justice*, where these are moral values promoted or respected sufficiently only by *desert*.[10] The primary intuitive nudge in this direction comes from considering what's wrong with the scapegoating sometimes associated with pure forward-looking accounts of blame, that is, why is it immoral to blame the innocent? The answer is that doing so is either unfair or unjust. Hanging the innocent man in the classic "Sheriff in a Small Town" counterexample to act utilitarianism is an obvious injustice.[11] Blaming your son for what your daughter did is unfair. And for most theorists working in this zone, the injustice and unfairness are derived, at least in part, precisely from the lack of desert in each case. As Randolph Clarke asserts, "[T]o blame the innocent is to do them an injustice. The injustice...consists in the fact that they do not deserve blame. To lack this injustice, blame must be deserved" (Clarke 2023: 4). Desert is a necessary condition for the justice (or fairness, as some say) of blame, and blame has to be just or fair in order to morally justify its harms.

This is blame presupposing what many, following Pereboom (2001, 2014, 2021a), refer to as *basic desert*, which would provide a moral justification for blaming an agent for some action solely in virtue of the fact that the agent voluntarily and without excuse "performed the [wrongful] action, given an understanding of its moral status, and not, for example, merely by virtue of consequentialist or contractualist considerations" (Pereboom 2014: 127). Such a reason itself may be thought to have its source in either axiological or deontological considerations, but I won't worry about these in-the-weeds issues here (for discussion in the weeds, see McKenna 2012: ch. 6; McCormick 2023). What matters for my purposes is that, for an agent to basically deserve blame, it is nearly universally thought that that agent must have *free will*, itself thought to consist in the possession and proper exercise of certain (typically rather robust) metaphysical capacities, for example, the ability to do otherwise or the ability to be the

---

[9] See Bennett 2002: 148–51; and McKenna 2012: 134–41 and 158 for discussion of some of these costs.

[10] Lots of people to cite here, but the main players are Clarke 2013, 2016; Clarke and Rawling 2022; Macnamara 2020; McKenna 2012: chs. 6–7 and 2022; McCormick 2023; Nelkin 2013, 2014, 2016, and 2019a; Pereboom 2014 and 2021a.

[11] For the original objection, see McCloskey 1957.

GROUNDS 87

ultimate source of one's actions.[12] And it has been over the nature of these capacities, and whether their exercise can be squared with either determinism or indeterminism, that philosophers and theologians have been engaged in a never-ending metaphysical tussle for at least the past two thousand years. To undercut the motivation for this tussle, I will identify all of the general types of blame that various people at various times have insisted cry out for moral justification of the sort provided by desert. Then I will systematically investigate each type to see (a) whether moral justification of any kind is actually needed for that type of blame, and (b) if so, whether the moral justification is of the desert-providing kind. While the answers to (a) will occasionally be "yes," the answer to (b) will always be "no."

Types of "Harmful" Blame

The first category in which blame is thought by some to generate harms requiring moral justification via desert is purely attitudinal blame. The leading candidate here is, of course, *anger*. This is the emotional core of both resentment and indignation. I may be slighted-angry at you for some injury but not express it to you (or anyone). You may never even find out that I held that attitude. In such cases, I'm not actively causing you any *pain*. Nevertheless, some theorists think, this sort of blame can still harm, perhaps in the way that privately held racist or sexist attitudes can harm the targets of those attitudes, even if those targets never find out. If so, that could make purely attitudinal blame unjust or unfair if undeserved.

Second, now that I've included mockery in the pantheon of blame, it needs to be included in our investigation, for the obvious reason that it *stings* (or at least aims to do so). Consequently, it would seem to cry out for moral justification, a justification that also seems to implicate desert. Indeed, wouldn't mockery of someone be unjust if undeserved?

Third, some *expressions* of anger (or other blaming emotions, like contempt or even disappointment) require moral justification, as they too can hurt. No one (except the perverse) likes to be yelled at, guilted, disdained, or be the object of their mom's disappointment, say. I ought not inflict these unliked states upon you without moral justification, it might well be thought, of a kind presupposing desert.

Finally, there's the most familiar form of morally worrisome blame, namely, sanctions, or what many think of as punishment, which explicitly and deliberately

---

[12] And this is precisely why skeptics like Pereboom, who introduced the notion of basic desert, are skeptics, as they don't believe humans ever meet the robust conditions required for the kind of free will ostensibly grounding basic desert. See Pereboom 2014 for the most extended defense of this idea. See also Caruso 2016 and 2021, as well as Dennett and Caruso 2021.

88   THE ARCHITECTURE OF BLAME AND PRAISE

aims at hurt, suffering, or setbacks in its target. This is the form of blaming treatment that has most enduringly motivated the metaphysical search for desert-capacities ostensibly found in the possibility of robust free will. One cannot, it is thought, be justly punished (retributively) if one doesn't deserve it, and one doesn't deserve it if one couldn't have done otherwise, say, or if one weren't the ultimate source or sole author of one's actions (see, e.g., Campbell 1957; Strawson 1994).

In the remainder of this chapter, I will explore the first two categories, and I will reject the notion that any moral justification, let alone desert, is needed for their normative grounding. Rather, fitness does all of the requisite normative work. I won't get to the final two categories until Chapter 9, as I'll need to do some preparatory work in the two intermediary chapters.

If the Blame Fits...

Start with purely attitudinal blame. Suppose you have wronged me and I'm angry with you in response, but I never reveal my anger in any way, and you never find out about it. There are no downstream effects, no change to our relationship. Internally, I angrily "shake my head," but then we just go on. I blame you, it seems clear, albeit totally privately. Could this purely attitudinal state require a moral justification ultimately grounded in desert?

The position that I will take as my default starting point—in which the answer is "no"—has two parts. The first has its source in a suggestion floated by Joel Feinberg in his groundbreaking discussion of desert: "[P]ersonal desert...is...to be likened to, or even identified with, a kind of 'fittingness' between one person's actions or qualities and another person's responsive attitudes" (Feinberg 1970: 82). The view I have urged in previous work is the stronger of Feinberg's two formulations, that talk of "desert" is just to be *identified* with (or reduced to) talk of "fittingness" (Shoemaker 2015: 221–3). That is where I will start here too. The second part of my default view draws from a conceptual commitment that I think many people share (even if many philosophers don't), which is that moral concerns about justice or fairness apply only to our *treatments* of other people, not to any of our mere attitudes about them as such.[13] Insofar as purely attitudinal blame doesn't treat anyone in any way, concerns about justice or fairness—and thus a

---

[13] I'm well aware of the burgeoning epistemology literature about morality's alleged encroachment on beliefs and other attitudes. While not explicitly about our *blaming* attitudes toward others, these arguments could be relevant to our discussion, so I'll deal with them later in the text, as well as in Chapter 7. I think my statement here is still true, though, that many *people*, if not philosophers, hold that you don't violate demands of justice (e.g., what we owe to each other) with mere attitudes, i.e., morality has no jurisdiction over one's mind (see Sher 2021 for explicit defense of this view).

non-derivative form of desert extending beyond fit—are inapplicable to it.[14] It is only *expressed* anger, contempt, or disdain to which justice or fairness might apply. Merely evaluating someone incorrectly alone is surely not a matter of injustice or unfairness, it seems, so purely attitudinal blame requires no desert-beyond-fit (see also Brink and Nelkin 2022 for a view like this).

This is, I think, a fairly natural and plausible default position. Can we be moved off of it?

Initial pushback comes from those who do indeed think that the moral language of injustice or unfairness (and so desert) can apply to mere emotional blaming responses. Perhaps I admit to my therapist, "I've been so mad at my father for all these years, but I've finally realized, given his own emotionally cloistered upbringing, just how unfair that is: he doesn't deserve my anger." Or perhaps I tell you that I have contempt for what I thought was a shared friend's callousness to someone, and you quietly note to me that that's unjust—undeserved—because she's been undergoing stress and depression over her beloved partner's recent death.

But both of these are pleas for *excuse*, and both can be reduced entirely to the language of fit without remainder. In other words, in both cases, to say that these are "undeserved" responses is to say nothing more than that their appraisals are actually *incorrect*: my father didn't really slight me after all, as he was just doing his emotional best in the only way he knew how; and the "callousness" I thought I saw in our shared friend was really just emotional husbanding, as a coping maneuver, rather than anything blameworthy. To say that these responses are "unfair" or "unjust" would be no more than a rhetorically dramatic way of pointing out their inaccuracy.

And yet isn't there *something* unjust or undeserved in privately blaming someone when that appraisal is inaccurate (unfitting), something more than the inaccuracy itself? Suppose that, in each of the above cases, where the targets had clear and compelling excuses, one continued to angrily blame them regardless: "Yeah, my dad isn't to blame, I can now see that, but I still resent him," or "Yes, I see that she was grieving and wasn't really being callous, but I'm still angry at her nevertheless." Is there anything more to these attitudinal blaming appraisals, though, beyond mere *recalcitrance*, a kind of irrational hangover of an emotion in the face of judgments contrary to the emotion's appraisal?[15] Is there really anything unjust or undeserved thereby?

---

[14] Feinberg, in the same passage, says that on the desert-as-fittingness view, "modes of treatment" expressing fitting attitudinal appraisals would be deserved, then, "only in a derivative way, perhaps as a "natural or conventional means of expressing the morally fitting attitudes" (Feinberg 1970: 82). For discussion, see McKenna 2022.

[15] For detailed discussion of emotional recalcitrance, see D'Arms and Jacobson 2003, as well as 2023: 67–8, 92–3, and 107–8.

90 THE ARCHITECTURE OF BLAME AND PRAISE

As I've noted, it's certainly not the case for any other of our natural emotional appraisals that they implicate justice or desert. Continuing to grieve a close friend's death, even after you find out they are still alive, while irrational, is neither immoral nor undeserved. Continuing to be amused by a string of words you thought were funny but that were actually a threat is irrational but not immoral or undeserved. And the same is true of continuing to fear what you thought was a threat but that was merely a joke. So why think there's anything different about continuing to angrily blame someone who's innocent?

Articulating that difference has in fact been the aim of some recent philosophical work. So, for example, in drawing on some ideas in Feinberg, Randolph Clarke says, "We generally dislike being blamed when we are aware of it, and blame of which one remains unaware [as in purely attitudinal blame] is still the kind of attitude that we generally dislike being the object of" (Clarke 2023). T. M. Scanlon (2018: 121) has noted that we have reason to care how others regard us, even if we're never aware of it. And Rima Basu explicitly remarks that "we care not only how people act towards us and what they say about us, but also the attitudes they hold of us" (Basu 2019a: 2504). Perhaps, then, unfitting anger is to be differentiated from other unfitting emotional appraisals in virtue of the fact that the former contravenes our cares about how we would like people to think about us, and it's in the contravening of these cares where we locate its harm and immorality. Private slighted-anger, then, can be unjust if not deserved. There is thus more to the aptness of blaming attitudes than mere fit.

I disagree. The fact that I care about how others regard me, in and of itself, generates no normative constraint on whether and how they do so, in any context. It surely doesn't matter with respect to justice or fairness, for example, if people have incorrect attitudes about my factual properties even if I really care that they not believe incorrect things about me. For example, there's no injustice if people believe that I'm an inch taller than I actually am, even if I care a lot that they don't believe it.

And when it comes to more evaluative matters, what I care about being lodged in other people's heads can vary wildly from how I actually am (and so vary from what they're epistemically justified in believing about me). For instance, it may matter to me greatly that people regard me *poorly* in various skill domains, perhaps so that they will underestimate me. It may matter a great deal to me that my poker opponents think I'm a poker newbie, a "fish." Suppose, though, that they see through me and regard me instead as the skillful poker player that I am. The fact that I care otherwise is neither here nor there with respect to what they ought to believe, and so they certainly don't wrong me, in terms of justice or fairness, by their *accurate* appraisal of me.

Still, I admit that how others appraise us can be *hurtful*. Perhaps I overhear you, my friend, whispering to someone else that you find my paintings to be very amateurish. Or perhaps I stumble across your diary, in which you've revealed the fact that, despite how hard you've tried, you continue to be suspicious of Jews, and I am Jewish. This discovery could well be hurtful, even if you've always treated me with the utmost respect, and even if the hurt isn't a response to having been misled about your actual attitudes. Indeed, there's often something quite hurtful when we do find out how poorly some people actually think of us, so that even were it to remain totally private, the hurt*fulness* of someone's private blaming attitude toward us might still obtain, when unfitting, in a way that may seem to cry out for moral justification provided by desert.

The best description of what we're experiencing in such circumstances is, I think, *hurt feelings*. It would indeed be hurtful for a daughter to find out that her father thought she stole money from the family store (to use an example from Basu 2023a), when she didn't, and even if he treated her no differently. And it would hurt my feelings if I've been sober for several months, but you, my partner, immediately suspect I've been drinking again when you smell alcohol on my clothes, even though the truth of the matter is that someone spilled it on me at a party (the example is from Basu and Schroeder 2019).

If this is right, though, what renders hurt feelings themselves fitting is entirely untethered to immorality or desert.[16] The hurt of hurt feelings may aptly obtain *regardless of the accuracy of the evaluation that sparks it.* That's because hurt feelings aptly respond instead simply to a mismatch between what the hurt person cares about or hopes someone will think of her and what that person actually thinks of her, where what that person thinks is worse than what was cared about or hoped for (see Shoemaker 2019b: 140).

Suppose, for example, that I care a lot that you, a fellow philosopher, think well of me as a philosopher. Perhaps, though, I really am a philosophical idiot (this is not beyond the realm of possibility), and you accurately believe this of me after seeing several lame talks and reading several terrible papers. Were I to find this out, my feelings would be hurt, despite the accuracy of your evaluation. Hard truths hurt feelings.

But then desert-beyond-fit is unnecessary when it comes to believing justified and accurate truths about people, even if doing so is or would be hurtful.[17] And if desert is unnecessary for accurate appraisals that are hurtful in this way (in virtue

---

[16] This is the mistake, I think, at the heart of the popular moral encroachment enterprise: It aims to infer *wronging* and *blameworthiness* from the aptness of hurt feelings (and apologies), which actually entails neither. I say much more in critique of this enterprise in Chapter 7.

[17] There are qualifications worth making here. It may be that, as your very close friend or lover, I owe you the benefit of the doubt on many things, that I should be *slower*, perhaps, to believe bad things about you than others based on the same evidence (this goes to the alcoholic case of Basu and Schroeder 2019). This principle between those in close relationships surely only applies, though, when the evidence isn't yet decisive. But when the evidence is overwhelming, there's no more benefit in doubt. Suppose, for instance, that my partner has worked very hard at his sobriety for several years, but then he starts to come home a little wobbly on a regular basis. Perhaps my benefit of the doubt should extend a bit here, but after a while, the evidence renders continued benefit-of-the-doubt self-deception, which benefits no one.

92 THE ARCHITECTURE OF BLAME AND PRAISE

of the mismatch between the hoped-for and the actual), then I can't see why it would be necessary for *inaccurate* appraisals that are hurtful *in virtue of that mismatch as well*. Were I to angrily (but privately) blame you for something that you didn't do, even though I know you didn't do it, and my slighted-anger isn't merely recalcitrant, this could be hurtful, that is, it would aptly hurt were you to find out. But the aptness of your hurt would still be exclusively in virtue of the *mismatch* between your care that I regard you in a certain way (that I would appraise you as innocent, in this case) and how I actually regard you (as anger-worthy). And because the source of the hurtfulness is found in that mismatch, and not in your attitudes about me per se, there's no injustice or need for desert in play.

This point is brought out even more explicitly when we consider cases in which I care that you appraise me *incorrectly*. Perhaps I always feel guilty (because we're all sinners?), for everything I do, and it's important to me that you have slighted-anger toward me as well. But you refuse, as I am innocent (so you say). In this case, the fact that you appraise me correctly may be hurtful.

Some may still think it anger-worthy for someone—a close friend, say—to have resented me incorrectly for several years.[18] It *might* be, I admit, but we need to know more details of the case. If it turns out that he was *justified* in thinking me guilty, perhaps having been shown doctored surveillance footage, then my slighted-anger at him won't be apt, as he's not at fault. If, however, he'd simply taken the word of someone he shouldn't have, or he'd gotten himself to resent me out of jealousy or spite, then these are indeed anger-worthy attitudes, but they are so only in virtue of his *poor quality of will*, his motivating failure to take me and my interests sufficiently seriously (more on this point in the next chapter). His mistaken resentment *as such* isn't what's anger-worthy, then. This is just like if I resent you for maliciously causing me an injury, it's not the injury as such that I aptly resent you for, as you could have done it by accident; it's the malice that matters. My slighted-anger now fits his slight, not because I didn't deserve his private resentment all these years, but simply because his ill-willed resentment slighted me, period. He could also blame me *correctly* with ill will, as in a case of *schadenfreude*. In that case, my slighted-anger would also fit. But in neither case would his blaming attitude *in and of itself* be unfair or unjust, though (even if it were hurtful), and so in neither case would it require desert for its normative grounding.

The natural position I started with, then, stands: Private emotional (or more generally attitudinal) forms of blame in and of themselves get their normative grounding from fittingness, and need nothing more. In and of themselves, they raise no questions of unfairness or injustice—and so no desert-beyond-fittingness—as they don't treat anyone any which way, and any hurtfulness they

---

[18] This is the sort of case pressed upon me by Doug Portmore.

GROUNDS 93

contain is either ungoverned by morality (as with hurt feelings) or is instead motivated by an always resentible—and desert-free—ill will.

So much for the first type of purportedly harmful blame, purely private attitudes. What about forms of blame that do involve treatments of others? What about, specifically, *mockery*? This is the second type of purportedly harmful blame up for discussion.

Mockery and the Mockable

The first item of the blame/praise system involving actual treatments of others that may be harmful is mockery-blame. Its positive counterpart, complimenting-praise, raises no urgent moral or desert-based worries, at least with respect to its specific targets.[19] But mockery stings, or at least it aims to do so, if only a tiny bit. It consists, after all, in deliberately drawing attention to someone's screw-up in a way that invites public ridicule. This treatment might thus seem to require desert-beyond-fittingness. Indeed, Descartes actually makes this requirement explicit, claiming that the justification for mockery—what he called "scorn," which is "a sort of joy mingled with hatred"—was found in perceiving, unexpectedly, the "small evils" in others, that is, to perceiving that they are "deserving" of it.[20] This idea may be manifest in our counsel to stop mocking someone: "Lay off, he doesn't deserve that!"

Even in the mockery zone, though, as with pure attitudinal blame, I continue to think that talk of "desert" reduces without remainder to talk of "fit." To say that someone doesn't deserve some mocking-blame means nothing more than that such mockery was unfitting, that is, it was (nothing more than) *incorrect* in virtue of the target's not having the purported "mockable" property to which attention was being drawn.

To see why, suppose that I mock you for someone else's flaw; you're innocent! Is it *unjust* or *unfair* for me to make fun of you as I did, given your lack of that mockable property?

No. The reason is that mockery-blame delivers its characteristic sting *only to the extent that its target actually has the mockable flaw being singled out for ridicule.* Punishing the innocent is unjust because the pains or setbacks of punishment are delivered *regardless* of that person's innocence. But in mockery-blame,

---

[19] They may raise worries about unfairness to *others*, namely, those who have done equally complimentable things but aren't in fact complimented for them. Here the unfairness may be thought to speak in favor of giving compliments to those who deserve them. But my treatment of mockery will carry over to compliments: Desert talk in this subdomain is entirely reducible to fittingness talk, so that one has a *pro tanto* reason of fit (and nothing more) to compliment the complimentable (whoever they are).

[20] *The Passions of the Soul*, Article 178; see also Hazlett, in Morreall 1987: 76.

94 THE ARCHITECTURE OF BLAME AND PRAISE

I aver, the mockery's sting can be delivered only if it zeroes in on and highlights some recognized *truth* about the mocked person, that is, only if the mockery is fitting.[21]

To illustrate, suppose that you are sitting in the stands of a basketball game in which I'm playing, but you are rooting for the other team. I make a long three-pointer without so much as disturbing the net, but from your angle it looks like what you now shout out, in the familiar sing-song style: *"Air ball! Air ball!"* This won't bother me in the least; indeed, I'll find *you* a bit mockable yourself for making such a mistake. There is surely no unfairness or injustice in your unfitting mockery of me, as there's just no sting delivered. But then suppose that, a few plays later, I accidentally stumble into the referee, who then brings assault charges against me, and I'm then convicted by a corrupt jury and serve time. Now there *is* a seriously unjust setback that's been delivered, even though I'm innocent.

The difference between the cases comes from the source of pain or setbacks in various kinds of treatment. It's unjust for you to treat me in what you think is some evaluatively-called-for way only when that treatment delivers pain or setback that can be inflicted on me regardless of the accuracy of your evaluation. But mocking-blame's sting can be delivered only when its evaluation is accurate. There is thus no question of justice or desert in the absence of fit, no remaining moral value that fit alone can't capture.

This doesn't yet mean that there might not still be some extra value included when mocking-blame *is* fitting, extra value imported by "desert-beyond-fit." There's an argument style popular these days that might get us to that view, one that pumps intuitions in cross-world comparisons. There are two ways this might go. Some people compare the non-instrumental goodness in worlds in which the blameworthy are blamed with those worlds in which they aren't blamed (for just a few examples of this move, see, e.g., Bennett 2002: 147; Clarke 2013; McKenna 2012: 129). Others compare non-instrumental goodness in worlds in which the blameworthy are blamed with worlds in which the *non*-blameworthy *are* blamed (see, e.g., Portmore 2022: 53). In both cases, though, the "correct" intuition we're supposed to have is that worlds in which the blameworthy are blamed (or made to suffer, including feeling guilt) are better than their cross-world counterparts, the thought (often) being that the former worlds are more *just* than the latter.

---

[21] There is a complication here: some unfitting mockery can sting me if I *think* I have the quality for which I'm being mocked. And sometimes I can be brought to that incorrect thought by repeated mockery. Such cases do involve injustice, but it's not the injustice pertinent to desert; it is instead the epistemic injustice of having one's self-conception obscured. The cases I'm focused on, then, are just those in which the mocked party's vision is unobscured in this way. I'm particularly grateful here for discussion with, and friendly pushback from, Holly Kantin, Gunnar Björnsson, and Jada Twedt Strabbing, among others.

Perhaps, then, the same might hold for mocking-blame? Maybe worlds in which the mockable are mockery-blamed are somehow more just than their cross-world counterparts (of either stripe), so that the mockable *deserve* their fitting mockery?

I tend to have a hard time assessing cross-world comparison arguments, but my impairments don't much matter for this particular application.[22] For when it comes to mocking-blame, the strategy pretty clearly fails. Ask yourself: Is the world in which you mock someone who really did miss the shot (with "Air ball!") somehow *better*—in terms of justice, say—than either the world in which you mistakenly mocked the person who made the shot, or the world in which you didn't mock the person who missed it?[23] Given that there's no sting delivered in any of the alternate worlds, and given how weird it is to think about stinging mockery-blame as a matter of justice in the first place, it's difficult to see how the first world would be better than either alternate world in terms of justice. Indeed, it's hard to think of it as better in *any* terms, except that maybe there's non-instrumental betterness attached to worlds in which people make correct appraisals of others. Perhaps this is a kind of aesthetic goodness? Regardless, it's certainly not the moral goodness of justice (or fairness, for that matter), and that's all I need here.

Conclusion

This chapter began my discussion of the normative grounding of two categories of backwards-looking blame. First, the aptness of purely private blame is entirely and exclusively a function of fit, that is, accurate appraisal. When blame crosses over into treatment of others via mockery, desert-beyond-fit might be thought to have a better chance of being required, but that's not true either. The constitutive sting of mockery is instead still entirely a function of its fit. Desert-beyond-fit is unnecessary.

Nevertheless, there are two remaining categories of blame treatment I have yet to consider: (a) the expression of various blame/praise emotions, such as anger or resentment, and (b) actual punishment or interpersonal sanctions when meted out as blame. Desert might well be necessary in one or both of these categories. I will not take up this topic until Chapter 9, however, as first it's important to spend some more time discussing what precisely makes various responses fitting,

---

[22] For actual and excellent *philosophical* doubts about the cross-world move, see Nelkin 2019b; Macnamara 2020; Achs 2023.

[23] It's very important to note that I'm assuming here that the mockery-blame is issued without any ill will. Shouting "airball!" at a basketball game can be done, as can lots of other mockery, all in good fun (and yet sting nevertheless when it hits its target).

in both their other-directed and self-directed forms. For now, though, we've at least got a significant swath of the blame/praise system that's been rendered immune from concerns about desert, and that in itself is a big first step toward pushing the metaphysics of free will out of the blame/praise system.

The Architecture of Blame and Praise: An Interdisciplinary Investigation. David Shoemaker, Oxford University Press.
© David Shoemaker 2024. DOI: 10.1093/9780198915867.003.0006

7

Fitmakers

When our blame and praise are apt, they have the right targets. But "targets" is multiply ambiguous, between *recipients*, *activities*, and *aptness-makers*. Consider the following formula, which exhibits the variables that must be filled in when blame and praise are properly deployed:

One aptly blames/praises X for Y in virtue of Z.

All of the variables are, in one sense or another, "targets" of apt blame and praise. X refers to agents or persons, typically adult humans with fairly sophisticated capacities (though not always). When I blame, I blame *someone*.[1] Y refers to the event or state triggering my response, typically an action or attitude (though not always; sometimes it's a character trait). If you insult my mother, I'll blame you *for* that insult. If you write me a letter of recommendation, I'll be grateful to you *for* your generosity.

The Z variable is where most of the action is, theoretically. Filling it in provides the specific normative bases for blame/praise, namely, the properties that *render* those responses apt. These properties are hotly contested. Some competitors include reasons-responsiveness, deep selves, agent-causation, ultimate source-hood, forward-looking consequences, or others.

To this point I have discussed only our emotional blame/praise responses and our mocking/complimenting blame/praise responses. The aptness of both, I have argued, consists wholly in their fittingness (the correctness or accuracy of their appraisal), whereas desert is unnecessary for either. What I need to do now, however, is say more about the fitmakers in each case. What precisely makes these appraisals correct?

I will start with mockery-blame and complimenting-praise. To this point, I have labeled their fitmakers as, respectively, the *mockable* and the *complimentable*. But what do these properties actually consist in? It turns out that they are rather interesting (and symmetrical).

---

[1] On its face, this way of filling out the X variable is in tension with a no-self view favored by Buddhists (see Siderits 2011; Flanagan 2017 (233–52); Chadha 2017 and 2018). There are various ways out of this jam, though, including positing a very thin notion of the self to which actions/attitudes may be attributable (*à la* Flanagan 2017: 162) or allowing for the object of praise/blame to be some "mere" values or intentions. At any rate, this is a problem Buddhists have to solve, and I'm no Buddhist.

98   THE ARCHITECTURE OF BLAME AND PRAISE

What, though, about the emotional blame/praise responses? I have already said quite a bit about the fitmakers of slighted-anger and gratitude in Chapter 5. They are, respectively, slights and heights, actions and attitudes that manifest, respectively, poor and excellent quality of will. But I have yet to say very much about the nature of quality of will (QW), nor have I said anything about the fitmakers of the rest of our emotional blame/praise responses, including contempt, admiration, disdain, regret, pride, and more, other than to use their placeholder evaluative labels: the contemptible, the admirable, the disdainable, the regrettable, the prideworthy, and so forth. As it turns out, all of these emotional responses are rendered fitting by various qualities of will as well, albeit only with a pluralistic understanding of the "will." I will explain and defend this idea in the second section.

In the remainder of the chapter, I will defend my QW theory of the fitmakers of emotional blame/praise against several challengers. Some are old school, that is, they are familiar and longstanding challenges to QW theories of responsibility of a Strawsonian bent, such as mine. These are challenges appealing to moral luck, manipulation, and negligence. I won't have a lot new to say about these challenges, but it's at least important to note them and suggest lines of plausible response for QW theorists.

I'm much more interested in several new school challenges to QW theories, as these haven't really been discussed yet in the responsibility literature. There are three worth considering. First, corporations, many want to say, can be aptly blamed or praised for evil or good deeds, but they seem to lack any "quality of will" at all, or at least any quality of will remotely like ours. Second, there seem to be some cases in which it might be thought that we should *take on* responsibility and blame for some of our inadvertent—but not ill-willed—behavior. Finally, there seem to be some cases where morality encroaches on epistemology, where certain beliefs (or attitudes more generally) are thought to be wrongful and blameworthy even if one has good evidential reason to hold those beliefs, and where one does so without ill will.

In all three new school challenges, then, it looks as if poor quality of will may not be necessary to render slighted-anger fitting after all, suggesting that QW is not the fitmaker of emotional blame or praise that I think it is.

QW still is the relevant fitmaker, I'll argue, although there are nuances and complications aplenty. But before I make that case, a quick word about mockability and complimentability.

Mockability and Complimentability

Insofar as mockery-blame hasn't been discussed in the literature on responsibility before, I'm simply going to assert what I think are its fitmakers, and then note

FITMAKERS   99

how these carry over to its positive counterpart, complimentability. What's key to both is that they are, paradigmatically, responses to performances relative to some (typically nonmoral) standards, including aesthetic, athletic, culinary, epistemic, prudential, philosophical, and many more. Consequently, specific conditions on both mockability and complimentability will be determined, in great part, by the specific performance standards within those various normative domains. That being said, there are some general conditions that can be laid out for both. I'll start with mockery, where there are at least three.[2]

Remember, to mock someone is to make fun of them for some failure, in a way that could foreseeably result in their feeling the sting of embarrassment, shame, or even humiliation.[3] It's that sting that seemed to need moral justification. I argued in the previous chapter that only fitting mockery can generate that sting, and it's from that argument that we can garner some of mockery's more precise fittingness conditions.

The first condition is *truthiness*: the target of mockery must have (in the vicinity of) the quality for which they are being mocked. I can't aptly mock the fast for being slow, or the heroic for being cowards.

The second condition on fitting mockery is *publicity*. Mockery draws attention to some flaw for public consumption; otherwise, no sting would necessarily be attached. It's in having that flaw *exposed* that one's embarrassment is triggered, so the mockery, in order to be apt, must both be expressed and be aimed at that exposure.

While mockery aims to publicly expose flaws or failures, it can't just be any old flaws or failures. A third condition of apt mockery is thus that these flaws or failures be significant, that is, *ridiculous*. If you've come in second place in the Olympic finals of 100-meter dash by 0.001 seconds, you've failed to win, but there is nothing at all mockable about your performance. However, if you're entered in the 100-meter dash at the local charity event, and you trip coming out of the starting blocks and roll head-over-heels into the long-jump pit, then your failure is ridiculous enough to render you mockable.

Incidentally, this last condition is one of those that is the most heavily context-dependent, depending on both the specific performance standards of the particular normative domain, as well as who the mockers are. Golf pros or chess masters may mock each other for making mockable shots or moves that the rest of us mortals could only aspire to make.

There may be other aptness conditions for mockery, but these are, I believe, the most important ones. They also carry over directly to its positive counterpart,

---

[2] I draw some of this discussion from Shoemaker 2024: ch. 4.

[3] And the sting is, for some, merely subjunctive. I can aptly mock Biden or Putin without their being in the room or ever hearing my mock. But they *would* be stung (or that's what I'd be aiming for) were they there to hear my ferocious zings.

complimentability. For complimenting-praise to be apt, it too must be "truthy": the targeted agent must have the quality for which she's being praised (or have some quality in the vicinity). I can't aptly compliment the slow for being fast or the cowardly for being heroic. Complimentability also requires publicity: it must be expressed and intended to generate its buzz in the recipient.[4] Finally, complimentability requires something more from its target than a mere success relative to some standard; rather, that success must be, in some respect, significant (which is, again, very context-dependent), although because there are only warm fuzzies delivered by compliments, this may not be a very carefully patrolled condition.

These fitmakers for mockery-blame and complimenting-praise are not, as far as I can see, terribly controversial. They are drawn from my thinking about the types of reasons we give for and against both responses in various circumstances, especially when we disagree with one another about whether some response or other is, indeed, a correct appraisal of someone.[5] I welcome discussion on these matters, though, as they are new to the responsibility scene.

My views on the emotional blame/praise responses, however, are quite controversial. QW theories have been on the responsibility scene for a while now, where they've had plenty of opportunity to garner objections, and so they have. I turn now to lay out the general theory, in its most plausible pluralistic form, before responding to the objections, both old and new school.

Qualities of Will

QW theories have their source in Strawson's (1962/2003) "Freedom and Resentment," where QW is put forward as the gloss on the evaluative targets of naturally occurring reactive attitudes like resentment, indignation, guilt, and gratitude. The theory can be motivated by pairwise cases: If your foot lands on mine, causing me some injury, I'll naturally feel resentment, but it's likely to be suspended if it turns out that you did so by accident (as a way of righting yourself when a crowded subway jerks unexpectedly). If, however, I see the malicious grin on your face when doing so, my resentment will stick. There is no difference between the two cases in terms of the injury or pain caused. The only difference is in what that injury manifested: a poor quality of will in the latter but not in the former (Strawson 1962/2003: 79).

And indeed, argues Strawson, all of our successful excuses—pleas to get off the hook for some injury—are attempts to show that what might have seemed like poor quality of will really wasn't. "I didn't know," or "I was pushed," or "They left

---

[4] Again, subjunctively.
[5] I adopt a similar strategy—what my colleague Derk Pereboom has labeled the "argument argument"—in my discussion of the fittingness conditions of amusement in Shoemaker 2024: ch. 1.

me no alternative" are all attempts to show that the injury was one for which I wasn't actually resentment-worthy, in virtue of the fact that it didn't reveal any poor quality of will on my part. And so, in general, "the reactive attitudes are essentially natural human reactions to the good or ill will or indifference of others towards us, as displayed in *their* attitudes and actions" (Strawson 1962/2003: 80; emphasis in original).

But what is the *will* in "quality of will," precisely? This has been a matter of some debate. Some take it to be the *regard* we have for others or for the relevance of moral considerations (McKenna 2012: 59). Others take it to be about our *evaluative judgments*, in particular our judgments about the worth of various reasons (Scanlon 1986; Smith 2005). Still others, without using the term "will," see it as about our *character*, about various of our traits, dispositions, cares, or commitments (see, e.g., Hume 1960, Book II, Part III, sec. II, 411).

I have argued elsewhere that we cannot understand the full nature of responsibility without incorporating *all three* notions of "will" into its purview (Shoemaker 2015: Part One). The motivation for doing so comes from reflection on our wide array of emotional responses to manifestations of the practical agency of others, alongside an account of their characteristic evaluative targets. Slighted-anger— which includes Strawson's favored responses of resentment and indignation— targets slights, which is a gloss on insufficient regard. Regard, as I've argued elsewhere and earlier in this book, itself requires the capacity for and exercise of empathy. Its positive counterpart is gratitude, which appraises heights, where one's benefactor had a higher regard for one than one had any right to expect. As it too invites acknowledgment from its target, heighting requires the capacity for and exercise of empathy as well.

We don't just appraise agents' quality of regard, though. We also appraise their evaluative judgments. The paradigmatic emotional appraisals here are *regret* and *pride* (which are of course self-directed emotions, but they are the ones best illuminating the relevant other-directed versions). Regret's characteristic target is poor judgment, and in particular poor *decisions*, and it motivates policy change (Jacobson 2013: 104). Pride typically celebrates good decisions or judgment generally, and it motivates the reinforcement of one's policies. In both cases, for these responses to be appropriate, the target (oneself) must have the capacity to evaluate and respond to the worth of various reasons, which is a reasons-responsive or judgment-sensitive capacity (Shoemaker 2015: ch. 2).

Finally, appraisals of character are found paradigmatically in emotions like *disdain* and *admiration*, which are, very often, responses respectively to vices and virtues, aretaic predicates referring to various (un)worthy traits or dispositions. These responses are typically fitting in response to *patterns* of actions or attitudes, and they motivate self-improvement, either away from the disdainful or towards the admirable. The capacities required for one to manifest various qualities of character are simply the emotional dispositions constituting one's cares and

102 THE ARCHITECTURE OF BLAME AND PRAISE

the general evaluative stances constituting one's commitments (Shoemaker 2015: ch. 1).

Because each of these three referents of "will" requires a different capacity (or set of capacities), I have argued that they each mark out three different types of responsibility: *attributability*, which requires the capacity for the cares and commitments making up one's character; *answerability*, which requires the capacity for judgment about the worth of reasons; and *accountability*, which requires the capacity for empathic regard. Further, each type of responsibility is independent of the others (i.e., no type is necessary for any other).

One enormous advantage of this tripartite machinery is that it most plausibly explains the responsibility-status of many so-called "marginal" agents, those with various psychological disorders or mental illnesses. While monistic views are forced to defend the idea that these agents either are or aren't responsible, full stop, my pluralistic view accounts for people's *ambivalence* in response to such agents: they seem responsible in some ways but not others. The tripartite view predicts that those with clinical depression, for instance, are indeed both accountable and answerable, given their high empathic regard for others and their capacities to form evaluative judgments (often accurately), but they are not attributability-responsible for character traits like "laziness," as their inability to rouse various motivational states is a product of their illness, not their character. Psychopaths, on the other hand, may be attributability-responsible (for their cruelty or manipulativeness), but neither accountable nor answerable (given their impairments in empathy and in evaluating the worth of moral reasons).[6]

The emotional agential responses I've noted here—all of them—are part of the blame/praise system. To the extent that the tripartite view aims to capture *all* we mean when talking about responsibility, it should also capture all we mean when talking about the blame/praise system. And so, I think, it does. Blame and praise, in all of their basic emotional forms, at least, are rendered fitting when they are accurate appraisals of these distinct qualities of will: character, judgment, and/or regard. With respect to blame's and praise's acknowledgment-seeking forms, our slighted-anger to people is rendered fitting in virtue of their insufficiently good regard toward us, and our gratitude-praise is rendered fitting in virtue of their excellent regard. And within blame's and praise's non-acknowledgment-seeking forms, our contempt or admiration for people is rendered fitting in virtue of, respectively, their poor or excellent qualities of character, and our regret or pride (or their third-person analogues) is rendered fitting in virtue of, respectively, the poor or good qualities of judgment that were manifested.

---

[6] For application of the tripartite view to several "marginal" agents, see Shoemaker 2015: Part Two. I have put these verdicts in stark terms, but of course for real-life agents, the correct answers will come in much more hedged degrees.

On the pure version of the QW theory that I favor, *that's it*. Our emotional responsibility responses are apt (or not) entirely and exclusively to the extent that they are fitting, where this just means that they are correct or accurate appraisals of their various targeted qualities of will. This view has numerous detractors, though, so my aim in the remainder of this chapter is to provide a sustained defense of pure QW theories against several different attacks. The attackers all share the same simple strategy: to identify cases of fitting emotional blame or praise whose fitmakers aren't (exclusively) QW. The attacks have come from many quarters, some old school, some new school. We'll start with the older, more familiar, versions.

Old School Challenges and How to Thwart Them

Most of the old school challenges to QW theories have been generated by those interested in metaphysical approaches to responsibility, focused primarily on whether it, and the free will presumed necessary for it, are compatible with determinism.[7] They are these:

- **Moral Luck**: Pairwise cases of agents with identical QW generate different, seemingly fitting, blame responses depending on various (un)lucky features of the case, features that may include the agents' circumstances, the outcomes of their attempts, and how they've been built (including their histories). All of these features are presumably out of the agents' control and independent of their QW, so the differential blame responses can't be (wholly) in virtue of the agents' different qualities of will, as predicted by pure QW theories.
- **Manipulation**: Suppose that particular wills and their qualities might be externally installed or manipulated in agents. Intuitively, such agents would not be responsible or blameworthy, despite acting from poor qualities of will, say, so QW can't be the (exclusive) fitmaker for blame.
- **Negligence**: Sometimes perfectly good will is found in cases of negligence, where the negligence is still of a sort that seems to render blame fitting. The most tragic sort of case here is of the good and loving parent who forgets that his infant is in the car's back seat, sleeping, and so leaves her there in a hot car all day long…

Let's consider each of these versions of the challenge in turn. There are several responses available for QW theorists to worries about luck, but the best ones,

---

[7] I draw much of the material that follows (with an exception noted below) from Shoemaker 2023.

I think, come down simply to rejecting it. Blameworthiness, one might insist, remains exclusively a function of QW, so where two agents have identical qualities of will, their blameworthiness is in fact identical, regardless of luck in outcome, constitution, or anything else. This view is perfectly compatible with the psychological plausibility or predictability of different people responding differentially to those with identical qualities of will (perhaps as a matter of good or bad character), but it insists that the fittingness of having the same response for each remains the same.

For some, this is an inadequate answer, insofar as it fails to take sufficiently seriously (or fully explain away the reasonableness of) the differential responses in real life to outcome luck cases. Indeed, this is why T. M. Scanlon urges that it's QW *plus* the significance of the outcome for one's relations with others that matters for blameworthiness (Scanlon 2008: 128–31; Scanlon 2015: 105). If two people drive recklessly down a residential street, but only one of them hits a child who happens to run out, the parents of that child will no doubt blame that unlucky driver more than the lucky one, even though both drivers had identical qualities of will, given the significance the unlucky driver's poor QW had for *them*. And this seems a perfectly fitting response too.

Note, though, that it could well still be fitting for the parents of the unhit child to be just as slighted-angry at the lucky driver as the unlucky one. "You *could have* hit my child!!" is a perfectly reasonable angry response, and they might well yell at the driver from the roadside, shaking with horror at how close it all was and how it could have easily been a tragedy. Their angry blame may, as a result, be equal in "type and intensity" to that of the unlucky parents (Talbert 2022). The fittingness of slighted-anger surely admits of a *range* of angry responses, depending on particular people's specific sensibilities. Some may be roused to rage; others roused merely to clenched jaw. That one observer of outcome luck responds with more intense slighted-anger than another does nothing to undermine the very plausible possibility that both reactions are within a single but wide range of fitting angry responses nevertheless all rendered fitting exclusively by the QW they target (Talbert 2022 incisively explores this line of thought). Perhaps the significance of the action will tend, as a descriptive psychological matter, to kick up the intensity of the reaction in unlucky cases, but that doesn't at all mean that there's some property in *addition* to QW that's rendering slighted-anger fitting here.

The QW theorist can also deny constitutive luck. One plausible way is by noting that people's different histories can actually make for different current qualities of will. Two racists who have come by their racism differently—one deliberately, one via moral ignorance in formative circumstances—may actually have different qualities of will now, given their differential access to relevant reasons to refrain from their racist actions, say (see, e.g., Shoemaker 2015: 193–203; Talbert 2022). Another way is by differentiating cases of constitutive luck by appealing to "wrong kinds of reasons" for differentiating between expressions of angry blame. In other words, one might say of the two racists that both are equally and fully responsible and blame*worthy*, in virtue of their identical qualities of will, but that one should actually *blame* the ignorant one to a lesser extent, given various difficulties he'll have in recognizing the sorts of reasons of which he was ignorant (Smith 2005: 268–9).[8]

Manipulation cases are notoriously difficult to get just right (see, e.g., Pereboom 2001, 2014, and 2021a: 15–18 for many attempts to tweak his famous Four-Case Argument). They are meant to show how one's favorite compatibilist conditions can be met via manipulation, where the manipulation nevertheless renders the target not blameworthy. This would mean, in our case, ginning up a situation in which someone is manipulated into having the kind of QW that QW theorists say renders slighted-anger fitting, but where the fact of manipulation itself would intuitively render any and all blame *unfitting*. There's a very delicate tightrope walk that has to be undertaken here, though, one that requires getting the details of the manipulation case precise in a way that the target remains an actual agent, yet also isn't blameworthy. The more extraordinary the manipulation (e.g., moment-to-moment insertions or alterations of values or decisions from an evil neuroscientist), though, the less actual agency seems to remain. But if the manipulation is too subtle and ordinary (involving the kinds of nudges to the target's moods closely akin to the sort that may occur in everyday life, as when one's favorite team loses a game; see Pereboom 2014: 76), then it becomes much easier to hold onto the target's blameworthiness after all, at least after a bit of time (enough so that the newly installed QW settles in and becomes the agent's "own"; see Frankfurt 1988: 52–4; Scanlon: 1998: 278–9). QW theorists can plausibly push in either direction (see Shoemaker 2014 for my response to Pereboom's specific manipulation argument).

Negligence cases are tougher for QW theorists, I think, but certainly not insurmountable. The biggest challenge comes from "hot car" cases, in which loving parents forget that their napping infants (or dogs; see Sher 2006a: 286–7) are in the back seat, and they leave them in there for hours, resulting in tragedy. Here the challenge comes from the (stipulated) fact that the parents have *excellent* qualities of will, but they are nevertheless often viewed as blameworthy, by both some members of the general public and their own partners, a result which strongly suggests that poor QW isn't the fitmaker for angry blame in such cases.

There are a couple of moves available to the QW theorist, though. First, one might hold the line, maintaining that these parents are *responsible* for their negligence, but they in fact aren't *blameworthy*—fitting targets of blame—despite the

---

[8] I'm skipping circumstantial luck, or any other kinds, because most of the moves are likely to be similar. For rich and insightful discussion, again see Talbert 2022 for ways in which pure QW theorists can respond.

fact that some people (wrongly) blame them. That is, while they are responsible for the negligence, they nevertheless have an excuse—they honestly forgot—that gets them off the blame hook for it. This response is less than inspiring, however. More often than not, we do blame each other for forgetting some things. It doesn't tend to get us off the blame hook, as we *should have remembered*, and we were capable of doing so, having done so easily before (see Clarke 2014: 166). Ratcheting up the stakes in these infant cases should also increase the stringency of the demand to remember, rather than ease it.[9]

The QW theorists who have the best chance of thwarting the threat of tragic negligence are—surprise, surprise!—pluralists about the nature of the will whose quality is being assessed. With my tripartite machinery, for instance, we can say that these negligent parents are blameworthy in some ways, in virtue of some of their qualities of will, but not in other ways. They don't have insufficient regard, we might say; indeed, they have the highest respect and care for the interests of their charges. And they don't have poor quality of judgment, as they rightly evaluate their charges as worth caring for. But their negligence may reveal a poor quality of *character*: they aren't as good parents as one would want or expect. They aren't sufficiently *vigilant*. This is a character flaw, something that may well be disdainable or deeply disappointing. It surely could be aptly viewed that way by a grieving spouse or partner.

There is of course much more to be said about all three old school threats.[10] Indeed, much has been said, and I don't have much to add to it. I thus leave aside any more discussion of them in favor of exploring the new school threats to QW theories, as they raise a variety of fascinating and important new issues for responsibility theorists generally to contend with. They have been primarily advanced independently of metaphysical concerns about free will or determinism; rather, they are *moral* challenges, coming from the "normative" theorists, who, like me, are concerned almost exclusively with the fittingness conditions of our blaming and praising attitudes and practices. QW theories often explicitly aim to sidestep the traditional problems of free will and determinism, and that's one reason it is no surprise that they have multiple ways of avoiding the old school challenges just discussed. But the new school threats are, as it were, playing the same normative game as the QW theorists, so their threats are coming from *inside the house*! They are challenges to the necessity of QW for fitting emotional blame (and praise), and they often derive from thinking about institutions or close personal interactions in which there is a kind of "responsibility gap"— moral badness or wrongness without any identifiable bad agents or individual wrongers at their source—and, in particular, where social justice may demand

---

[9] Thanks to David Brink for this suggestion.

[10] For rich and insightful discussion of these threats, construed mostly as worries about free will, see several of the excellent essays in Russell 2017.

that we blame some people who are faultless-in-terms-of-no-ill-will, given blame's value in making both people and the world morally better.

Blaming BP: Corporate Blamability and Quality of Will

The first threat comes from thinking about corporations, which are often the targets of our blame, but which also seem to have no *will* for which there could be a relevant quality.[11] Start with the following famous case:

> On April 20, 2010, there was an explosion on the Deepwater Horizon drilling rig south of New Orleans in the Gulf of Mexico. Eleven workers on the rig were never found and were presumed dead. Two days later, a massive oil leak was discovered, which turned into the largest oil spill in history, lasting for five months and discharging nearly five million barrels of oil into the gulf. The effects on marine life and the environment were devastating.[12]

The rig was owned and operated by BP. I lived in New Orleans at the time, and everyone was angry. As it came to light just how egregious the mistakes and negligence were that led to the enormous loss of human, marine, and environmental life, we all got even angrier. And yet the precise *target* of all this anger seemed spectral, elusive. Where exactly was "BP," the villain? To whom or what should we direct our anger? One identifiable target seemed to be the numerous BP gas stations around the U.S., so many people protested and boycotted those stations. But BP had sold off its gas stations years before, which rendered this reaction, while understandable, feckless, and it wound up hurting a bunch of innocent independent small business owners.[13] And people had a hard time finding any other proper targets for their anger. So the anger simmered, but without a clear outlet it dissipated, ran out of steam.

This is the frustrating and confusing response I wish to explore, the result of a deep tension between two very compelling thoughts about corporations: On the one hand, it seems clear that corporations can be agents who are responsible and blameworthy for various harms they cause; on the other hand, it also seems clear that corporations can't be angrily *blamed*, at least in anything like the way other people can, that when we try and target them with our slighted-anger they seem to *disappear* as blameworthy and responsible agents. I will first show why there are powerful reasons supporting both thoughts. I will then show why the seeming

---

[11] I draw some material in this section from Shoemaker 2019a.
[12] For details, see https://en.wikipedia.org/wiki/Deepwater_Horizon_oil_spill.
[13] See https://www.npr.org/templates/story/story.php?storyId=127747890.

competition between the thoughts is merely apparent, that the presumed paradox may be dissolved by appeal to my tripartite machinery.

I find very compelling the view that corporations can be interpersonal agents who make decisions that are independent of those of their individual members. The clearest and most persuasive arguments for this view have come from Christian List and/or Philip Pettit in several places, in advancing and defending the "discursive dilemma" (Pettit 2000, 2001, and 2007; Pettit and Rabinowicz 2001; List 2006; List and Pettit 2011). Their arguments are fairly well known, and I won't rehearse them here. Rather, I'll just state a few important aspects of their view.

Corporations are under immense practical pressure to collectivize the reason of their individual deliberators, but doing so risks generating collective decisions that no majority—and perhaps not any single member of the collective—endorses. Once they collectivize reason, though, they become collective *agents*, entities that are "subject to mental predications of a non-metaphorical, non-summative kind" (Pettit 2001: 114; see also Pettit 2000). Among these mental properties are judgments, intentions, desires, and beliefs, all of whose content they can articulate. These collective agents make decisions, and they act on those decisions. They can have moral ideals to which they may be held. They can give their word and be held to it. They can be interlocutors. Indeed, they have personalities, and they are *persons* (Pettit 2001: 116–17). And finally, insofar as they are under their own discursive control, corporations are both free and (collectively) responsible, eligible for having their reasons for doing what they do scrutinized. But if they are responsible agents, then they must be both blameworthy and blamable when they do wrong. *BP here we come!*

And yet...when we actually try to angrily *blame* BP, as I noted, it's hard to find a precise target. Indeed, how can we gin up and sustain slighted-anger at an irreducible corporate agent? BP was clearly blameworthy, I grant. But if this sort of angry blame is rendered fit by poor quality of will, what is BP's will? *Where* is its will?

Perhaps this vague worry about blamability is overblown, or even false, though? The case against corporate blamability, of a certain sort, can be made quite clear and compelling by engaging with a dialectic that started with Michael McKenna's (2006) argument against corporate responsibility and blameworthiness, one that appealed to his own burgeoning conversational theory of responsibility. According to McKenna, ordinary exchanges between morally responsible agents are akin to conversations, where the things we do in this community express "agent meaning," an analogue of Gricean "speaker meaning" (Grice 1957), and these actional conversations are intelligible only within our particular interpretive framework: "When an agent acts, she does so within this context, and she must, if she is a competent agent, stand prepared to adjust her conduct or account for it at later points, with the understanding that her actions can bear meanings in light of this interpretive framework of action assessment" (McKenna 2006: 28–9). To be a morally responsible agent, then, one must be capable "of mastering a sophisticated interpretive framework of action assessment and appreciating how [its] actions might be interpreted within it" (McKenna 2006: 29).

These conversational capacities are what enable agents to grasp *"morally salient* reasons" (McKenna 2012: 82; emphasis mine), to have a kind of emotionally dispositive moral sensibility (for inspiration, see Russell 2004). To be able to be aptly held responsible via various emotions (e.g., reactive attitudes like resentment), McKenna thinks, one must be able both to understand and to speak that emotional language oneself, and that same emotional capacity is what also enables one to grasp and respond to the relevant moral reasons to which one ought to adhere. One must be able to resent in order to be aptly resented, for it is only via the former that one can recognize and respond appropriately to the latter's demands, perhaps with guilt or regret.

McKenna thinks that pure (irreducible) corporate agents lack these emotional capacities and so just can't be blameworthy. Their emotional incapacity would thus explain why we can't seem to angrily blame them. But we get to this point only by denying what nevertheless seems plain: corporate agents really do seem to be able to do (because they actually do!) blameworthy things. And indeed, Gunnar Björnsson and Kendy Hess, in a very insightful article, tell us how they can do so in McKenna's own terms: Corporate agents, they show, can actually have the *functional equivalents* of emotional, agent-meaning interpersonal exchanges with us (Björnsson and Hess 2017). They can be "indignant" at the wrongdoing of others and suffused with "guilt" at their own wrongdoing, at least in ways that are perfectly sufficient for morally blameworthy agency.

Corporate agents certainly have the functional equivalents of beliefs, desires, and intentions (which, again, are distinct from those of their individual members). They typically have a mission statement around which they organize plans, roll out products, advertise them, change how they are sold in light of consumer demands, and so forth. Corporations can be diachronically coherent. They have a point of view and predictably act to express it. It is a point of view that is *their own*, and not that of their individual members. Corporations are, for all the world, instrumentally rational agents (Björnsson and Hess 2017: 278–80).

But they are also, for all the world, *moral* agents. They may have moral commitments: to treat their employees, suppliers, and consumers with due regard, to be environmentally sensitive, and so forth. "Depending on what a corporation's commitments are, its actions can thus express straightforward analogs to good or ill will" (Björnsson and Hess 2017: 280). There is thus no reason to think that corporations have access to any fewer moral reasons than nonmoral reasons, and so no reason to think they won't have the kind of reasons-responsive sophistication McKenna worries they won't have. Indeed, to the extent that a corporate agent is constructed by individuals who themselves have access to moral reasons

110   THE ARCHITECTURE OF BLAME AND PRAISE

and so can contribute them to corporate deliberations, corporate agents may actually have access to *more* moral reasons than any individual member does.

But what of the *emotional* capacities seemingly necessary to recognize or respond to those moral reasons? What Björnsson and Hess argue is that corporations can have their functional equivalents too. They focus on indignation and guilt. There are several features associated with indignation: a belief that someone has done a moral wrong; an attentional focus on the wronging agent; motivations toward aggression, expression, and treating the wronging agent in a punitive manner; a tendency toward withdrawal of these motivations upon a recognition of the wronger's guilt or willingness to change; and an overall belief in the *fittingness* of these responses (Björnsson and Hess 2017: 283–4). They also survey a similar range of features associated with guilt, which they take to involve a belief in one's own wrongdoing, attentional focus on what one did, motivations toward changing one's ways, and a belief in the fittingness of these feelings and tendencies (Björnsson and Hess 2017: 284–5).

What matters, then, is "not whether corporate agents are strictly speaking capable of these emotions, but whether they are capable of moral equivalents of these emotions" (Björnsson and Hess 2017: 285). And it should by now be obvious that they are. Furthermore, even though the painful phenomenology of something like guilt can't be experienced by corporate agents, it would seem, all that's relevant about that phenomenology is simply its *motivational* and *epistemic* role: It motivates us to change our ways or to apologize, say, and it gets us to see what the right thing to do is. But corporate agents can be moved to change their ways or express apologies, and they can also identify the right moral reasons moving forward. So even though they lack ordinary emotional phenomenology, *that doesn't matter* for functional purposes (Björnsson and Hess 2017: 286–8). For all the world, then, pure corporations can be morally responsible persons, and, as such, they can be blameworthy and thus blamable.

Despite the force of this argument, it may still seem as if slighted-anger is inapt for corporate agents like BP, that they remain, in some important sense, unblamable. I think this is still the correct response, given that, in contrast to Björnsson and Hess, I will now argue that a certain kind of emotional phenomenology *is* necessary for being the proper target of slighted-anger, and corporations lack *that*.[14]

What I've argued repeatedly throughout the book is that what slighted-anger demands from its target is, most fundamentally, remorseful empathic acknowledgment. I have yet to say much about what remorse itself is, though. I believe it is best described as a distinctly *ruminative* emotion, defined by its action-tendency to think over and over again about a loss in value one caused (see Thomas 1999: 130).

---

[14] See also Sepinwall 2017, who argues for a very similar conclusion about corporations lacking the crucial phenomenology of *guilt*.

The remorseful agent typically relives the events he caused again and again, bemoaning his damage. When the value-loss one causes was in a fellow human being, though, remorse consists in the painful empathic acknowledgment of how one made that person feel from that person's perspective. This pained-empathic-acknowledgment-motivating-rumination is remorse's defining feature.[15]

A wrongdoer may manifest such acknowledgment in a variety of ways (via admission of fault, apology, etc.), although those actions may also mislead. But given our incredible facility at reading the subtleties of others' emotional experiences off their faces and body language (Frith and Frith 2007), we often just "know it when we see it." Sincere remorse really is hard to fake. Once we see it, forgiveness becomes appropriate.[16] Presumably, then, being a fitting target of the slighted-anger that forgiveness foreswears is for one not to have been in the state of empathic acknowledgment that such slighted-anger demands in the first place.

As should by now be clear, though, this is a purely phenomenological state that has no functional equivalent in corporations. The phenomenology of remorse is not about practical motivational or epistemic considerations; that is, it is not (merely) instrumental in getting us to do something or providing us with knowledge of some sort. It rather consists in a *pure perceptual stance*: What slighted-anger demands is that slighters come to *see and feel* what they did to us from our perspectives. While you can act *as if* you have felt remorse, and so apologize, make amends, and so forth—and while these intentions and actions do have clear functional equivalents in corporations—were we to find out that these activities masked your *lack* of sincere remorse, our reason for dropping slighted-anger would disappear (see Shoemaker 2021).

This is the type of blaming exchange with which we are most familiar in our interpersonal human lives, but it is a type of exchange that cannot take place with pure corporate agents, given their incapacity for the phenomenological component of remorse. To the extent that corporate agents cannot *feel* remorse—cannot empathically acknowledge us—we cannot sensibly demand it of them. But insofar as slighted-anger consists in precisely this demand, we now have a clear explanation of why corporations aren't slighted-angry-blamable. And insofar as they are not slighted-angry-blamable precisely in virtue of lacking the capacities to adhere to the same demand for acknowledgment whose violation triggers slighted-anger in the first place, they don't seem to be fitting targets of slighted-anger at all. The reason is that they *do* in fact lack the capacity for a specific

---

[15] Guilt is in this neighborhood too, of course, but the difference is found in their defining action-tendencies, I think. Whereas remorse is ruminative and can attach to all sorts of values one damaged, guilt typically motivates relationship-repair, as its primary appraisal target is of oneself as having damaged a relationship, in particular. But I'll say much more about guilt in the next chapter.

[16] I am officially neutral here on whether the "appropriateness" of forgiveness means one has a reason to forgive, one has an obligation to forgive, one has a permission to forgive, or one would merely be a kind of asshole *not* to forgive.

112 THE ARCHITECTURE OF BLAME AND PRAISE

quality of will, namely quality of *regard*, which requires empathic mechanisms that corporations simply lack.

A brief summary of the dialectic is called for. McKenna's conversational theory implies that irreducibly corporate agents cannot be responsible and blameworthy because they lack QW. The Björnsson-Hess response, however, urges that corporations can be responsible and blameworthy in virtue of having the functional equivalents of the emotional capacities McKenna thinks are necessary for QW. But the centrality of the phenomenological features of remorse to our ordinary interpersonal blaming lives reveals that, because there's no functional equivalent to it in irreducible corporate agents, they still lack the *right sort* of QW to be blamable with slighted-anger.

Does that mean, then, that they aren't blameworthy? No. While they aren't slighted-anger-blameworthy, they might yet be blameworthy *in a different way*. And here's where a major new advantage of my pluralistic understanding of responsibility and blameworthiness is revealed.

The type of blame that I think fits for pure corporate agents is primarily of the *protest* variety. I discussed this view in Chapter 2. I argued there that it isn't adequate as a functional theory of the entire blame/praise system, as it has nothing clear to say about praise, and it also has a hard time accounting for several examples of blame without protest. Nevertheless, protest is surely *one* of the ways that we sometimes signal our commitment to various norms, so some protest certainly belongs in the system. Indeed, the value of including protest as one way of blaming is that it captures well many non-emotional instances of blame, as well as instances where no communication uptake is or can be secured by the blamed party. Indeed, these are instances pertinent to the blame of corporations. There is, for one, no need for emotional exchanges between us and corporate agents in order for us to successfully protest them. In doing so, we stand up for ourselves by repudiating their actions, and this protest can be successful whether or not the corporate agent itself "gets it" (see Hieronymi 2004; Smith 2013; Talbert 2022). Being *protestable* does not require that the protested agent be able to understand, appreciate, acknowledge, or change in light of it. But if protest is indeed a type of blame, then corporate agents can easily be blameworthy and blamable under its rubric, even if they aren't under the rubric of slighted-anger.

Protest may of course demand things of protested agents, but what it demands in any event is *action*: "Change what you're doing," it may demand, or "stop treating us this way!" But corporations *can* secure uptake of *those* demands; as we already know, they are agents, and they are capable of actions, so they are also capable of responding to protest's demands for action in a way that they can't respond to slighted-anger's demands.

Protest-blame fits the case of corporate wrongdoing quite well, in a way that slighted-anger does not. It thus also fits well into my pluralistic model of responsibility. Let me briefly say how, although the answer might already be obvious.

On my model, corporate agents are *answerable* but not *accountable*.[17] Pure corporate agents can judge as to the worth of various reasons, make decisions, and execute those decisions—or at least, following Björnsson and Hess, they can do all the functional moral equivalents of these things. This is all that's necessary for them to be able in principle to respond to the fundamental answerability question, "*Why did you do that?*" Answerability is the natural domain of protest-blame. Protest delivers a criticism of its target's evaluative judgment and decision-making, an expression of disapproval for agents who can, in principle, answer its fundamental question (but do so poorly). These are agents who must be capable of, essentially, discursive control (reasons-responsiveness), and they must be able to act in ways expressive of policy change. Corporate agents are capable of all of this.

Slighted-anger, by contrast, is appropriate instead exclusively for the *accountability* domain, where what's targeted is poor quality of *regard*, which is at its root the capacity for emotional empathic acknowledgment. Corporate agents lack this empathic capacity. This explains why slighted-anger feels so inappropriate for them: They are not capable of acknowledgment, but slighted-anger seeks just that, and so they remain beyond its grasp. Corporations, at least in this respect, are like psychopaths and narcissists.

Consequently, corporate agents may be blameworthy and blamable in terms of answerability but not blameworthy or blamable in terms of accountability. And if we are pluralists about the "will" in "quality of will," then QW remains necessary for blameworthiness in *both* cases; it just refers in some cases to quality of *judgment* (answerability), while it refers in other cases to quality of *regard* (accountability). QW theorists can thus defend against the threat from corporate agency, albeit only, I think, by being pluralists about the different qualities of will rendering fitting different types of blame.

Taking Responsibility for Faultless Behavior

The second new school challenge to QW theories comes from a relatively recent way of filling responsibility "gaps" in our interpersonal lives, one that urges some people to *take* responsibility for some unfortunate outcomes that aren't actually their fault.[18,19] Elinor Mason's example is of Perdita, who borrows a friend's

---

[17] They may also be attributability-responsible, insofar as they at least manifest commitments across time, which are features of the kind of character expressions that render fitting aretaic appraisal emotions like contempt, disdain, and admiration.

[18] Once again, some material from this and the next section is drawn from Shoemaker 2023.

[19] Wolf 2001 talks about the virtue of taking responsibility in some domains, and Enoch 2012 says we have a moral duty to do so sometimes. I will focus on Mason's account, which focuses in a more plausible way on the *fittingness* of doing so, and thus it is an explicit attack on pure QW theories.

114   THE ARCHITECTURE OF BLAME AND PRAISE

sentimentally valuable necklace, and then, through no real fault of hers, loses it. That is to say, she took due care, she wasn't careless, she didn't knowingly do anything stupid with it, and so forth. In telling her friend that she lost it, though, she rather callously says that, while of course she'll buy her a new necklace, blaming her isn't appropriate, as she didn't have any bad will: "[I]t was just one of those things" (Mason 2019a: 249).

This sort of response would be rather maddening, Mason rightly claims: "The problem is [Perdita] focuses on her own conscience, rather than on the other person" (Mason 2019a: 249). Once that switch is made, then pleading for forgiveness and experiencing genuine remorse is the way it would be fitting for Perdita to respond to her friend, despite her lack of bad will, and that is just what it means to take responsibility for losing the necklace (Mason 2019a: 250). To feel remorse is to feel badly about actions that are one's *own*, and the disposition to feel it in taking ownership even for "faultless" actions is a constitutive part of being in personal relationships.[20]

One might think that taking responsibility for such things is a matter of politeness, a way of greasing the wheels of relationships and getting past various inadvertent screw-ups. That would make Perdita's "apology" and "remorse" merely strategic play-acting, but they wouldn't be admissions of *true* responsibility or blameworthiness. Mason disagrees, advocating an ambitious view that "there is no reason to think the blameworthiness we take on is any less real than quality of will-based blameworthiness" (Mason 2019a: 260). Indeed, what is the point, after all, of a Strawsonian QW view? It's to emphasize that "our responsibility practices are socially constructed, and worth keeping because they regulate and rationalize our relationships" (Mason 2019a: 260). But among the things that regulate and rationalize our relationships are not just our qualities of will toward each other but also how we deal with inadvertent injuries. In these latter cases of "ambiguous agency," "the broader reasons that we have for our responsibility practices might be brought to bear more directly" (Mason: 2019a: 261). In other words, we might counsel taking responsibility, independently of QW, given its role and value in the construction and preservation of our personal relationships. This, Mason claims, is to "disrupt the standard view of what would count as the wrong sort of reason in this context" (Mason 2019a: 261).

But this is *precisely* the wrong sort of reason with respect to blameworthiness. It would be akin to making up a new rule to juice up the action in the middle of a boring baseball game (two strikes and you're out!), so as to promote more directly the values involved in playing and watching such games. Perhaps the rules committee can study the issue after the season, but even if they change the rules later,

---

[20] This is why remorse wouldn't be apt for losing a necklace you'd rented from a store, say. It's only in personal relationships that *feelings* of a certain sort are necessary. See Mason 2019a: 252–7.

they have to be respected in the meantime *during* games. To change baseball rules mid-game just isn't, well, cricket.

There are several other worries about the account that QW theorists can voice in defending their view. First, Mason's theory seems implausibly asymmetrical, on its face inapplicable to positive analogues of ambiguous agency. Imagine someone whose "faultless" inadvertence yielded some benefit to someone, so they "took responsibility" for it, feeling a swell of pride and inviting the praise of others. This strikes me as quite inapt, precisely because they lack a genuinely praiseworthy QW. Indeed, in some cases one can imagine it as a version of "stolen valor."

Second, it likely seems to many that Perdita couldn't really have *faultlessly* lost the necklace. If you've borrowed such a sentimental item from someone, the standards for what counts as "due care" for it are rather significantly ratcheted up (as in the baby-in-the-backseat case): Perdita ought to have been keeping track of where it was at all times, and she ought to have been noticing where she placed it on the counter, how she wore it, whether it was properly clasped, and so forth. It's thus hard to imagine that it simply disappeared without her having failed to live up to the ratcheted-higher standards of due care, despite what she asserts. And taking due care (or not) is of course a component of QW.

Third, even were we to have a more compelling case of truly faultless inadvertent harm before us, what it would do is render applicable an expectation for *owning up to it*, for feeling badly about having been involved in such a chain of events. To fail to do so would be callous. But now we are in Bernard Williams's lorry driver lane: This person's failure to adhere to the expectation about owning up to such misfortunes (even though she's not at fault *for* the misfortune, by stipulation) could itself be grounds for a couple of kinds of blame. She could be attributability-responsible for her poor quality of (callous) *character*, and she could also be accountability-responsible for her poor quality of regard in blithely failing to acknowledge her body's role in causing tragic events (for which she nevertheless wasn't at fault).[21] Neither of these targets of blame would render her faultless inadvertence *itself* blameworthy, though.

This last point drives home the fact that one may often have powerful (wrong kinds of) reasons *not* to take Masonian responsibility for cases of ambiguous agency if it meant that one would thereby be rendered the fitting target of various real blaming responses *from others*. Mason focuses only on the self-directed blame (remorse) that is ostensibly rendered fitting when one takes responsibility for inadvertent harms. But if Perdita really did lose the necklace inadvertently and went on to take responsibility for it, coming to feel genuinely fitting remorse, why shouldn't her friend also take seriously that Perdita has rendered herself truly responsible—truly blameworthy—for having lost it? It would then be fitting for

---

[21] I'm grateful to Itay Melamed for discussion of this last possibility.

her friend to be *slighted-angry* at Perdita, perhaps to shun her, to change her relationship with her, to protest her action, or more. But that hardly seems fair! These ought to remain ways of responding to actual wrongdoing or slights, but Perdita allegedly didn't do anything wrong (not even counterfactually), nor is her general moral orientation supposed to be thought objectionable in any way. It is this implication for other-blame that starts to make the view itself seem morally objectionable.

Once again, the QW theorist can defend against the challenge.

Racist and Sexist Beliefs

Turn finally to a recent challenge to QW theories that comes out of intriguing work by Mark Schroeder, Rima Basu, and Erin Beeghly, among others (Beeghly 2015 and 2021; Basu 2019a, 2019b, 2023a, and 2023b; Basu and Schroeder 2019; Schroeder 2018). I will mostly focus on Basu's version. Consider a "supposedly rational racist," named Spencer, who is a restaurant server holding the presumably racist belief that "black diners don't tip well," but who believes it in light of empirical evidence that suggests precisely such a verdict (the case and quotes are from Basu 2019a; the empirical evidence is from Lynn 2008). It seems that Spencer might be evidentially justified in his belief that a particular black diner in his section won't tip well, given the actual average racial disparities in tipping practices. This seems to be a morally wrongful and blameworthy—racist—belief, though. So how could a rational and evidentially justified belief be wrongful and blameworthy? Where and what exactly is the wrong here?

One natural thought is that the wrong is actually located downstream from the belief, found in the harmful consequences risked by holding such beliefs. Perhaps Spencer, for instance, won't treat his black customers as well as his non-black customers. Nonetheless, being harmed isn't necessary for being wronged, as the famous case of one partner secretly cheating on another presumably shows. Furthermore, as many people of color know, even if security guards in pricey stores don't actually *do* anything to them when they shop there, the guards' sometimes obvious *beliefs* that they'll probably steal can hurt, and so seem wrongful and blameworthy in and of themselves. Finally, we could just stipulate that Spencer won't in fact treat his customers any differently from those who don't have the belief. Even so, there still seems to be blameworthiness here.

One might try to locate the wrong *upstream* from the belief, then, in the racist background epistemic framework in which we all share essentializing views of others. But it's hard to see how a biased framework, especially if it's one we all share, could be wrong in and of itself. Indeed, how we are oriented to and see the world is in many—perhaps all—respects filtered through our various commitments and cares, and these are surely all biased in one way or another without rendering the resulting beliefs shaped by them *immoral* (Basu 2019a: 2507).

Furthermore, argues Basu, racist beliefs don't require any *hot irrationality*, a nasty attitude or unwarranted belief about members of the targeted groups. Spencer's case reveals this point: He's somehow wrong and blameworthy, despite his cold *and reasonable* belief about black diners (Basu 2019a: 2509–12).

Finally, one might try to resist the thought that beliefs themselves can wrong anyone, given the fact that we lack *control* over them. But this attempt won't help a pure QW theorist, given that many don't think control is even required for blameworthiness in the first place (see Scanlon 1998: ch. 6; Hieronymi 2004; Smith 2005; Talbert 2022). Further, as Basu plausibly notes, we do at least have some *indirect* control over many of our beliefs, likely a sufficient amount to ground the ordinary sort of blameworthiness for beliefs we often assign in everyday life. And we *do* assign blameworthiness for beliefs, it seems, quite a bit in everyday life (Basu 2023b).

So we seem to find ourselves with the conclusion that holding stereotyping beliefs can be immoral, in and of itself, and that such believers can thus fittingly be blamed, regardless of their QW. One can be a goodwilled (or at least not a bad-willed) racist, someone nevertheless blameworthy simply in virtue of holding certain beliefs in and of themselves (and even if they are held for good reason).

How to respond? First, it's not at all clear what the wrong actually consists in in these sorts of cases (reasonable and goodwilled racist believers). Basu doesn't spend any real time on this, primarily because she is more concerned to clear away objections to the general view.[22] Nonetheless, it all seems to start with this data point: "We care what people believe about us" (Basu 2019a: 2505). When we believe something about someone who cares that we *not* believe that thing of them, it can hurt, even wound. And this is one indication that we are in immoral or wronging territory: "The feeling of being wounded is arguably a sign of a directed wrong" (Basu and Schroeder 2019). One illustration that I mentioned in the previous chapter (altered a bit from Basu 2023a) comes from a father, running a family convenience store, who believes his daughter might have stolen money from the till (when, it turns out, he'd been giving a discount to some patrons without noting it on the receipts). His daughter, upon finding out that he believed this of her, is deeply wounded. And the other example previously noted (from Basu and Schroeder 2019) is of a husband eight months sober who comes home from a department party smelling of alcohol because someone spilled a drink on his jacket. He can tell from his wife's eyes that she immediately believes he's started drinking again. This too would be hurtful, given how hard he's worked.

---

[22] Although in Basu 2023a, she allows that identifying the precise nature of the wrong has been a more serious problem for views of moral encroachment than defenders have wanted to admit.

118   THE ARCHITECTURE OF BLAME AND PRAISE

In addition, when our hurtful beliefs are found out, we tend to *apologize* to those we've hurt. This too is ostensibly a sign of a directed wrong. In both cases above, the father may apologize to his daughter, and the wife may apologize to her husband, and it seems their apologies make sense only to the extent that they viewed themselves as having wronged their family members.

Consequently, as Basu writes:

> These two conditions—that the belief is one that the subject feels wounded by, and it's not unreasonable to seek apology for that belief—are central to explaining that it is the *belief* itself that wrongs. That is, these conditions locate the wrong in the belief itself, not in anything upstream or downstream...from the belief. (Basu 2023a: 4; emphasis in original)

Unfortunately, neither hurt nor apology does the trick. Start with hurt. Yes, we care what others believe of us, and yes, when people believe things of us we care about them not believing, it can hurt. But that fact doesn't at *all* imply that our belief is wrongful or blameworthy. Hurtful doesn't entail wrongful, a point I made in the previous chapter but that is worth reemphasizing here. Suppose you mistakenly think I'm more of a friend to you than I am—I consider us decent work colleagues, nothing more, and I never (mis)led you to believe otherwise—so when you find out that I've planned a weekend getaway with some of my other friends without including you, you may well be hurt. Or suppose you, my partner, don't believe my novel-in-progress is any good, and I overhear you telling that to someone else.[23] Or suppose you and I go on a blind date, and at the end I overhear you whispering to your friend on the phone, "I just don't think he's all that interesting."

These are all cases of hurt feelings, rendered apt by the mismatch between what the hurt person cares the hurter believes about her and what the hurter actually believes about her (where the latter is worse than what was hoped for). But in none of these cases has the believer done *anything* wrongful or blameworthy (see Shoemaker 2019b for many more examples and discussion). You can't get wrongfulness or blameworthiness from mere hurt feelings.

You can't get wrongfulness or blameworthiness easily from apologies either. People apologize for all sorts of non-wrong and non-blameworthy things. Just ask the British. Less glibly, we may apologize for accidentally bumping into someone, for being unable to keep a promise because we had an allergic reaction to a bee sting, for failing to recognize an old friend who's lost weight, for the actions of our children, for the leg-humping of our dogs, and much, much more. And we also apologize for hurting someone's feelings with hard truths, even though we delivered them with kindness: "I'm so sorry, but I just don't like you in that way." None of these apologies implicate immorality or blameworthiness.

---

[23] This is the premise of the recent film *You Hurt My Feelings*.

Neither hurt nor apology is anything like a reliable indicator of directed wrong or blameworthiness. But if these activities aren't available to draw from, then it's hard to see precisely what else one could draw from to establish the ostensible immorality of belief alone (without begging the question), let alone how *goodwilled* beliefs could wrong, and so this threat to QW theories disappears.[24]

In a different paper, Basu suggests one last possibility, that living in a racist world requires radically increased moral care in the formation of our beliefs (Basu 2019b). For example, a white person back in 1975 believing that a black man at a social club was a staff member might well have been epistemically justified, given the actual odds, and such a belief might in fact have been *true* in such a case. But even so, insists Basu, to believe this proposition *on the basis of his skin color* is paradigmatically racist—and so immoral. As a result, she argues that some moral considerations can in fact count as *evidence* against the formation of various beliefs (Basu 2019b). We owe it to our fellows, especially our fellows who have been subject to ongoing devaluation, oppression, and disrespect, to do right by them in our beliefs. These obligations obtain even for those who are ignorant of various injustices (and so lack a poor QW). As she puts it, in referring to how she'd not been taught anything about the removal of many oppressed minority children in Canada from their homes for the sake of assimilation:

> An account of doxastic morality that holds people responsible and morally blameworthy for the predictable consequences of our limited epistemic opportunities might be perverse. But, these wrongs at the level of the believer must be balanced against the fact that we must also do justice to this ongoing wrong that occurs when history is erased or forgotten. The wrong to First Nation, Inuit and Métis children is not just a wrong in how the Canadian government acted. If we do not accept responsibility and blame for our beliefs that are the result of forgetting or miseducation, we continue to contribute to a terrifying epistemological reality for the First Nation, Inuit and Métis peoples: we devalue their lives and experiences. (Basu 2019b: 18)

Thus can blame for otherwise reasonable-belief-with-good-will be called for, even though doing so may be "perverse" and "wrong," given the costs to social justice of not doing so.

This challenge urges a cost-benefit analysis in favor of committing the "wrong" of blaming individuals for their doxastic immorality even if they have a

---

[24] Others have argued that beliefs might wrong when they are disrespectful, or when they would violate demands of mutual recognition or proper ways of relating to others (see, respectively, Marušić and White 2018; Smith 2011). Note that both of these objections are aimed at, basically, attitudes motivated by *ill will* (or insufficiently good will), and so, if those attitudes are blameworthy, they would be so in virtue of the ill will they manifest, and these are reasons a QW theorist would actually embrace. What's distinctive about the Basu project in particular is that it's an attempt to find wronging and blameworthiness even where there *is* no ill will (as in the "supposedly rational racist").

sufficiently good QW in so believing, as it's ostensibly outweighed by the benefits of expressing respect to our oppressed fellows. But to urge blame in terms of the first-order costs and benefits of doing so is to adopt a version of the forward-looking justifications for blame that has long been rejected, especially amongst QW theorists, in part for its inhumanity (see, e.g., Strawson 1962/2003: 89 for this strong language). Indeed, once we divorce QW from blameworthiness for the sake of expedience, there is nothing preventing us from divorcing accurate attributions as well from blameworthiness—that is to say, *scapegoating*—for the sake of expedience. In other words, to the extent that its positive contribution to social justice would warrant blaming some people of good will for their immoral beliefs, so too might it contribute positively to social justice to blame some people who are merely perceived (mistakenly) to hold immoral beliefs, making them scapegoats for social justice. But surely attributing blameworthy beliefs to innocent people for the sake of social justice is itself unjust. Because it involves using innocent people as a mere means for the benefit of others, it's a deeply objectionable form of disrespect.

And so too would be any practice of blame that is exclusively governed by considerations of first-order social costs and benefits of blame, where the blame practices are thought justified independently of anyone's poor QW. To blame me for my good-faith efforts at belief formation that nevertheless run afoul of certain moral constraints, even if blaming me is done for the sake of social justice, is to use my ignorant self's pain in being blamed as a means for the betterment of society. That's unjust and disrespectful—immoral—full stop. If you can't blame innocent people for the sake of social justice, neither can you blame *non-culpable* people for the sake of social justice, where their non-culpability is a function of their having no objectionable QW.

Wrong kinds of reasons are rife here. Slighted-anger fits slights. And slights deliver *pro tanto* reasons: If someone slights you, you have a reason of fit to appraise what they've done as such by responding with anger. This reason obtains regardless of what other reason-generating value domains—like social justice—may be in play. Consequently, while considerations of social justice may well counsel *blaming* someone without a poor quality of will for their belief formation practices, they are the wrong kinds of reasons for counseling the blame*worthiness* of that person, insofar as fitting slighted-anger is purely a matter of correct appraisal of slights, which remains exclusively about QW.

Of course, perhaps I've misunderstood the points being made here. Perhaps the idea instead is that we simply have to take greater care in our belief formation when it comes to members of historically oppressed or marginalized groups. Basu actually concludes her article with the following lines:

> To practice the virtue of wokeness is to exercise a kind of indirect long-term control over how we engage in inquiry, what sources we attend to, when we stop

inquiry and when we extend it, what evidence we look for and how we evaluate it, etc. Just as we are responsible and can be held accountable for the development of our moral character, I suggest that there is an epistemic virtue of wokeness that we are responsible and can be held accountable for, and that bears on the development of our epistemic character. It will be hard to sustain and develop this epistemic virtue, but it's not easy being a good person. (Basu 2019b: 19)

This way of putting it, however, is *all about quality of will*! It's about the virtue of *attending* properly, of *evaluating* evidence in the right way, of how and for what reasons we *develop* our epistemic character. But this is no challenge at all to QW theories (or even control-based theories); indeed, it seems to rely on them, as these activities are themselves all evaluable in terms of how seriously we take the interests of our fellows. This conclusion thus seems to undercut the more provocative claims made in the rest of the papers by essentially affirming a QW theory after all.

Conclusion

None of these challenges—old school or new school—to QW theories of emotional blame's fitmakers truly threaten the theory. One key to the defense is pluralism about the "will": sometimes it's about character, sometimes about judgment, sometimes it's about regard, sometimes it's about two of these, and sometimes it's about all three. Of course, I can't survey every single case of ostensibly fitting emotional blame or praise to see if this is the right target. Instead, I offer this as a theory that explains quite a lot, and it remains to be seen whether there are indeed challenges out there to it that might in the end be more successful than those I've surveyed here. Until then, I'm cautiously optimistic that the pluralistic QW story remains the right story of emotional blame's and praise's fitting targets.[25]

The Architecture of Blame and Praise: An Interdisciplinary Investigation. David Shoemaker, Oxford University Press.
© David Shoemaker 2024. DOI: 10.1093/9780198915867.003.0007

---

[25] My only hesitation here comes from my previous writing about hurt feelings, which seem sometimes to be responses to responsible agency that have a blame-like cast, but that don't necessarily target poor QW (see Shoemaker 2019b). I leave it to others, though, to suss out whether hurt feelings are indeed blaming responses when we have them.

8

Directions

Until this point, I've been focused almost exclusively on blame and praise directed at others. This is standard methodology in philosophy and psychology. The assumption, at least for philosophers, has been that once we figure out the nature and conditions of other-directed forms of blame and praise, they will simply carry over to the self-directed forms. In other words, there's nothing distinctive about self-directed blame and praise: it's just standard issue blame and praise aimed in a different direction.

This assumption is false. There are some essential differences between other-blame and self-blame, and these differences call for additions to our architectural design. These additions also come with new normative conditions, which I will detail as well.[1]

Athletic Self-Blame

Tom Brady is often referred to as one of the greatest American football quarterbacks of all time. His ability for pinpoint passing, taking hits without fumbling, identifying weaknesses in defenses, and simply finding ways to win was unparalleled. And yet every once in a while he seemed very unhappy with himself. After throwing an interception, even in a meaningless game, he would sometimes wail and moan, even falling to his knees and pounding his helmet with his hands or, in a few cases, viciously tossing his sideline iPad to the ground. He was obviously blaming himself.

There are many other familiar examples: Serena Williams, behind in a tennis match, used to scream at herself, pound her racket, and stomp her foot; Tiger Woods would stare in shock and then mutter to himself for missing a putt; Lionel Messi may cover his eyes or pull his jersey over his head after missing a crucial penalty kick. And this sort of response is not the exclusive purview of elite athletes. The weekend golf "duffer" who shanks her iron shot, the aging academic who misses an easy layup in a departmental basketball game, the bar denizen playing pool who scratches on the 8-ball—regular folks like us also clearly blame ourselves for our competitive failures.

---

[1] I draw some of the material that follows from Shoemaker 2022b.

DIRECTIONS 123

In theorizing about blame, philosophers and psychologists tend to draw from the interpersonal, overt, and directed paradigm: blame is taken to be a response, depending on the specific theory, to someone else's ill will, moral wrongdoing, or relationship impairment, and it consists in demands, invitations, conversational moves, communiques, protests, and/or relationship modifications.[2] But while some of these overt, directed, interpersonal features might seem to be present in some cases of self-blame, they are quite hard to find in cases, such as those we've surveyed, of athletic self-blame. The athletes haven't done anything *to* anyone else, let alone anything for which any others could legitimately blame them.[3] They didn't manifest a poor quality of will, they didn't damage any relationships, they didn't violate any of their fellows' demands, they didn't make any "threatening" claims, and they haven't engaged in any moral wrongdoing. And what does their self-blame consist in? Well, we know what it *isn't*: They aren't making conversational moves with themselves, they aren't communicating a demand for acknowledgment from themselves (they already know what they did!), they aren't protesting their threatening behavior, and they aren't modifying their relationships with themselves (what might that even mean?). Athletic self-blame constitutes a surprisingly serious prima facie counterexample to theories that take other-blame to be their paradigm.

Recently, though, a few enterprising theorists have advanced and defended the idea that self-blame is actually more fundamental than other-blame, and that we can and should understand other-blame in light of it.[4] Understanding the athletic cases, then, should simply be a matter of applying the more fundamental notion of self-blame to that specific instantiation of it.

As I will show first, though, such a move won't work, precisely because it relies on a crucial misunderstanding about the emotional nature of self-blame that is, unfortunately, maintained widely in the literature. I will then go on to take a fresh look at self-blame by *starting* with the athletic cases, arguing ultimately for the view that they have very different paradigmatic emotional cores from other-blame, and that as a result we cannot understand either form of emotional blame in terms of the other.

---

[2] See, e.g., McKenna 2012; Watson 2004; Smith 2013; Scanlon 2008.

[3] Perhaps the professional athletes at least have failed their fans or the team owner? Fans surely don't have a claim on an elite athlete's perfect performance. I myself don't think they have *any* kind of accountability claim on athletes except, perhaps, that the athletes put in a good faith effort in accordance with the rules, which might be the same claim the owners have on them. But I just can't see how one could think that Tom Brady violates any obligation to his fans when, in trying his hardest, he nevertheless throws an interception. This may *disappoint* his fans, but it can't fail or betray them. Of course, we can get rid of all the fans in the cases of the everyday golfer and pool player, and when it comes to the professionals, we can focus just on cases of self-blame they may engage in on the practice field or when working out alone to make the point. Thanks to Dana Nelkin, Randy Clarke, Angie Smith, and Sandy Reiter for discussion.

[4] Carlsson 2017 and 2019 is the leading example; Duggan 2018 takes a somewhat similar tack; Clarke 2013 and 2016 is a forerunner only in some respects; Graham 2014 is an ally, but again, only in some respects.

124   THE ARCHITECTURE OF BLAME AND PRAISE

Emotional Blame

When theorists talk about the "blaming emotions," they typically share several assumptions in common. First, their focus is often exclusively on the Strawsonian Holy Trinity: resentment, indignation, and guilt.[5] Resentment and indignation are taken to be the paradigmatic emotional forms of "other-blame," both of them "cognitively sharpened" forms of anger (D'Arms and Jacobson 2003; Pereboom 2014: 179). Guilt, then, is taken to be the paradigmatic emotional form of "self-blame."

A second common assumption is that these blaming emotions really just differ in terms of their standpoints and targets, an assumption that comes straight out of Strawson as well. Resentment he calls *personal*, a reaction to poor quality of will manifested toward *us*, where we have been the victims of some "injury or indifference" (Strawson 1962/2003: 83). Strawson describes indignation as the paradigmatic example of "sympathetic or vicarious or impersonal or disinterested or generalized analogues of the [personal] reactive attitudes...reactions to the qualities of others' wills, not towards ourselves, but towards others" (Strawson 1962/2003: 83). And he completes the picture by pointing out, "Just as there are personal and vicarious reactive attitudes associated with demands on others for oneself and demands on others for others, so there are self-reactive attitudes associated with demands on oneself for others" (Strawson 1962/2003: 84). And here we arrive at self-directed reactive attitudes that include "feeling guilty or remorseful or at least responsible" (Strawson 1962/2003: 85).

There are nuances and interesting wrinkles in Strawson's own account that have gone underappreciated.[6] Nevertheless, most Strawsonians have gravitated toward the now-consensus view that resentment constitutes emotional blame's second-personal mode, a victim's response to the offender who injured or slighted her; indignation constitutes emotional blame's third-personal mode, someone else's response to that offender (which could be any member of the moral community, in principle); and guilt constitutes emotional blame's first-personal mode, an offender's response to him- or herself in light of the offense.

A third shared assumption amongst emotional blame theorists in the Strawsonian tradition is that all three blame emotions mutually entail one another. This means that (a) if it's appropriate for me to resent an offender for injuring or slighting me, then (b) it's also appropriate for you (and others) to be indignant toward this offender, *and* (c) it's appropriate for the offender to feel guilt for what he did.[7]

---

[5] Strawson 1962/2003: 77–89; Wallace 1994: 20–5, 51–2; Fischer and Ravizza 1998: 5–8; Darwall 2005: ch. 4; McKenna 2012: 71–3; Franklin 2013; Carlsson 2017: 92; and many more.

[6] For careful and insightful discussion, see Sars 2022.

[7] This point is explicitly in Carlsson 2017: 102, but it's suggested all over the place, including in Wallace 1994, Darwall 2005: 66–70, and McKenna 2012: 64–6.

DIRECTIONS 125

Given the mutual entailment and symmetrical structures of their representative emotions, emotional self- and other-blame are thought to be characterizable under a single umbrella theory. As noted earlier, most people theorize first about other-blame, and then they simply apply their findings to self-blame, but this method leaves them vulnerable to the serious prima facie counterexample of athletic self-blame. Does the recent movement to start with self-blame thus do any better?

Guilt Mongers

The movement has been spearheaded by Andreas Brekke Carlsson, in a few important papers (Carlsson 2017 and 2019). I will call him and those inclined to follow or offer variations on him the *Guilt Mongers*, because their fundamental claim is that *emotional self-blame is just guilt*, and "an agent is blameworthy in virtue of the fact and to the extent that he deserves to feel guilt" (Carlsson 2017: 91), where guilt necessarily involves suffering, that is, "the pain of recognizing what you have done" in wronging someone (Carlsson 2017: 91).

On Carlsson's view, resentment and indignation, even if they demand guilt, can be apt while remaining private, and when they are kept private they don't necessarily cause pain to anyone. That means they don't necessarily call for any moral justification (as pain-causing typically does).[8] Guilt enjoys no such privacy shield, though: to feel guilt just is to feel its pain. Being caused to feel the pain of guilt thus needs moral justification, which presumably has to come from, yes, its being *deserved* (Carlsson 2017).[9] Now to deserve guilt requires that one meet more robust control conditions than is required by resentment or indignation, which may suggest a disanalogy between self- and other-blame. Carlsson, however, argues instead that we can preserve the analogy between self-blame and other-blame by taking deserved guilt to be "the basic notion in our conception of blameworthiness" (Carlsson 2017: 103, drawing in part from Clarke 2016). The more fundamental appeal to guilt then reveals what makes resentment and indignation appropriate: Someone is other-blameworthy for something—that is, someone is an appropriate target of another's resentment and indignation for that thing—if and only if that someone deserves to feel guilt (self-blame) for it (Carlsson 2017: 104). Consequently, when resentment and indignation are experienced and expressed, they count as other-blame in virtue of their guilt-mongering aims (Carlsson 2017: 105).

---

[8] Obviously, those who think purely private attitudes can harm disagree. See the discussion of such attitudes in Chapter 6.

[9] There are others who have run a line like this about guilt and desert, including McKenna 2012 and Clarke 2013 and 2016.

How might this approach apply to our athletes? It just doesn't. Instead, it should be obvious that most athletes who blame themselves for their poor performances typically don't feel anything remotely like guilt about it. Consider: If I am playing by myself and miss a 2-foot putt for par, or if you scratch on the 8-ball while playing some barroom pool with a friend, we may blame ourselves, but it will be utterly without guilt. This is true too in the high-profile athletic cases. When Serena Williams broke her racket during tournament play, she wasn't experiencing or expressing guilt! Consequently, if the self-blame-first strategy is a guilt-first strategy, it fails to account for many obvious cases of athletic self-blame.

One might insist that the account of blame being proposed, both self- and other-, pertains only to *moral accountability*, the kind of blame in which we hold others and ourselves to account for violations of moral demands and expectations in sanction-ey ways. Thus it can sidestep the athletic cases insofar as they don't involve moral violations, and no one else has any standing to blame the athletes either.

There are real difficulties with this move (and I will deal with the move more generally in the final section of the next chapter). First, it's very tough to articulate a principled difference between the moral and non-moral domains. Moral foundations theory has, over the last twenty years, thoroughly undermined the biased Western view that morality is entirely and exclusively about rights and claims about harm and fairness; it also includes, for many around the world, norms pertaining to authority, loyalty, purity, and other values (see Haidt and Joseph 2004 and Graham et al. 2013, among many others). And once those other moral foundations are included in the mix, finding a unifying principle or value underneath them all has proven elusive (see, e.g., Sinnott-Armstrong and Wheatley 2012).

More to the point, though, some athletes may in fact think of their self-blame as a matter of moral accountability, where they have failed to live up to certain self-set moral *ideals*, standards of excellence to which they hold themselves. Indeed, they may feel that they owe such excellence to their fans, so that failures to live up to those ideals strike them as failures of moral accountability. We can't rule this out by fiat. Even so, these failures aren't something to which they respond with *guilt*.

We can avoid these problems altogether by following Douglas Portmore in expanding the emotional repertoire of self-blame to include, beyond guilt, *regret* and/or *remorse* (Portmore 2022).[10] Now most of the athletes we are considering probably aren't feeling remorse either. But they are likely feeling *regret*, and regret is painful in its own right, sometimes as painful as guilt. Consequently, we could

---

[10] I should stress that Portmore is not a Guilt Monger, for he thinks he is developing a conceptual account of blame proper that applies equally to self- and other-blame (and so he doesn't think one form of blame is more fundamental than the other).

construe the more expansive Guilt Mongering view to be that, to the extent that these athletes are blaming themselves aptly, they must be representing themselves as blameworthy and are aiming to cause the blame-pain of regret in themselves. But insofar as aptly aiming at (self-)pain requires moral justification, their pain must be deserved to render their regret-mongering justified. We can then continue to understand other-blame on the analogy with self-blame, as still foreseeably aiming to instill *self-directed emotional pain* (be it guilt, remorse, or regret).

With this tweak, the Guilt Mongers' general approach, and its application to athletic self-blame, looks more promising. Unfortunately, it makes the mistake of many other accounts of blame by misunderstanding the relation between the self-directed emotions and blame more generally.

Blame and Guilt

Here's the problem: *Guilt just isn't a form of blame, let alone self-blame.*[11] Guilt is instead best understood as a *response* to blame, both self- and other-. More carefully, guilt is a response to *being* blamed. But of course it isn't a response *only* to being blamed; it may also respond directly to one's perception of one's own wrongdoing (or ill will, or failure to meet a legitimate demand, etc.), without its having been spurred by blame of any kind (including self-blame). I can (aptly) feel guilt without having been blamed by anyone, including myself.[12]

This makes guilt an uneasy—unholy?—member of the Trinity. Let's assume, as is plausible, that indignation and resentment are the paradigmatic emotional cores of other-blame. When expressed to a wrongdoer, they may best be described (especially by the Guilt Mongers) as *guilting* the wrongdoer, that is, as drawing her attention to what she did and aiming for her to feel guilt as a result. But that's explicitly to aim for her to have the proper *response* to their blame. They don't feel

---

[11] The conflation is everywhere. See, e.g., R. J. Wallace: "To hold myself responsible for a moral wrong [i.e., to blame myself], for example, it is sufficient that I should feel guilt about my violation of a moral obligation that I accept...[R]esentment, indignation, and guilt are backward-looking emotions, responses to the actions of a particular agent...they are essentially *about* such actions, in a way that exactly captures the backward-looking focus of moral blame....*Once blame is understood in terms of the reactive emotions*...we...have a natural and appealing explanation to hand of what unifies the sanctioning responses to which the stance of holding people responsible disposes us" (Wallace 1994: 67; second emphasis mine). See also McKenna 2012: 72: "In moral contexts, guilt is the self-reflexive emotion whereby one holds oneself morally responsible and blameworthy for doing wrong. In short, it constitutes self-blame." See also Carlsson 2019: "To blame oneself in the accountability sense is to feel guilt." Finally, see Portmore 2022, who gives "fitting guilt" as one example of self-blame (the others being regret and remorse, as just noted).

[12] Of course, we do say things like, "I blame myself, I just feel terrible for what I did." But this simply means that I *take* the blame, that is, I accept any blame there is for what I did *by* feeling the appropriate guilt.

128 THE ARCHITECTURE OF BLAME AND PRAISE

guilt in guilting her, after all. So other-directed blame certainly doesn't consist in guilt.

Perhaps, then, only self-directed blame consists in guilt. But again, if the proper aim of (all) blame, as the Guilt Mongers would have it, is to *guilt* the offender, that is, to get her to feel guilt, then if I'm blaming myself, my blame can't consist in my guilt. If my aim in self-blame is to get myself to feel guilt for my own wrongdoing, then the blame itself can't consist in what it *aims* for. Imagine this absurd conversation: "Why do you feel guilt?" "I'm blaming myself." "To what end?" "So that I will feel guilt." My guilt in such a case would have to be a response to my guilt*ing* myself. But guilting isn't guilt, and so neither is self-blame.

But isn't guilt a stinging and costly (insofar as hard to fake) signal of my commitment to some norms, norms I've violated? Surely when I feel guilt, it (typically) sends off signals (via pained expressions, gnashing of teeth, etc.), conveying otherwise hard to glean information about me and my striving to patrol norms to which I'm committed. If so, doesn't guilt fall under my functionalist rubric of blame after all?[13] No. Recall from Chapter 2 that most of blame's actual signaling costs are risked by the fact that it stings. But "stings" is ambiguous, between its aim and its effect. Blame aims to sting. And when blamed, one is (typically) stung. It's being stung that contributes to norm maintenance: when your anger or mockery stings me, I'm much more apt to toe the normative line I crossed. The sting mockery-blame delivers typically consists in embarrassment, shame, or humiliation, but clearly none of these are instances of blame; they are simply responses to being mocking-blamed. The sting that slighted-anger delivers typically consists in guilt or remorse. But this too isn't an instance of blame's *stinger*; it's just what being stung (by acknowledgment-seeking slighted-anger) feels like. And it's also the feeling that typically motivates us to toe the normative line.

So if self-blame isn't guilt or remorse, what is it, then? As should be obvious from the athletic cases, it is a kind of *anger*. This is one respect in which self-blame remains analogous with other-blame's paradigms—resentment and indignation—as they too are types of anger. And this should feel familiar and plausible: We get angry at ourselves for our screw-ups on a regular basis (or at least I do, as I screw up regularly), and we do so across all normative domains, not just in the domain of "moral accountability," but also in prudential, aesthetic, culinary, epistemological, and, yes, athletic domains.

Blame's most familiar, paradigmatic emotional core, both self- and other- is anger. This fact might seem to suggest, then, that other-blame and self-blame really only differ in terms of their directions after all, that they are, in their core content, identical. Yet here's an odd little puzzle suggesting otherwise.

---

[13] Thanks to Doug Portmore for raising this question.

Hypocrisy and Self-Blame

If self-blame were fully analogous with other-blame, identical in core content and differing only in direction, then a familiar complaint against some instances of other-directed blame should apply all the time against every instance of self-blame.[14] But it never does. So self-blame is not fully analogous with other-blame.

That, at any rate, is the abstract argument I will now fill in and develop. Suppose that we are friends. I tend to lie to you on a regular basis about fairly trivial things (e.g., that I saw a concert I never really saw, that I'm taller than I in fact am), and I do so without apology or guilt. While you know this fact about me and don't like it very much, you put up with it, as we have been friends for a long time. One day you lie to me in the same fashion that I regularly lie to you, and when I find out, I self-righteously and angrily blame you for doing so. Your response to me will—and likely should—be: "Who are *you* to blame me?! You do this all the time!"[15] I'm a hypocrite, of course, and my hypocrisy renders my anger at you "off" in an important way, making it something you may rightly ignore, even if what you did was in fact blameworthy.[16]

Here is the oddity: If self-blame and other-blame were essentially identical in content, differing only in their directions, then self-blame should ground a charge of hypocrisy *in its every instance*. That's because if the blamer is one and the same person as the blamed, then the blaming-self is unapologetically guilty of having done precisely what the blamed-self did. So were I to angrily blame myself for slighting someone, I-the-blamed ought to be able to challenge me-the-blamer with the familiar complaint of hypocritical other-blame: "Who are *you* to blame *me*?" But this is just silly; such a charge never arises and seems inapt besides. And yet we obviously engage in lots of seemingly apt self-blame. So self-blame and other-blame can't be, directions aside, essentially identical in their core content.[17]

This puzzle resonates with Plato's remark in the *Republic* that the notion of self-control, taken literally, is "ridiculous," as the "stronger self that does the controlling is the same as the weaker self that gets controlled, so that only one person is referred to in all such expressions" (430e–431a). Plato's solution was to render

---

[14] I received, and am grateful for, helpful feedback on the ideas in this section from the readers of PEA Soup in response to my post of August 2019, https://peasoupblog.com/2019/08/the-puzzle-of-hypocritical-self-blame/. I'm also grateful to Kasper Lippert-Rasmussen and Thomas Pink for helpful discussion and pushback.

[15] For the "Who are you?" form of the objection to hypocrisy, see Tognazzini and Coates 2018. This is merely one dramatic way of putting a hypocrisy charge to someone.

[16] For the term "offness" to describe hypocritical blame in as neutral terms as possible, I'm grateful to Eric Brown. See his 2020 dissertation, "The Offness of Blame: A Defense of Universal Standing" (Tulane University).

[17] Since I made this point in Shoemaker 2022b, Todd and Rabern 2022 published "The Paradox of Self-Blame," which sets forth the situation I've just described as a paradox. Their solution is to argue that self-blame is thus inappropriate. This strikes me as overly revisionary, especially given the availability of the solution I'm about to outline.

130   THE ARCHITECTURE OF BLAME AND PRAISE

the phrase intelligible by distinguishing between different parts in the soul of a person, so that a self-controlled soul is one in which the naturally better part of the person (reason) controls the naturally worse part of the person (appetite).

So too, in trying to explain why there can't be hypocritical self-blame, we might try to distinguish between different parts of the soul, a (naturally better?) blaming part and a (naturally worse?) blamed part. And indeed, this is precisely what Adam Smith urges:

> When I endeavor to examine my own conduct, when I endeavor to pass sentence upon it, and either to approve or condemn it, it is evident, in all such cases, I divide myself, as it were, into two persons; and that I, the examiner and judge, represent a different character from that other I, the person whose conduct is examined into and judged of. The first is the spectator, whose sentiments with regard to my own conduct I endeavor to enter into, by placing myself in his situation, and by considering how it would appear to me, when seen from that particular point of view. The second is the agent, the person whom I properly call myself, and of whose conduct, under the character of a spectator, I was endeavoring to form some opinion. The first is the judge; the second the person judged of: But that the judge should, in every respect, be the same with the person judged of, is as impossible, as that the cause should, in every respect, be the same with the effect. (Smith, *Theory of Moral Sentiments*, Part III, Chapter 1)

Regardless of Smith's final assertion, though, the judger and judged *are* one and the same person! Taking up one's behavior from different perspectives does not literally divide one.[18] Consequently, the "person judged" still ought to be able to legitimately demand of the "judge," "Who are *you* to blame me?!" Furthermore, while there is something phenomenologically plausible about Plato's picture of a wrestling match between reason and appetite in the face of temptation, there is no such phenomenological wrestling in self-blame. Indeed, when I blame myself for something, the thorough *unity* of blamer and blamed is what feels most striking.

Alternatively, then, we might appeal to Alfred Mele's explanation of self-deception, a phenomenon which on its face is also puzzling: In self-deception, I have somehow brought myself to simultaneously believe both p and not-p (Mele 1987: 121–2). Mele's solution is that in such cases I might have caused myself to be deceived unintentionally, and, further, that this can be a function of motivated irrationality, a desire to believe something against evidence that I might easily have absorbed and deployed in my belief-formation were it not for the desire in question (Mele 1987: 136).

---

[18] Thanks to Richard Moran for discussion.

DIRECTIONS   131

Nevertheless, self-blame isn't, or isn't necessarily, irrational, and it's not necessarily a function of motivated reasoning. If I have slighted someone else, then I *do* have a *pro tanto* reason to feel slighted-angry at myself (as do all others have a reason to feel slighted-angry at me). Indeed, we often talk as if self-blame is both rational and appropriate. Yet surely we don't think the self-blamer is a hypocrite. So what gives?

The answer, which you may have already foreseen, draws from the discussion in Chapter 5: Angry other-blame and angry self-blame are, paradigmatically, *different types of anger*. Recall my case for there being two types of anger, slighted-anger and goal-frustrated-anger. I differentiated between these two types in order to give the competing motivations and appraisals historically associated with anger their due: Sometimes we're moved to confront people by our anger and sometimes we're moved by it simply to overcome frustrating goal-blockages, and these different motivational impulses can occur independently or together. I also differentiated the two types in order to make sense of very different appraisals sometimes associated with our anger: While we adults often angrily appraise what others do to us as slights, angry babies aren't doing any such thing; they are instead just angrily crying in response to not getting something that they want. Finally, there are different things being sought by each type of anger. My slighted-anger at you seeks empathic acknowledgment; my goal-frustrated anger just seeks—hopes for—blockage-removal.

This important distinction is further bolstered in plausibility once we see how easily it can be wielded to dissolve the puzzle of hypocritical self-blame: The paradigmatic angry core of other-directed blame is slighted-anger, and the paradigmatic angry core of self-blame is goal-frustrated anger. Hypocrisy can attach only to the former.

To explain, in other-directed cases, when I hypocritically blame you, I-the-hypocrite am blaming you with slighted-anger. I am appraising what you did (lying to me, in this case) as a slight—you have raised yourself above me, taking yourself to count, normatively, more than I do—and my action-tendency is to confront you with a demand for remorseful acknowledgment, a demand for you to painfully appreciate from my perspective how you made me feel in slighting me this way, so that our normative equilibrium may be restored. But given that I have also done, unapologetically, what I'm slighted-angry at you now for doing, my blame of you is hypocritical, in the sense that I'm demanding remorseful acknowledgment from you for doing the very same thing which I myself have *not* remorsefully acknowledged having done. I have thus placed myself above you (via a slight which persists), upsetting our normative equilibrium already, while demanding that *you* be the one to restore it. But I'm the reason we are out of normative whack with one another, so I thus lack some kind of standing, right, or authority to make any such demand from you until *I've* restored that equilibrium (via apology and sincere remorse, say).

132   THE ARCHITECTURE OF BLAME AND PRAISE

Goal-frustrated anger makes *no* such demands; indeed, it can't, as much of our goal-frustration is in response to non-agents. But when it is in response to agents, for pure goal-frustration-*without*-slights, it simply wants the frustration to stop, wants the blockage to go away. Because that's all that goal-frustration anger seeks (hopes or wishes for), it has nothing to do with normative equilibrium, and it has no authority or standing requirements whatsoever. *Anyone* has standing to hope, wish, or ask that someone frustrating their goals (without slighting them) stop doing so.

So what does this activity have to do with self-blame? Why is goal-frustration anger its paradigmatic emotional core? What does it look like? And don't we nevertheless get slighted-angry at ourselves? I aim to answer these questions by actually starting my investigation explicitly with cases of athletic self-blame.

"Yer Gonna Make Me Give Myself a Good Talkin' To"[19]

The most plausible construal of the paradigmatic emotional core of self-blame is that it is "talking angrily to oneself." In laying out this view, I draw from findings in the empirical literature about a phenomenon labeled "self-talk," which has remarkable effects on athletes and has been studied widely in the athletic domain by theorists of sports psychology, competitive anxiety, exercise, and cognitive behavioral therapy.

Here is how the concept of self-talk is operationalized in the literature: "(a) verbalizations or statements addressed to the self; (b) multidimensional in nature; (c) having interpretive elements associated with the content of statements employed; (d) is somewhat dynamic; and (e) serving at least two functions; instructional and motivational" (Hardy 2006: 84). This is meant to capture a phenomenon with which we should all be intimately familiar. Just think back to your last bout of exercise and the ways you might well have coaxed yourself to get through it (e.g., "Just ten more reps, you can do it!").

What are the effects of self-talk on the studied athletes? As demonstrated repeatedly, it can dramatically increase their motivation and mental toughness (Hatzigeorgiadis et al. 2008; Hardy 2006: 88). Positive self-talk (as in "That's it!" or "You're doing great, keep it up!") can actually increase physical endurance, staving off exhaustion significantly longer than for those in non-self-talking control groups (Blanchfield et al. 2014). And, very importantly for our purposes, *negative* self-talk (e.g., "That was terrible!" or "What are you *doing*?") can increase both motivation and performance *equally as well* in some athletes (Van Raalte et al. 1994; Van Raalte et al. 1995; Hardy 2006: 88).[20]

---

[19]   From Bob Dylan's "You're Gonna Make Me Lonesome When You Go."

[20]   For some athletes, however, negative self-talk correlates with decreased motivation and performance. Unfortunately, the phenomenon of negative self-talk remains understudied, and it seems that many psychologists view it, almost a priori, as dangerous or imprudent for athletes to engage in.

DIRECTIONS   133

Self-talk has also begun to be studied outside of the athletic domain. In both its positive and negative expressions, it has been found to reduce shyness (Coplan and Armer 2005), and even pain (Girodo and Wood 1979), and there is a well-documented link between self-talk and the formation of various emotions (Lazarus 1982; Hardy, Hall, and Alexander 2001). One can, of course, talk oneself into emotions like anger and fear by repeatedly refocusing one's attention on the anger- or fear-making properties. But one can also regulate one's emotions, and increase one's emotional intelligence generally, by deploying self-talk (Lane et al. 2009).

I believe that self-blame's paradigmatic emotional core is *negative self-talk*, which is itself an expression of goal-frustration anger. The action-tendencies of goal-frustration anger are toward eliminating or bypassing a blockage, and they don't care one whit for any agential *why* (i.e., quality of will) at the source of the blockage. And because the *why* doesn't matter, the reflexive nature of the anger cannot generate the charge of hypocrisy, a charge that sticks on someone only in virtue of their insufficiently good will in disrupting the normative equilibrium. But quality of will is irrelevant to goal-frustrated anger, which focuses instead simply on the *fact* of goal-frustration and how to overcome it, not on any of the *reasons* someone may have had for frustrating that goal. That's why questions of standing, authority, or hypocrisy don't arise.

Goal-frustration anger has precisely the same content and plays precisely the same role as negative self-talk, according to the psychological literature: In angrily criticizing yourself for frustrating your own goals, you are motivating yourself to get around self-caused obstacles and to improve your performance. Self-talk is thus crucially *forward-looking*: It aims explicitly to keep your head in the game, to get you to try harder, and to expand your physical limits. These good consequences may be achieved, the empirical research tells us, by either positive or negative self-talk. When it is negative ("Keep your stupid head still when putting!"), it's an extremely familiar form of what we can only describe as self-blame.[21] The anger involved isn't about accusing and guilting, though; rather, it is about *coaching* and *constructing*. But obviously this makes it a very different form of emotional blame than the slighted-anger of other-blame that I have been investigating to this point in the book, which is instead backward-looking, tracks the *why* (quality of will) of agential activities, responds to and appraises slights, motivates confrontation, and seeks empathic remorseful acknowledgment.

At the beginning of Chapter 6, I explored the difference between backward-looking and forward-looking justifications for blame and praise, and I noted that I thought most blame and praise are backward-looking. At this point, I can clarify

---

I think the cases of Tom Brady and Serena Williams are powerful counterexamples to that thought, however.

[21] It should also be obvious that I think the best construal of self-*praise* is positive self-talk, although I won't go into it much here, as there's really nothing more to say about it than that.

134 THE ARCHITECTURE OF BLAME AND PRAISE

that this is indeed true, so I think, but only for other-directed blame. When the blame is directed to oneself, the opposite is true: most of it is forward-looking, justified by its presumed good effects in removing goal-frustration. This fact yields a complicating nuance to the mutual entailment thesis: To the extent that your apt blame of me entails that my blame of myself would also be apt, their fundamental grounds may be different, as your blame of me may be apt in virtue of fitting what I *did*, whereas my blame of me may be rendered apt in virtue of *what it may motivate me to do or become.* This is an intriguing result, I think.

Nonmoral Self-Talk

The self-directed goal-frustrated anger I've been discussing is certainly present in the cases of athletic self-blame with which I began. But it extends to many other domains, albeit mostly nonmoral ones (another contrast with other-directed slighted anger).[22] In some recent psychological work, subjects were asked to think back to times when they had been angry at themselves, and these responses were studied in comparison with memories subjects had about when they had felt anger at others, as well as when they had felt shame or guilt at something that they themselves had done. While shame, guilt, and other-directed anger all tended to have predominantly moral overtones, self-directed anger simply did not. That is to say, people who got angry at others typically appealed to moral language, saying that "what happened was unfair and morally wrong" (Ellsworth and Tong 2006: 581), and people who felt shame or guilt also said "that they were morally wrong" (Ellsworth and Tong 2006: 582). But while people who reported having felt *angry* at themselves did believe they'd done something wrong, they did "not see the situation as involving a moral violation" (Ellsworth and Tong 2006: 581–2). This point is borne out by the kinds of examples subjects repeatedly gave for what they remembered causing their self-directed anger: "hitting one's head against a shelf, locking oneself out of the house...losing keys, getting a bad grade" (Ellsworth and Tong 2006: 579). This in fact explains why the overwhelming action-tendency of self-directed anger in the psychological studies was "wanting to get out of the situation" (Ellsworth and Tong 2006: 582). And the most natural response to this kind of self-directed anger, then, is not guilt, shame, or remorse; it is, rather, *embarrassment* (which, interestingly, is also often a

---

[22] It also extends to some cases of *other*-blame too, although I won't go into any detail about it in the text. But the anger of actual coaches to players, of fans to artists who "sell out," and of chefs to their line cooks is often goal-frustrated anger as well. As such, it also has the characteristics of negative self-talk I've discussed here regarding self-blame: It too is about coaching and constructing, it is forward-looking, and it often generates the kinds of responses akin to those of self-directed goal-frustration anger that I'm about to discuss, namely, a kind of sheepish embarrassment. I'm grateful to Alexander Velichkov for raising and discussing this issue with me.

DIRECTIONS   135

response to mockery-blame from others). This is why people often try to keep self-directed anger private, or to avoid being seen during such episodes: They want to hide their embarrassment, to avoid others seeing the kind of stupid goal-frustration they caused themselves (Ellsworth and Tong 2006: 582).

Moral Self-Blame

The most familiar emotional form of self-blame is negative self-talk, primarily nonmoral, forward-looking, goal-frustrated anger. This is how the elite athletes I've mentioned enjoin themselves to greater performance. But it is how we ordinary schlubs enjoin ourselves to greater performance too, across many normative domains. In recognizing our prudential, culinary, aesthetic, philosophical, epistemic, and athletic failings, we may angrily talk to ourselves in an attempt to rouse our motivation to overcome the blockades we ourselves have put in the way of achieving our own goals.

But why is this pretty exclusively a *non*moral phenomenon? It's because there is something distinctive about the moral domain—the domain of slights, guilt, and remorseful acknowledgment—that has a curious psychological upshot when we try to blame ourselves for slighting others. When anyone recognizes a slight, that person has a *pro tanto* reason, no matter who he or she is, to feel slighted-anger at the offender on behalf of the slighted agent. Consequently, when you yourself slight someone else, you have a reason to feel slighted-anger at yourself. But we slight others a lot. If so, then shouldn't there be a lot of cases of fitting self-directed slighted-anger, that is, of *moral* self-blame? And why wouldn't *that* kind of self-blame fall victim to the hypocrisy puzzle? In other words, if I have a reason to feel slighted anger at myself for slighting someone else, then when I adhere to that reason, why can't my blamed self object to my blaming self, "Who are *you* to be slighted-angry at me?"[23]

I have three replies. The first is an important descriptive psychological point: It turns out to be very difficult actually to *feel* self-directed slighted-anger, or, once felt, to maintain that feeling. That's because the moment you discover that what you did was a slight, and so the moment you recognize that reason to be slighted-angry at yourself, *that discovery is actually just the dawning of remorse*, the moment when you typically begin feeling the painful empathic acknowledgment of what you put your victim through, which meets—*and thus undercuts the point of and reason for*—slighted-anger's acknowledgment-seeking demand. Once you have recognized what you did to someone else *as a slight* (which you presumably didn't see as such when you did it, as people don't typically aim to slight others,

---

[23] Thanks to an anonymous referee for pressing me to address this question.

136 THE ARCHITECTURE OF BLAME AND PRAISE

at least under that description), there's nothing left for your self-directed slighted-anger to fittingly *seek*. It can't fittingly demand acknowledgment, for that demand is already being met, and it can't fittingly protest a threat, for that threat is already being removed, and it can't fittingly aim to communicate anything because you already know the message. To have a reason to feel self-directed slighted-anger *is just* to have a reason to guiltily or remorsefully acknowledge one's slight in a way that, at least for those with functional emotional sensibilities, seems instantly to meet its aims by *replacing* slighted-anger with guilt or remorse.[24] Rationally fitting moral self-blame is self-effacing.[25]

My second reply is a bit more psychologically speculative: To the extent that we are angry at ourselves for slighting someone, I think, it's often *goal-frustrated* anger, of the "I can't believe you did that!" form. Slighting people often frustrates our goals. I briefly noted earlier that we don't usually act motivated by a desire to slight someone, under that description. Rather, we are typically motivated to do things we'd describe as being in our interests, or as the best course of action. When it turns out that my pursuit of those ends injures someone, where I wasn't taking their interests sufficiently into account when I was earlier deliberating what to do, then I recognize what I did to them *as* a slight, and the fact that I slighted them, given my general goal to be a morally good person, is frustrating in a way that aptly generates goal-frustration anger at myself.

Now what's important and fascinating here is that the action-tendency of goal-frustration anger is to eliminate or overcome the source of the frustration, which, in this case, is my slight of someone. I can best eliminate or overcome that slight by apologizing, offering recompense, and *remorsefully acknowledging what I put that person through*. In other words, goal-frustration anger can spur us to do precisely what slighted-anger (from others) demands of us. This is obviously why goal-frustrated anger and slighted-anger may be conflated in the self-directed case, as they both ready us for similar kinds of action.

So my first two replies to the question of why self-directed slighted-anger isn't hypocritical rely on some interesting facts about human moral psychology, that it's really hard to feel it, at least for long (because it's self-effacing), and that what we may think is slighted-anger often isn't (it's goal-frustrated anger instead, albeit with a similar direction of motivation). Nevertheless, some people surely do feel

---

[24] Sometimes, of course, it's not so instant. After all, if I have seriously slighted you, causing you lasting pain or damage, then there's no way I can instantly acknowledge the full extent of your harm. For me to fully appreciate what it was like for you to live with my foul deed, I may have to "feel your pain" for a long while. In the meantime, then, I may be angry at myself while also remorsefully acknowledging what I did. However, in such cases, this ongoing self-directed anger typically turns into the *goal-frustrated* kind (akin to what I'm about to note in the text), as I'm prevented from fully and quickly appreciating what I put you through, so I'm angrily coaching myself to keep working at it. Many thanks to Andreas Brekke Carlsson for thinking through this point with me.

[25] Indeed, this is why I suspect that so many have conflated self-blame with guilt/remorse, as at least the reasons for self-directed slighted-anger are essentially identical to the reasons for guilt/remorse.

self-directed slighted-anger. Why aren't they thus hypocrites? The answer is that, technically, they are, but there are far greater concerns afoot in such cases, involving a bizarre, irrational, or downright pathological psychology, sufficiently worrisome in any event to swamp minor concerns about hypocrisy.

There are two ways such cases might go, only one of which seems psychologically plausible. In the first, someone could be *fittingly* slighted-angry at herself for slighting someone, yet not feel any remorse or guilt (which would ordinarily replace the slighted-anger), even though she's capable of doing so. She thus would be demanding remorseful acknowledgment from herself *for reasons she recognizes as compelling* (thus the "fit" of her slighted anger), but without simultaneously recognizing those to be the very same reasons to feel the remorseful acknowledgment she herself is demanding that she feel. This seems psychologically bizarre to me, however.

(Or maybe she's *incapable* of guilt or remorse but capable of slighted-anger? This seems to describe some psychopaths, who get angry at others for what they take to be slights, but who don't respond with guilt or remorse when they slight others. But psychopaths also seem incapable of slighted-anger at *themselves*. This again is easily explained if the reasons for self-directed slighted-anger and for emotionally painful acknowledgment just are identical, so if they can't recognize reasons for the latter, they can't recognize reasons for the former. So once again, it's hard to conceive of the psychological possibility of feeling fitting slighted-anger at oneself without guilt or remorse.)

The second way one might feel self-directed slighted-anger is quite conceivable, though, as people certainly do it. It is to feel *unfitting* slighted-anger in the form of self-flagellation, as *punishment*. Consider first an other-directed case. Suppose you remain slighted-angry at someone who slighted you in the past but who has since come to manifest sincere remorse and done everything possible to address and make up for the slight (e.g., acknowledgment, apology, compensation, relationship-repair, etc.). She has effectively erased the slight, and so eliminated your having any reason for slighted-anger any more at her. If you continue to feel it nevertheless, your anger is unfitting and so is recalcitrant, that is, it is *irrational* (D'Arms and Jacobson 2003, 2023). But if you nevertheless continue to *express* it to your former slighter, you have moved from the irrational to the immoral, as you are flagellating the no-longer-guilty: You could only be aiming at her pain at this point, as you've already gotten her acknowledgment.

Fortunately, with respect to unfitting and recalcitrant other-directed slighted-anger, you can keep it to yourself. But if you yourself are the slighter, you cannot. Suppose, then, that you are slighted-angry at yourself despite already having fully empathically acknowledged what you put your victim through, and your victim has fully forgiven you as a result. Your reason for self-directed slighted-anger has now been completely eliminated, so if it persists, you are just carrying out an immoral punishment on yourself—beating yourself up. This sort of self-blame

138 THE ARCHITECTURE OF BLAME AND PRAISE

has three key features: (a) it highlights your helplessness—your lack of personal control—insofar as there's nothing left that you can do to rectify, replace, or change what you did; (b) as a form of punishment, it carries with it the clear overtones of desert that the Guilt Mongers (wrongly) thought all self-blame has; and (c) coincident with the previous two features, it is directed to your *character*, attributing negative traits to you as a person as a result of what you've done.

This type of self-blame is, as we know from Chapter 3, what psychologists call *characterological*, as opposed to *behavioral*. Behavioral self-blame focuses simply on your behavior, not on who you are, and it aims at getting you to do better in the future. That's just goal-frustrated angry self-talk. Characterological self-blame, though, is the provenance of all sorts of psychological hazards, some of which were detailed earlier. It strongly correlates with depression, low self-esteem, self-harm, PTSD, maladaptive coping in victims of sexual assault, and suicide (Janoff-Bulman 1979; Pagel, Becker, and Coppel 1985; Swannell et al. 2012; Bryant and Guthrie 2007; Ullman 1996; Baumeister 1990). It is destructive and unhealthy, and even if there were magically some right kinds of reasons in its favor, they would easily be outweighed, all-things-considered, by these "wrong" kinds of reasons against it. These hazards are, once again, dramatically illustrated by the case of the pitcher Donnie Moore, who couldn't stop blaming—punishing—himself for giving up that game-winning home run in 1986, culminating in his suicide. This is self-flagellation taken to its most unfitting and unhealthy extreme.

Two Brief Paragraphs on Self-Mockery

How does blame-as-mockery fit into this picture? Can you mock yourself? Of course you can! It's called self-deprecating humor, making fun of yourself for some failure or flaw. You may do so publicly or privately. Recall that, because mockery seeks no acknowledgment, it has no standing requirements: *Anyone* has standing to mock your mockable flaws, and the domain of "anyone" includes you. Consequently, self-mockery contains no hypocrisy puzzle either, nor does it call for us to draw any special distinctions within the domain of non-acknowledgment-seeking blame. As with non-acknowledgement-seeking complimenting-praise, you can direct it at yourself without a problem.[26]

Mockery is often also, in its self-deprecating form, forward-looking, in a way that other-directed mockery is not. The self-deprecator is often aiming to highlight their own faults and failures as a way of preempting others from doing so,

---

[26] I am of course referring to self-deprecating versions of mockery, not the much more destructive self-defeating versions, which are less about self-mockery than self-denigration for the sake of (only) others' pleasure.

as a way of controlling the narrative, and also as a way of reminding themselves to avoid those faults or failures in the future. In other words, it too is a form of self-talk. But when it's also done with good humor, it amuses everyone around the self-mocker, and in so doing it can generate sympathy, warmth, friends, and even mates (Hay 2001; Greengross and Miller 2008; Nihonmatsu, Okuno, and Wakashima 2017). These are all excellent ways of advancing what are typically anyone's goals.

Conclusion

The charge of hypocrisy would always arise for angry self-blame if it were fully analogous with angry other-blame. However, as this charge never arises (or is utterly swamped by more serious concerns of irrationality or pathology), there's an important disanalogy between them (beyond their different directions). Even though they both consist in a kind of anger, other-blame's paradigmatic version is slighted-anger, whereas self-blame's paradigmatic version is goal-frustrated-anger. The former is an acknowledgment-seeking, backward-looking form of blame, but the latter isn't. Further, psychologically feasible self-directed *slighted*-anger is self-effacing, irrational, or downright pathological. This explains why those who have tried to characterize self- and other-blame in light of each other have failed, for they are just two different emotional animals.

All of this adds yet more complexity to our overall architecture, but that's just the cost of our finally taking seriously the multiple directions blame and praise can take, as well as what those different directions might require for their normative grounding.

The Architecture of Blame and Praise: An Interdisciplinary Investigation. David Shoemaker, Oxford University Press.
© David Shoemaker 2024. DOI: 10.1093/9780198915867.003.0008

9

Sanctions

Blame isn't necessarily punishment. When I disdain you for being a jerk, mock you for your deflated souffle, or talk angrily to myself after scratching on the 8-ball, I'm blaming but not punishing. When I prudently keep my blame of the hulking Jon Cena to myself, blame my dead dad for his emotional coldness, or excoriate Putin (to my wife) for invading Ukraine, I'm punishing none of them.

Nevertheless, some examples of blame do seem like punishment. If you, my friend, reveal an embarrassing personal secret to my enemies at a party, I may give you the silent treatment. If you, my colleague, talk over me at department meetings, but I'm in charge of scheduling, I may assign you an 8 a.m. class. If you diss my mother at the bar, I may punch you in the nose. And if you, my spouse, cheat on me, I may take a golf club to your precious Corvette.

The blamers in this second set of examples all impose some setback, pain, or suffering on someone as a retributive response to a perceived bit of wrongdoing. This sure sounds like punishment. We sometimes view such measures as apt. It then seems only natural that a fully adequate story of their aptness conditions would have to appeal to desert.

Indeed, it is punishment—legal, criminal, and interpersonal—that has motivated the most serious and longstanding worries about free will, and about free will's (in)compatibility with determinism. The most pressing concern has come from considering the possibility of God's eternal damnation of sinners. How could such a sentence possibly be just if those punished didn't deserve it? And such questions have carried over squarely onto earthly punishments as well. How could the death penalty, or life in prison, possibly be justified, or just, unless deserved?

In my discussion thus far of the specific normative grounds of various categories of blame (in Chapter 6), I considered only two: pure private attitudes (e.g., slighted-anger, gratitude, admiration, or contempt), and non-acknowledgment-seeking forms of blame (mockery-blame and complimenting-praise). What I tried to show was that all they need to be rendered apt is fittingness—accuracy of appraisal—but no desert or even any moral justification at all. But if punishment is really a part of our blame/praise system, then mere appeal to fit to render its instances apt will likely seem woefully inadequate. That's because punishment *really* harms, and it deliberately and coercively aims to do so. It thus seems to cry out most loudly for moral justification, where said justification seems like it has to make some kind of reference to the punished agent's deserving it, either by

SANCTIONS 141

having been able to avoid doing the dastardly deed, or by having been the ultimate source of the deed, and these both sound like fairly robust metaphysical capacities, ones it may not be possible to have unless determinism is false, say, or unless we could change the past or have special libertarian agent causal powers, etc. That is to say, punishment seems to invite some high-powered and messy metaphysics into our tidy responsibility home.

In this chapter, I aim to keep such metaphysics homeless.[1] I do so via a two-step process. First, I will argue that punishment actually has no legitimate place in interpersonal life, so even if it does require desert, it is irrelevant to the interpersonal blame/praise system on which I have focused in this book. Punishment is its own special normative beast, and there are some powerful reasons to continue excluding it from our interpersonal lives.

However, even if punishment as such has no legitimate place in the blame/praise system, *sanctions* of various sorts seem to. These sanctions may include hurtful expressions of various emotional appraisals (e.g., yelling and guilting done out of slighted-anger), but they may also include some of those activities mentioned above, for example, giving someone the silent treatment, withdrawing friendship or trust, or refusing to help someone who has wronged you. These sanctioning activities, even if they don't count as punishment, seem as if they do require moral justification, a justification going well beyond fittingness, and consisting in or requiring desert. My second aim in this chapter will thus be to show why that's not true. While many of our interpersonal sanctioning treatments do require some moral justification, it's not at all of the sort that implicates desert. In order to accomplish this task, I will draw from important work in experimental economics and social psychology.

Punishment, Authority, and (A)symmetry

Moral and criminal blame are actually quite different normative enterprises.[2] Criminal blame consists wholly and exclusively in punishment. A guilty verdict, while surely unwanted and capable of destroying lives on its own, isn't blame. It's the coercive carrying out of a *sentence* for a guilty verdict that constitutes the state's blame. And the state's blame of convicted criminals takes the paradigmatic form of punishment, which coercively denies people things to which they'd ordinarily have a moral right, namely, liberty, or the avoidance of harm, suffering, or particular sorts of setbacks.[3]

---

[1] Unhoused?   [2] This section draws some material from Shoemaker 2013.

[3] What if we switched to a radically different model post-sentence, say, of quarantining criminals, under an analogy to what we have to do sometimes to promote public health? (See, e.g., Caruso 2016 and 2021.) Then, I think, we are no longer engaged in criminal *blame* at all (and I think advocates of the public health model would happily agree). Indeed, this is the sort of reframing of how the state

142   THE ARCHITECTURE OF BLAME AND PRAISE

Punishment is the point of this state practice, and an essential condition of its normative legitimacy (if it has any) is that the state stands in an *asymmetrical authority relation* to its citizens. Citizens are subjects of the state. This is a relation that doesn't obtain in ordinary interpersonal morality between normative equals. The closest analogy to state punishment in non-state interactions occurs in families, between parents and children. Parents punish their children—by spanking, grounding, and/or issuing time-outs—for violations of the rules of the household. The legitimacy of their doing so depends on their having authority over their children, and only their children are the proper subjects of that authority: I can't ground my neighbor's children, no matter how annoying they may be. The authority relation is also asymmetrical: Children do not have the authority to punish their parents, even when their parents violate the rules of the household or wrong their children. The fundamental aim of parental punishment of children is to set back their interests or withhold liberty or other goods, goods to which ordinarily they'd have some kind of right.

There are other non-state arenas in which punishment takes place: in the military, where soldiers are made to "drop and give me twenty"; in schools, where students are suspended or expelled; on the job, where workers may be fired or suspended without pay; and on sports teams, where coaches may bench players or require them to run laps. These cases are analogous to state punishment insofar as the punisher stands in an asymmetrical authority relation to the punished. They take place in special normative domains in which someone is in charge of others who are legitimately subject to being governed by that authority. And, most importantly, the authority's responses have as their fundamental aim *precisely* those setbacks. True, the setbacks may be delivered in ways we also find in some forms of interpersonal blame—as an expression of the authority's anger or as a demand for some form of acknowledgment—but those aren't necessary components. Coaches discipline players without seeking any empathic acknowledgment, and parents can (and perhaps ought to) give their children time-outs dispassionately.

Now contrast these sorts of cases with paradigmatic instances of interpersonal moral blame. Suppose I discover that you, someone I thought was my friend and ally, have been making fun of me behind my back to my enemies. In blaming you, I may be moved to confront you, express my anger and hurt, or call you names and swear off seeing or dealing with you again. However, what I cannot legitimately do is *punish* you, at least in a way that's analogous to the cases above. I simply lack the authority to spank you, ground you, give you a time-out, make you run laps, sit on a bench, or do push-ups, and my attempt to do any of these things would be laughable. That's because *you are not my subject.* We are instead

---

should respond to criminals that sidesteps all worries about desert as well (which is partially why desert skeptics like Caruso embrace it). This desert-avoiding result could also be obtained by thinking about punishment strictly on a self-defense model (see, e.g., Quinn 1985; Farrell 1989).

moral equals, bearing a symmetrical relation to one another within the moral community. So while I may have the authority to make certain *demands* of you as a fellow member of that community, I don't have the requisite authority *over* you to legitimately carry out anything more if you fail to comply. I cannot, in other words, *coercively enforce* my demands, as I lack the standing to deprive you of anything to which you would otherwise have a right. (You don't have a right, for example, to my being pleasant around you or to my not getting upset with you.) So while I may rail and pout and bluster and cry and condemn you (again, all things against which you have no moral right), I simply lack the relevant normative authority to punish you. At most, what we have is the authority to *demand*, but not *exact*, certain things from each other.[4]

Punishment has no legitimate place in interpersonal life: We lack standing to coercively deprive people of things to which they'd otherwise have rights. While punishment *may* require desert to be justified in institutional life (or in non-institutional authority-over domains), that is not pertinent to our discussion here, which remains focused on interpersonal blame between normative equals. We can thus leave any desert worries that may attach to punishment behind.[5]

Nevertheless, and despite the slick conceptual argument just laid out, we often *do* deliberately aim to set back people's interests within our blaming practices. It may not hurt, as such, to be assigned an 8 a.m. teaching schedule, but it's surely a setback to one's interest in sleeping in. So too, when my partner gives me the silent treatment, it sets back my interests in communicating with her. Now in neither sort of case have any of my moral rights been violated: I have no right against teaching 8 a.m. classes, and neither do I have a right to my partner's being communicatively forthcoming. But why aren't these treatments *close enough* to punishment to suggest that we engage in a lot of "punishment-adjacent," or "punishment-light," practices in our interpersonal lives, practices that occasionally also feel like they are apt responses to norm violations? If so, then surely they require moral justification going well beyond fittingness, justification consisting in or itself requiring desert, don't they?

---

[4] Do I at least have the authority to *guilt* you, to aim at inducing the pain of guilt in you for the wrong you did to me? (See Portmore 2022; Achs 2023.) No, not if my *aim* is for you to feel pain. We have a right against people directly aiming to make us feel, without our consent, unwanted pain. But I don't have a right against feeling guilt as such. Why not? What guilt motivates is something like relationship-repair, I think, and it often does so *via* the empathic acknowledgment that slighted-anger demands. Slighted-anger thus doesn't *aim* at any emotional pain, though. Rather, the pain of guilt (and remorse) is, between normative equals, a *foreseen but unintended side effect* of the acknowledgment that slighted-anger demands (Fricker 2016; Shoemaker 2018b). This sort of unintended side effect garners moral justification fairly easily (if it even needs it), given the value of the acknowledgment aimed at, as long as the pain is proportional to the valued aim. But if I am *guilting* you, I'm directly intending to make you feel unwanted pain, without your consent, and that's immoral. Note also that guilting people isn't a form of punishment, which involves, further, the authority and ability to coercively *ensure* the aimed-for setback. But I can't ensure that you feel the pain of guilt; I can only try to get you to feel it through various psychological ploys.

[5] And again, I think it's perfectly possible to design a criminal justice system that leaves desert behind as well. See Chapter 9, n. 3.

144 THE ARCHITECTURE OF BLAME AND PRAISE

Label these interpersonal, non-rights-violating treatments not *punishments*, but the more neutral and encompassing *sanctions*. As Pamela Hieronymi writes, "To sanction someone is to impose something unpleasant or unwanted upon that person in response to his or her violation of some norm, demand, or expectation. That is to say, sanctions are consequences that are *created* and *attached* to certain failures" (Hieronymi 2021: 230; emphasis in original). Clearly, all punishments are sanctions, but not all sanctions are punishments. We are thus interested in potentially legitimate cases of sanctions between normative equals, the imposition of something unpleasant or unwanted on someone in response to a violation of some sort (whether demanded or not) which does not depend on an asymmetrical authority relation, either directly or derivatively, and doesn't involve coercive enforcement or rights violation. Where might we find them?

Games People Play

There's a vast literature, in both experimental economics and social psychology, investigating how people strategically interact with one another, where what's almost universally labeled "punishment"—but what I've just urged is more neutrally labeled as "sanction"—is deployed. In several famous types of economic games, players may keep or distribute money in a variety of ways and for a variety of reasons, and when their decisions are deemed improper in some way, other players, including sometimes non-playing third parties, may opt to sanction them. Understanding when and why this occurs is part of the aim of the experiments. What's especially valuable about them, as Shaun Nichols notes, is that, because they "involve interactions between individuals in novel scenarios," they help reveal "how people think about punishment [*sic*] in interpersonal interactions rather than how they think about institutionalized forms of criminal punishment" (Nichols 2015: 121). And this is precisely the sort of thing we are interested in now as well (where the first mention of "punishment" in Nichols's remarks can be replaced with "sanctions").

The main lesson learned from all of these games is taken to be that people are overwhelmingly *retributive*. They deliberately aim to sanction players whose decisions they deem unfair or unjust, and they do so regardless of any forward-looking considerations, regardless of utilities they might receive, lessons that might be learned, or communication that might be taken up. Those who sanction other players often lose money thereby—they *pay* to "punish"—both in the short term and in the long term.[6] And they do this is in one-off games, where

---

[6] But note, of course, that none of the players had any antecedent right to any money at all, so the imposition of a "burden" here is by no means the coercive enforcement of actual punishment. It's simply the carrying out of a dispreferred consequence.

they'll never play the same players (or even the game) again; they do it as third parties who aren't even playing the game; and they do this even when the sanctioned party is unaware that they've been sanctioned (and the sanctioner knows this).[7]

Not only do people act retributively in these games, but they think they *should*. That is, they are explicitly acting under a retributive norm: money, they think, should be deducted from "greedy" or "selfish" players precisely and solely because of what they did (Nichols 2015: 125).

These seem clear-cut examples of what we were looking for: non-institutional and non-rights-violating sanctioning between normative equals. These responses are also closely correlated, it turns out, with *slighted-anger*. To see why, consider the ultimatum game, which is perhaps the most famous and widely investigated of the experimental economics games. There are two players in this game, the proposer and the responder. The proposer starts off with a set amount of money and is instructed to propose a division of the money between the two. If the responder accepts the proposer's division, they both get the proposed amount of money. If the responder rejects the division, nobody gets a thing. When proposers make a highly inequitable offer (proposing, say, that responders get only 10–20 percent of the money), responders overwhelmingly reject it, basically turning down free money. And they do so often because they are *angry* at what they take to be the proposer's unfair proposal (see Pillutla and Murnighan 1996; Bosman and van Winden 2002; Hopfensitz and Reuben 2009; Fehr and Gachter 2002; discussion drawn from Nichols 2015: 127). In such games, then, people seem to be expressing their slighted-anger via sanctions, in accordance with what they take to be a retributive norm.

Retributive sanctions, even of the non-punishing sort, seem to require some kind of moral justification. And while other justifications or responses have been offered, the classic justification appeals to basic desert: the responder is justified in sanctioning the stingy proposer simply because he deserves it.[8] This is of course the view of Kant and lots of contemporary theorists of responsibility (see, e.g., Pereboom 2001 and 2014; McKenna 2012: chs. 6–7; Dennett and Caruso 2021; McCormick 2023; Clarke 2023; and many others).

I agree that sanctions of this sort require moral justification. What I deny is that the moral justification required needs any appeal to or connection with desert.

---

[7] I draw from Nichols 2015 the many citations relevant here. For some famous results about basic retribution amongst economic game players, including in one-shot games, see Fehr and Gachter 2002; de Quervain et al. 2004. For results about third-party sanctions in economic games, see Fehr and Fischbacher 2004. For results about communication or "moral education" not being on the minds of sanctioners, see Nadelhoffer et al. 2013.

[8] See the discussion of alternatives to desert justifications in Nichols 2015: 131–9.

I begin with the important but overlooked datum that the people in these economic studies are *playing games*, and everyone knows it.[9] They also know that games have rules, either explicit or implicit, and that even moves technically within the rules sometimes contravene the "spirit" of the game. So some moves are viewed as acceptable—allowed by the rules or the "spirit" of the game—and some aren't, and when game players make an unacceptable move, one that contravenes those rules or the game's spirit, penalties are called for. If someone violates explicit rules, there are often clear penalties attached. And when someone violates the spirit of the game, even if it's technically allowed by the rules, penalties may also be called for, as such moves *just aren't cricket*: they are, as it were, dishonorable.

When we're playing a money-division game, just as if we were playing a cake-dividing game, the "honorable" game move is to divvy up the money more or less equally, even if the rules allow extremely inequitable offers. Violation of the spirit of this game calls for a penalty, just as does the explicit violation of rules in other familiar games, best exemplified in sports.[10] An egregious soccer foul in the aptly named *penalty box* of the pitch awards a penalty kick to the fouled team. Throwing a cheap check at another hockey player gets you a seat in an actual penalty box as well. Holding a player's jersey in American football has the consequence of moving your team backwards 10 yards.[11]

We might thus say, then, that the so-called retributive norm in games is less about retribution (which has a robust moral connotation) than it is about simple *rules enforcement*. And while it's often done in these games out of slighted-anger, it surely need not be. Third parties, after all, likely don't act out of anger; rather,

---

[9] Both the value and the frustration of engaging in empirical inquiry in economics is that there's a no-deception requirement. In social psychology, by contrast, a researcher can deceive subjects willy-nilly (as long as human subjects' research boards approve it).

[10] Importantly, then, *inequitable* distributions don't necessarily imply the morally charged label of *unfair* distributions.

[11] Daniel Dennett also sometimes appeals to games to defend his metaphysically thin notion of desert:

> The penalty kicks and red cards of soccer, the penalty box of ice hockey, the ejection of players for flagrant fouls, etc., all make sense; the games they enable would not survive without them.... Free will skeptics should consider if they would abolish all these rules because the players don't have real free will. And if they would grant a special exemption for such penalties in sport, what principles would they cite for not extending the same policies to the much more important game of life? (Dennett and Caruso 2021: 13–14)

Dennett is defending a thin notion of "desert" across both games and life, however, whereas I'm aiming to show that appeals to desert of any kind are unnecessary. But we are likely on the same team, as my target is really any metaphysically *robust* sense of desert, and if there are thinner ones available in talk of games, that may be just fine. Dennett doesn't talk at all about "fittingness," though, so it's hard to know for sure whether he'd be okay with eliminating all desert talk in favor of fit, which is what I've been arguing for. He also doesn't say anything to explain how his talk of games and penalties actually extends to the "game of life," but that actually takes some doing, as I'm now going to attempt to show in the text. (Thanks to Gregg Caruso for discussion.)

they act as *referees*, and referees need not—indeed, should not—be angry in handing down penalties.

This explanation accounts for all of the experimental data in a clean and simple way. Proposing a wildly inequitable division of money in the ultimatum game triggers a bad consequence: it results in the loss of all your (and everyone's) money. This penalty flag is thrown in response to rules/spirit violations whether the game is one-shot or ongoing, without regard to utility or any future lessons or other goods, and regardless of whether the penalized player knows that she's been penalized.

But this explanation does something more: It eliminates any need to appeal to desert (or any other moral justification) to ground such interpersonal sanctions. In sporting games like those mentioned, knowledge, intention, motive, and control—all the features typically appealed to as conditions of desert—are (mostly) irrelevant to the justification for penalties. Perhaps you didn't know about a new rule that says jersey-pulling counts as holding and you pulled down an opponent by his jersey. The penalty still applies. Suppose you were moved to hold the opponent's jersey to prevent him from being hit and injured. The penalty still applies. Suppose you accidentally grabbed that jersey to keep yourself from falling. The penalty still applies. Without knowledge, intention, motive, or control being relevant to the legitimate application of such penalties, there can't be any legitimate worries about whether the holder basically deserved to be penalized.

All of this is close to what occurs in the economic games as well. When proposals are made, responders don't necessarily seek to determine whether the proposer had some kind of control over the making of the offer or had knowledge of what he or she was doing, and so they aren't seeking to determine whether the proposer *deserves* the penalty in question in response to some kind of malicious motives, say.[12] Indeed, a similar pattern of rejection of proposals is found in those responding to offers by what they know are randomized computer outputs (see Peterburs et al. 2017).

These results may or may not feel intuitive.[13] Put yourself in the place of these players. Suppose that you're a responder, and your proposer offers a 10/90 split, that is 10 percent for you, 90 percent for her. Now imagine a variety of scenarios. Imagine first that the proposer was motivated to do so out of good will: she thought you'd be happiest with only 10 percent. I suspect that her goodwilled motive won't affect your reject response. Imagine next that your proposer doesn't really know the "spirit" of this game, and so has no clue that people reject wildly

---

[12] A significant number of people (nearly 20 percent) reject inequitable offers regardless of the intentions of the proposer or whether the proposer had any choice at all in making the offer. See Ohmura and Yamagishi 2005.

[13] In my informal discussions with friends and colleagues, some people lean one way, some another.

148 THE ARCHITECTURE OF BLAME AND PRAISE

inequitable offers. I again suspect that her lack of knowledge won't affect your reject response. Finally, imagine that your proposer got mixed up when typing in her offer (assuming it was not face to face), so that what she accidentally proposed was a 10/90 split, rather than the 90/10 split she had intended. This information also may not affect your rejection response ("no money for either of us!"). Sure, were you to find this out, any slighted-anger you'd felt would likely (and should) be quashed, as it's no longer fitting (the proposer didn't slight you), but the reject response to the offer itself may well still stand. In all these cases, even if it's not an unfair (slighting) offer, it's still an *inequitable* one, and it may simply not matter what the intentions, motives, or levels of knowledge or control were behind it. The sanctioning response here would then strictly be for *behavioral outcomes.*[14]

I think this insight about economic games has incredibly important ramifications once we re-enter the more realistic world of everyday interpersonal interactions.

Out of the Laboratory: Grading

Pamela Hieronymi gets us closer to real life by discussing grades. Poor grades are sanctions, as are late penalties. As grading systems are sanctioning (and incentivizing) systems, there is a moral value in play that has to guide their institution and imposition: *fairness.* This sort of sanction (and reward) system serves to incentivize timely submissions, but insofar as it also may impose a burden, that burden has to be avoidable in order for the system to serve its incentive function. But the kind of avoidability at issue here doesn't require robust free will or desert; rather, it's merely about the availability of adequate opportunities to avoid the penalty. Were a teacher to announce that a ten-page writing assignment was due in five minutes, with penalties attached for all late submissions, it would be unfair, insofar as students wouldn't have an adequate opportunity to write it in time.

But now consider a fairly instituted assignment with an attached late penalty: students have been given several weeks to write a paper, due at 9 a.m. on Friday. The late penalty is there in order to make sure students all have the same deadline, and that they've had the same amount time to work on it; in addition, it provides the teacher with enough time to grade it. Suppose, then, that a conscientious student nevertheless faultlessly oversleeps on Friday. Indeed, we can crank up the faultlessness: perhaps all three of her properly set alarms failed to go off. She may still be fairly penalized for turning her paper in late. As Hieronymi notes, "[S]ometimes making an exception is, itself, burdensome, and so it is sometimes

---

[14] Experimental results about intentions here are mixed. Some people do vary their responses based on their assessments of the intentions of the proposer. See Ohmura and Yamagishi 2005 for some discussion.

possible to fairly incur a sanction through bad luck" (Hieronymi 2021: 256). A late penalty is a penalty for lateness, period, and it can apply (fairly) even for specific inadvertent failures. This is true when, as Hieronymi notes, the costs of investigating particular excuses and then making exceptions for some are higher than the costs risked by the penalty. A teacher who has to investigate the excuses offered by her students has to know what "conscientiousness" capacities are and how her students are capable of exercising them, as well as whether slightly-less-than-conscientious students get off the hook for faultless behavior too, or even slightly-less-than-slightly-less-than-conscientious, and on and on. The costs of investigating the validity of excuses here are way higher than the costs of imposing late penalties across the board, for what are essentially just behavioral outcomes (late submissions).

What this means is that desert is not necessary to the fairness of some grading sanctions. The fair imposition of sanctions in these sorts of systems is instead simply governed by the moral principles governing *any* voluntary actions that affect the interests of others (e.g., "Do unto others..."). We must "treat all symmetrically while doing adequately well by all" (Hieronymi 2021: 232–3), and the risks or actualities of incurring a burden within a fairness-governed sanctioning system must be weighed against the overall value of the system.

Is this now the sort of example we've been looking for to demonstrate that desert is also unnecessary for the legitimate sanctions we deliver to one another in our interpersonal lives? Not yet. That's because even if a late penalty isn't a "punishment," per se, it is quite obviously a case of an asymmetrical authority-over relationship, so it may be too closely akin to "punishey" coercive enforcement to count as a model of legitimate sanctioning treatment *between normative equals*. But Hieronymi's case does inch us closer to what we want. So are there sanctioning systems akin to these grading systems that nevertheless have a *symmetrical* authority structure in interpersonal life? There are, in fact, plenty.

Real Life Sanctions

"Oh man, my wife is going to kill me," says a husband to his friend at the bar after realizing that he's stayed well past the time that he was supposed to be home to make dinner for the family. Now this is (hopefully) overblown rhetoric, but he knows full well that he'll likely face some sanctions when he gets home, including perhaps some icy remarks, yelling, the silent treatment, or a dispassionate hand-off to him of all the typically shared responsibilities for the evening and next day (dishwashing, getting the kids into bed or out of bed in the morning, driving them to school, etc.). These are interpersonal sanctions, none of which threaten his basic moral rights (i.e., she won't really kill him, or torture him, or swing a golf club at him), and none of which are coercively enforced (they can only be demanded), so they aren't illegitimate forms of punishment. He was well aware of the potential imposition of the sanction, and while it typically had been sufficient to incentivize him to get home on time (when his independent desire to do so was insufficient), sometimes, as with today, it wasn't. But the imposition of a sanction on him could still be quite fair. He violated a rule of their family "game," and he knows that his partner is going to throw a penalty flag in response to his violation when he gets home.

Now suppose that he immediately "gets it," that he knows full well as he leaves the bar, and well before he gets home, that he messed up, and so he redoubles his commitment to get home on time from there on out. Nevertheless, the delivered sanction may still be both apt and something he *views* as apt. That is, even though the threat of the sanction has an incentivizing function, its actual deployment is still purely retributive, a response to his norm violation, period. In itself, it doesn't aim at any future benefit, like his already redoubled commitment. It may also be delivered without any slighted-anger, as in, "You know what time we have dinner around here, mister, and you know what the penalty is for missing it." This too seems an apt response and he is likely to view it as apt, saying, "Yup, you're right, I screwed up, and so I'll take all the responsibility for the kids tonight and tomorrow."

Now here's the punchline: It might be fair for him to be penalized in this way for cases in which his lateness was *faultless*, a matter of bad luck. Perhaps instead of being at the bar he stopped at a park on the way home for a quick nap (with plenty of time to spare). He sets three alarms, as did the conscientious student, but, for some bizarre reason, none go off. Upon waking, he looks at the time and says to himself, "Oh man, my wife is going to kill me." He may enter the home sheepishly, saying, "I'm sorry, I had to take a nap after work, but all my alarms failed to go off." But the costs of investigating the excuse may, as with the student, be higher than the imposition of a fair sanction, and he may completely accept this: "Yup, I'll take over all the childcare duties tonight and tomorrow." This may simply be the way the game operates in their family.

Now this isn't to say that the penalty is *entirely* a function of behavioral outcomes. Return to the sports cases for a moment. If a soccer defender accidentally kicks the leg of a striker inside the penalty box, the defender's team is penalized by the awarding of a penalty kick to the opposition. But if the defender is *pushed* by someone on the striker's team so that his leg hits the leg of the striker, there's no penalty. So some inadvertent leg-kicking is penalized and some isn't. It just depends on the game. (I'll say more about roles occasionally played by intentions, motives, and excuses in sports in the next section.)

In this light, then, contrast the oversleeping case with one in which the husband was instead caught up in an enormous traffic jam while coming home at the proper time, a jam so sudden and huge that it makes the evening news, which his wife watches. If he texts her from the jam, attaching pictures from his stuck car, she (likely) won't penalize his inadvertent lateness, as she doesn't have to spend any costly time investigating whether his excuse was legitimate. But now suppose that he has missed his daughter's last five basketball games, and he promised her last night that he would absolutely not miss the next one, scheduled for tonight. Yet he's caught up in that unexpected traffic jam and misses it. His daughter may well not let him off the hook once he finally gets home. Further, her expressions of disappointment, anger, or the silent treatment may all be perfectly apt sanctions for him, *and he knows it*. But father and daughter are playing a different game with each other than are husband and wife.[15]

We engage in this sort of legitimate sanctioning in many of our interpersonal domains. It doesn't threaten basic moral rights, it is not coercively enforced, and it doesn't require asymmetrical authority. It's instead a simple matter of penalizing violations of the understood rules or spirit of the specific interpersonal games we are playing with one another. We have the authority, depending on our relationships, to call fouls on one another, and to throw penalty flags. We can't coercively enforce them, of course; that's the rubric only of some asymmetrical over-authority distinctive of punishment. Indeed, the late husband is free to simply ignore the penalty flag his wife has thrown and go to the den to sulk, drinking the night away. But if he fails to accept the penalty, his wife certainly doesn't have to play the marriage game with him anymore (which is another penalty).

I think a model like this is the best explanation for the normative grounding of the legitimate sanctions we dish out to one another within most, if not all, of our interpersonal lives. We play lots of different games with each other. The games I'm playing with my colleagues are just different than those I play with my friends, my children, my parents, and my partner(s).[16] I'm not trivializing these relationships by saying that we are playing "games" within them. Rather, what I'm trying to emphasize is that these relationships involve interpersonal strategic interactions that are governed by rules, both explicit and implicit, and with a "spirit" whose violations are dishonorable, "just not cricket." Violation of the rules or spirit of these games triggers sanctions, which may be aptly called for and viewed as apt by all in the exchange, depending on how the game has been set up. What matters is that these sanctioning systems themselves are governed by fairness. If so, then the imposition of individual sanctions may well be apt even for those whose violation was something they were unable to avoid at the time, a matter of bad luck. This means that these sanctioning systems do not depend for their normative grounding on desert.

---

[15] I am grateful to Carl Ginet for spurring me to discuss this sort of phenomenon.
[16] And of course the specific games and their rules may differ wildly as well between different specific friends, children, parents, and partners.

152 THE ARCHITECTURE OF BLAME AND PRAISE

Here are just a few examples where this description should feel very familiar:

- You hear about me having talked trash behind your back at a party, so you ignore me and my emails for several days.
- You are repeatedly obnoxious to me on Facebook, so I unfriend you.
- We are planning on co-authoring a paper for a new volume of essays, but you fail to do any of your work for it on time, so I back out of the project and cancel it with the editor.
- I pound on our shared wall when you, my neighbor, play loud thumping music after midnight, and when it keeps up, I report you to the building manager.
- You, my partner, have cheated on me, so I take the kids and we move to my sister's house for a while.
- You, my neighbor, mow your lawn early on Sunday mornings, despite my asking you to stop, so I discontinue my neighborly practice of bringing in your mail and looking after your plants while you're away.
- After the chair repeatedly ignores my suggestions at a department meeting, she asks me to serve on a time-consuming hiring committee, to which I sarcastically and pointedly reply, "Oh *now* you care what I think?"

Note that none of these examples fit very easily under the rubric of *payback*,[17] just like my calling a foul on you in our pickup basketball game doesn't involve my getting back at you. Rather, in both cases, the rules of the game are simply being policed via penalty, where the penalty (and method of calling it) is *itself* within the rules and spirit of the game. No one ought to get their hands cut off if they commit a foul or come home late. Of course, the precise rules for penalizing clearly differ, sometimes wildly, across relationships, communities, cultures, and eras, and they may also be seriously morally problematic (e.g., norms differentiating how women versus men may "aptly" sanction or be sanctioned, or norms urging differential sanctions for people of different races or ethnicities). But that they vary, or that they may be quite problematic in their current form, does not detract from the main point here, which is simply about the normative grounds of the sanctioning structures that, I think, make up most of our interpersonal lives. Some sanctions can in fact be a morally justified part of our blaming practices, fair impositions of setbacks to other people's interests that are apt without any appeal to desert.

---

[17] In contrast with what Martha Nussbaum mistakenly thinks is slighted-anger's aim. See Nussbaum 2015 and my reply to her in Shoemaker 2018b.

The Objection from Excuse

There remain many instances in which dishing out sanctions in the above-listed cases might strike us as unfair, cases in which familiar excuses obtain precisely because the blamed agents seemed to have lacked the capacities to avoid doing what they did (and so, one might well think, the sanctions are unfair precisely because *undeserved*). Suppose my neighbor has been taking some new medication that unexpectedly causes compulsion. Perhaps he is so assailed by strange thoughts in the middle of the night about his lawn's overgrowth that he simply must mow it *now*, at 5 a.m. Surely were I to find this out, it would be unfair of me to sanction him by no longer watering his plants or bringing in his mail while he's away, where the unfairness is precisely attuned to the fact of his compulsion, something which renders him incapable of doing otherwise.[18] One might thus think that my view tramples over, or fails to do proper justice to, the role of excuses in our lives, where these excuses are pleas against treatment that's undeserved.

Answering this challenge enables me to provide some additional details of the view, which allows that *of course* excuses still obtain in our interpersonal "games," but which still resists the connection to desert, at least of anything like a robust metaphysical kind.

Return to actual games for a moment, of the official sporting variety.[19] Suppose a member of the offense in an American football game tugs the jersey of an opposing player during a play. Normally this is a holding violation, resulting in a 10-yard penalty against the holder's team. If he tugged on it to right his balance while tripping over his own feet, his team would still get a penalty. If he didn't know that tugging was a violation, they'd still get a penalty. And if he did it because his new medication unexpectedly compelled him to tug on colorful jerseys, *they'd still get a penalty.*

However, if he momentarily faints from the heat and, while falling to the ground, his hands whack or tug the opponent's jersey, his team won't (or shouldn't) get a penalty. Handballs in soccer are similar: If a defender is fainting and falls to the ground, then even if her hand is in a weird position when a kicked ball strikes it, she won't be penalized. Why not? *There was no violation.* In neither case did anyone *commit* a violation, in other words, and that's because they didn't *do* anything; their bodily movements were a product of their fainting, which isn't

---

[18] I'm grateful to an anonymous referee for the challenge presented via this sort of case.
[19] I've had playfully hostile pushback from several philosophers who are sports fans, claiming that I've simply gotten the story about sports and desert wrong. I haven't, but I'm glad they've pushed me to say why, which I'm about to do. Thanks to Gunnar Björnsson, Matt King, and Manuel Vargas for their sporting complaints.

an action, and so it also can't be a violation. In these sorts of regular penalty cases, if what a player does is hold an opponent's jersey, then "I didn't know!" or "I didn't mean it!" simply don't excuse.

So too in some relationships such pleas don't excuse either. As long as the expectations within the relationship are fair, so that all are treated adequately and symmetrically, some strict liability of this sort for mere voluntary behavior may be tolerated. It doesn't matter that his three alarms didn't go off during his nap, the fact that dad was late to dinner is enough to warrant a penalty flag. It may not matter if your stress at work kept you from noticing your partner's new haircut, you may be penalized for failing to say something about it. And it may not matter, when you mow your lawn at 6 a.m., if you didn't know that people in your neighborhood like to sleep in; some will throw penalty flags your way.

But of course mere voluntary behavioral outcomes aren't the only activities penalized in sports. Some serious violations can get players kicked out of the game, and they may be the ones on which the desert-defenders may now try to focus. In soccer, there are deliberate fouls, "dangerous play," and entering the opposing technical area "in an aggressive or confrontational manner."[20] In football, there is "targeting," which involves tackling an opponent by leading with the crown of one's head into their head or neck. In basketball, there are "flagrant fouls," which are typically for deliberately aiming to bring down a player rather than going for the ball.

In these cases, some of the aforementioned excuses are relevant. For example: "I didn't mean to!" When intent is built into the rules, surely a lack of intent must excuse, right? Well, not always. In assessing these excuses, referees have an incredibly tough job, as it may seem that they have to read intent entirely off of body and facial language in a flash (it may be slightly easier when they have access to video replay). So sometimes the costs of making an exception—granting the excuse—may themselves simply be too burdensome to be worth it. In such cases, it may not be unfair to penalize the faultless.

Now precisely because intentions are themselves often so hard to suss out, especially in the heat of a charged athletic environment, what rules committees do instead is to spell out, as carefully and in as much detail as possible, what bits of *behavior* are most likely to constitute some intended action. So when a tackling football player's helmet meets the helmet of his tacklee, that behavior in and of itself may be enough to get that player kicked out, regardless of intent (e.g., even if what he actually intended was to make a clean tackle, but he just missed).

Indeed, this is precisely the sort of case that occurred in December 2023 with a very physical basketball player in the U.S., Draymond Green. In defending against an opponent, he was pushed toward the out of bounds line, and he turned around

---

[20] See the FA Cup's Laws and Rules of the Game here: https://www.thefa.com/football-rules-governance/lawsandrules/laws/football-11-11/law-12---fouls-and-misconduct.

quickly with his arms flailing wildly. One of his arms smacked the opponent hard in the face, and the opponent went down for a good five minutes. Green was almost immediately kicked out of the game for a flagrant foul, and he went without complaint, apologizing profusely afterwards, where he also noted that flailing his arms like that is just what he does to attract referees' attention to call fouls against him.[21] Let's take him at his word. If that's really what he was doing, it still doesn't matter. His unintentional smack was fairly penalized, even though it was inadvertent, even though he was faultless.

So too more serious penalty flags in interpersonal games may also be thrown for faultless behavior, even when intention is typically baked into the violated expectations. Our interpersonal equivalents of "targeting" or "flagrant fouls" may include a kind of deliberate cruelty in how we talk to one another. Certain words or ways of speaking typically express contempt or disdain, of the kind that corrodes relationships. But one can speak to one's friend or partner using such language, perhaps in the heat of the moment or simply unthinkingly, *without* the ill intent, and so without meaning to express contempt or disdain, and yet still be guilty of a "flagrant foul," whose penalty may consist in the silent treatment or even the dissolution of the relationship.

It's worth thinking for a moment about sports rules committees, which often amend or tighten up the rules in the offseason. Why change or add rules? It's because they are aiming to move the game closer to some envisioned ideal, creating a sporting contest that is, at the very least, athletic, competitive, and entertaining. All three values are necessary here, and committees have to balance them against each other.[22] But a crucial guiding value for this balancing act is *fairness*. Committees are looking to tweak rules in a way that will keep the game fair, so that all are treated symmetrically and are being adequately well done by. The aim is to set up the game so that, when it's been played and the rules have all been enforced, *whatever* outcome they generate is fair. This is what the political philosophers call pure procedural fairness.

This means that what they build into the rules *sometimes* includes features, such as intentions or a kind of control or even quality of will (motivations), that philosophers have taken to be crucial for desert. But those built-in features serve only an instrumental end, as they are taken to be the best way of generating fair and sporting outcomes, and, crucially, how those features are defined or specified within a game is still often in terms of mere behavior and may differ across different games or sports. There may also be instances in which it's compatible with a fair procedural outcome for some players to be penalized for inadvertent

---

[21] You can watch the incident here: https://www.youtube.com/watch?v=qktx_T4AOPM.

[22] If you emphasize the first two only, you get rhythmic gymnastics or curling. If you emphasize only the latter, you might have Colosseum style Christian-versus-lion matchups (or some of the early days of Ultimate Fighting).

156   THE ARCHITECTURE OF BLAME AND PRAISE

violations of rules that include these features (as when one inadvertently commits and is sanctioned for an "intentional" or "flagrant" foul).

And this too is how our interpersonal games go. While we don't typically have official "rules committees," we are often negotiating the rules with each other informally. Sometimes we maintain that only voluntary behavioral outcomes matter, so that blaming penalties for violations are a matter of strict liability. Sometimes, though, we bake intentions and control into the rules of our games, but they are only instrumental to one of our guiding relationship values, fairness (in the set up of the sanctioning system). They may also be interpreted behaviorally (we may inadvertently commit an intentional or flagrant foul in a relationship), how they are defined and enforced differs across different relationships, and they may also still be ignored in some cases where the costs of making an exception are too high.[23]

The one significant difference between most sports/games and our interpersonal sanctioning systems is that quality of will plays a much greater role in the latter, a position I argued for and defended in Chapter 7. But it does so, I think, only insofar as it is the fitting target of certain purely *emotional* responses, such as slighted-anger and gratitude. These emotions are irrelevant—or should be irrelevant—to sports refereeing, where the referees are mostly third parties.[24] Victims of fouls may scream and beg for a penalty to be thrown, but they aren't the ones whose determinations matter. Yet in our interpersonal lives, we are both the referees of norm violations (and supersessions) and their occasional victims (and beneficiaries). When we are victimized as a product of someone's ill will, say (or when we are responding on behalf of someone else to whom it's occurred), our emotional blame and praise will be fitting in virtue of the manifested quality of will, and any sanctioning penalties (or rewards) we throw as well (which may simply consist in expressions of those emotions) are importantly *independent* responses.

Their independence is illustrated by cases in which we may continue to dole out blaming sanctions even when our reason for slighted-anger has been undermined. We've already seen it with our oversleeping father. His partner may well believe that his alarm didn't go off as he slept at the park, and so not be slighted-angry with him at all, but she may nevertheless implement a burdensome sanction for his lateness, period: He still has to take on childcare responsibilities for the next twenty-four hours. Or perhaps your crying infant regularly keeps you up at night and so has you turning in things late at work, overlooking important

---

[23] It's important to note here that fairness can't be the only moral value guiding legitimate relationships. One could have a fair sanctioning system set up for a relationship constituted by a bunch of toxic norms. What I'm doing is simply articulating the general normative structure of interpersonal relationship sanctioning systems as such, not providing all the relevant moral values properly grounding the norms of these systems.

[24] In some sports, such as golf, players are expected to referee themselves.

information on forms, or not arriving to crucial committee meetings on time. Perhaps I'm your manager, and I'm slighted-angry at your shoddy work, at your failure to uphold your obligations. Once I hear, though, that there's no poor quality of will at its root, any slighted-anger I'd been feeling should fade away. But I may nevertheless still aptly *sanction* you, perhaps by giving you different duties (ones that don't require such concentration), removing some responsibilities from your plate, and not investing my trust in you. These may be costly sanctions; they may embarrass you and cause your colleagues to trust you less as well. But these sanctions may also be fair, despite your bad luck, and even though your excuse aptly gets you off the hook *for slighted-anger*.

What renders fitting emotional, acknowledgment-seeking blame (and praise) is quality of will, whereas that's not what renders fitting sanctions (or rewards), which may be fairly imposed utterly independently of quality of will.[25] Of course, there isn't always a sharp divide here.[26] And different relationships have different rules. For some, accurate quality-of-will-based excuses will get parties off the hook for both blaming attitudes and sanctions. For others, quality of will may just be irrelevant to whether the sanctions should be imposed, a strict liability relationship. And where expressions of slighted-anger are the sanction, then presumably such expressions ought not be made where the anger itself is unfitting (due to some good quality-of-will-based excuse).

But in any event, *none* of these responses requires desert.

"I admit there are multiple types of responsibility, but the type *I'm* interested in is..."

Since arguing in my book *Responsibility from the Margins* that there are three independent types of responsibility—attributability, answerability, and accountability—I've heard the above line spoken informally by many responsibility theorists: "Fine, Shoemaker, you've convinced me that there are these other types of responsibility, but the one *I'm* interested in, the one that matters, the only one in need of any real investigation and justification, is *accountability*." For instance, say some, the kind of responsibility that has been the historical focus in the free will debate has surely been about the justification for holding people to account by blaming them in various sanctioning ways. The "milder" forms of response that I had argued were fitting appraisals of attributability and answerability (respectively, attitudes like disdain/admiration and regret/pride) just

---

[25] I haven't said much about rewards, which I take to be the rough positive counterpart of sanctions, but it seems even clearer in those cases that quality of will is just irrelevant to whether someone, say, should be rewarded or credited for winning some race or doing a good deed.

[26] And I'm again grateful to an anonymous referee for emphasizing this point.

158   THE ARCHITECTURE OF BLAME AND PRAISE

aren't thought to be blaming responses of the "right" or "worrisome" sort, insofar as they aren't necessarily attached to any real sanctions, at least in the way that our methods for holding one another accountable ostensibly are. Consequently, they think, there's less pressing interest or need to investigate the agential conditions for those other types of responsibility.

There are many problems with this stance. First and foremost, it's one-eyed, claiming to deliver the most important goods about "Responsibility" as if there really is just one thing there, or there really is just one *mattering* thing there. But this approach prevents us from recognizing and vindicating the widespread *ambivalence* we have toward so-called marginal agents, who are far more plausibly—and inclusively—described as being responsible in some ways but not others, and so are the proper target of *some* blame/praise attitudes but not others (Shoemaker 2015: introduction).

Another problem is that this approach downplays or ignores the genuine and deep practical interest that we *do* have in those other types of responsibility. Those who are contemptible or admirable give us serious practical reasons, respectively, for being less or more like them, for withdrawing from or engaging with them, insofar as they are revealing important information about their practical identities. People who are the apt targets of contempt are people to get away from, and such reasons form the motivating core of much of our interpersonal lives, counseling what parties we'll attend, who we'll trust or do business with, who we'll steer our children away from, and much more. This effect is of significant practical value and ought not be poo-pooed.

The main problem I want to focus on here, however, is that those still under the grip of the "classic free will problem," which they think directly implicates desert, have been focused on investigating and justifying what turns out to be a very small subset of the vast blame and praise system, the subset of interpersonal sanctions. But most of our blame/praise system actually doesn't involve sanctions. None of the pure emotional responses constituting numerous forms of blame or praise necessarily involve sanction, including anger (of both the slighted and goal-frustrated variety), resentment, indignation, gratitude, disappointment, sadness, contempt, disdain, admiration, and pride.[27] Aspects of the praise system, when fitting, need no moral or metaphysical defense.[28] Blame expressed to third parties may not sanction anyone at all. And some blaming treatments of others, such as mockery-blame, may indeed sting, but apt mockery targets only the mockable, and what's mockable is exclusively grounded in fit, not desert.

---

[27] What about the pain of guilt or regret? As I argued in the previous chapter, neither one is blame; they are rather apt *responses* to blame.

[28] One of course has to be mindful of *over*praising children, as that may tend to generate little narcissists, but that's a matter of inapt or over-praise, and our aim is to see if some kind of metaphysical or moral defense is needed for otherwise *apt* praise of the right amount, and the answer is no.

SANCTIONS 159

So the world of blame/praise is far wider than the world of (legitimate) sanctioning treatment. Theorists who claim that the latter is the only responsibility domain that's important, the only one that merits our metaphysical focus, must admit that it's a relatively small subset of the world of blame and praise. Why should such a small domain merit such big attention? Well, their answer will be, this is the only domain in which our treatments really *harm* each other, and so this is the domain that requires special moral justification. I agree that this domain needs a moral justification. But it can be found entirely in the fairness of the sanctioning system. When sanctions like these are legitimate, they are just about rules enforcement, where expected penalties may be delivered by victims or bystanders in response to rule or spirit violations that are themselves within the rules or spirit of their particular interpersonal games. And, importantly, these are also the sanctions whose imposition may be fair sometimes even if the target lacks the ability to avoid them. They too, therefore, require neither metaphysical defense (because free will/desert is unnecessary) nor additional moral defense (because they are already part of a fair sanctioning system).

All of this, I believe, leaves *nothing* for the metaphysicians—the desert-mongers and the control freaks (to deploy some affectionate trash talking)[29]—to wring their hands about, at least in the world of interpersonal morality and the blame/praise system within which we find ourselves. Instead, all we need to appeal to in order to ground these attitudes and practices is either *fittingness* or *fairness*. That is to say, our role as responsibility theorists boils down to investigating what makes our blaming evaluations *fitting* or our sanctioning systems *fair*, in order to properly guide the games people play. And that's it. So even if the only type of responsibility you claim to be interested in is accountability, you *still* don't need to worry about free will or desert. Indeed, if I've succeeded here, then responsibility of all stripes has now been completely freed of free will and has finally deserted desert.

The Architecture of Blame and Praise: An Interdisciplinary Investigation. David Shoemaker, Oxford University Press.
© David Shoemaker 2024. DOI: 10.1093/9780198915867.003.0009

---

[29] Some of my best friends are desert-mongers and control freaks!

Conclusion

The Architecture of Blame and Praise

The blame/praise system is wildly variegated. It resounds throughout our interpersonal lives in a multitude of forms, emotions, grounds, targets, directions, and domains. If we start to think in addition that there are numerous asymmetries between blame and praise, we may feel deflated, thinking that there's just no *there* there in the end, no unified and coherent set of responses that could provide any real insight into "the" nature of responsible agency. All we're left with, it may seem, is a fractured disunity that runs well beyond the capacities of any corralling theory. This initial verdict might depress philosophers and thrill psychologists. Neither is the right reaction, however. There is a coherent unified structure to this system after all, and it can indeed inform us about responsible agency. In this conclusion, I'll briefly attempt to remind you of the details of both thoughts.

The architecture of blame and praise is, yes, enormously complex, but its many forms and manifestations are still unified by the system's overall function, namely, norm maintenance. Those who participate in the system contribute to this function, characteristically, by delivering stings and buzzes to norm violators and superseders, as well as by costly signaling of their own commitment to patrolling various norms. This is the structure and function of blame and praise across all practical domains: We engage in blame and praise wherever there are standards against which we can appraise people for their various failures and successes. This activity includes the domain of morality, sure, but it also includes every other normative domain you can think of: prudential, aesthetic, culinary, academic, etiquettal, epistemic, athletic, comic, and much more. In each of these domains there are, basically, performance norms, and to the extent that my stinging or buzzing appraisals of people within them signal my commitment to those norms and their maintenance (signals typically with both signaling and competence costs), those appraisals are part of the blame/praise system.

At the end of Part One, I included a table representing the mostly descriptive work I'd done to that point, the result of my investigating and dissolving the seeming asymmetries found within the system that initially threatened its coherence. I found that, once we introduced mockery to the system, and once we distinguished between two general types of blame/praise—between those that are fundamentally acknowledgment-seeking and those that aren't—a much more orderly and coherent system was revealed. I reproduce Table 5.1 here for convenience, now labelled Table C.1.

CONCLUSION   161

Table C.1 The first sketch of an architecture of blame and praise (descriptive)

	Blame	Praise
Acknowledgment-Seeking *(whose paradigmatic forms are symmetrical with each other)*	Paradigmatic Emotional Form: *Slighted-Anger*	Paradigmatic Emotional Form: *Gratitude*
Non-Acknowledgment-Seeking *(whose paradigmatic forms are symmetrical with each other)*	Paradigmatic **Expressive** Form: *Mockery* Paradigmatic **Non-Expressive** Emotional Forms: *Disdain, Contempt, Disappointment*	Paradigmatic **Expressive** Form: *Complimenting* Paradigmatic **Non-Expressive** Emotional Forms: *Admiration, Pride*

What I promised would be filled in by the end of Part Two of the book included the following additional parts: non-emotional forms of blame/praise (e.g., sanctions and rewards), other- and self-directed forms, and the normative grounds of the system's component parts. I began (in Chapter 6), by exploring the grounds of the unexpressed emotions in both the acknowledgment-seeking and the non-acknowledgment-seeking forms of blame/praise. These required *fit*—correct or accurate appraisal—and nothing more to be rendered apt. Where some responses required expression, as in mockery and compliments, their aptness too was entirely a function of fit (mockability or complimentability), not desert.

I then defended the view that the specific fitmakers for our purely emotional forms of blame/praise are a function of the target's quality of will (QW). The most familiar emotions here are slighted-anger and gratitude, and their fitmakers are, respectively, *slights* and *heights*. These are violations or supersessions of norms in what most theorists take to be the domain of *moral* responsibility, so they have been well discussed (or at least moral blame has). I was thus interested to see if QW would remain the exclusive fitting target of emotional blame in the face of several threats, both old school and new school. I concluded that all such threats could be thwarted. Corporations, inadvertent harmers, and "supposedly rational" racists and sexists are all off the hook for slighted-anger, which is a fitting response to poor quality of *regard*. But I also reminded readers of my tripartite machinery, which easily allows for other types of blame (and praise) to apply to such agents. One could, for instance, fittingly *protest* corporate wrongdoing, as corporations are at least answerable for their decisions (if not accountable) in a way that also enables them to make better decisions in the future. So too, one could conceivably reproach-without-anger inadvertent necklace-losers or "supposedly rational" racists, where the aim would be to tap into proleptic mechanisms that could ultimately generate in their targets the reasons they previously lacked. Again, I didn't make much of this point in Chapter 7, but I nevertheless include such responses as part of the full

162 THE ARCHITECTURE OF BLAME AND PRAISE

architecture in Table C.2 at the end of this chapter. They can, when they meet the functional conditions of the system, fall under the rubric of non-angry, but still acknowledgment-seeking, forms of blame. Their positive counterparts are likely responses such as cheering for, honoring, or encouraging in a way that also seeks a kind of acknowledgment, although I haven't really said anything about those either.

My in-depth discussion of self-directed blame revealed yet more distinctions within the blame/praise system. What we saw by starting with the athletic cases was, first, that self-blame just isn't guilt (or regret or remorse), as it's virtually always been held to be. Rather, it's most typically a kind of anger. But the fact that there's no such thing as hypocritical self-blame revealed that the kind of anger typically felt in self-blame is just different from the anger in other-blame. Other-blame's emotional paradigm is slighted-anger. But self-blame is mostly a matter of negative self-talk, so its angry core is of the goal-frustrated type. Self-blame, alongside self-praise (positive self-talk), is mostly about coaching, about performance improvement, so it is fundamentally forward-looking (as opposed to other-directed blame/praise, which is fundamentally backward-looking). When self-directed anger *is* moral, targeting one's own slights of others, it is typically self-effacing, melting quickly into guilt or remorse in the psychologically healthy. Where self-directed slighted-anger remains, it is typically an inapt, illegitimate, or immoral form of self-punishment.

Punishment, in fact, was left out of the descriptive discussion altogether in Part One. I saved it for the end of the book so as to connect it up explicitly with the primary motivation philosophers have had for doing a metaphysical deep dive, namely, the worry that the punishing, harmful aspects of the blame/praise system can be morally justified only if people deserve to be punished, and they can only deserve it if they have free will of some robust sort. While one might thus allow that some emotional responses and mocking treatments could be apt solely in virtue of being fitting, surely when we aim to cause others suffering and painful setbacks via our blame of them (albeit not through praise), we must have a more serious moral or metaphysical defense available.

My aim in Chapter 9 was to show that this worry is unfounded, at least for the interpersonal blame/praise system, for two significant reasons. First, punishment, as such, isn't a legitimate part of that system, as it requires an asymmetrical authority relation, one which isn't found between normative equals. Sanctions, however, are indeed found within the blame/praise system between normative equals. Can they be rendered morally permissible without appeal to desert? Yes, I argued. Sanctions are part of incentive systems that make up our interpersonal relationship "games," and as such, the only moral value they require is *fairness*, where this simply means that all people playing them are treated symmetrically

CONCLUSION 163

and have adequate opportunities to avoid the sanctions. The sanctions in these interpersonal games are merely penalties, then, for violating the rules or "spirit" of the game. Consequently, being the target of such penalties doesn't require desert; some penalties may fairly be imposed for inadvertent failures, where the costs of making an exception or granting an excuse exceed the burdens incurred. What counts as a proper penalty (as well as what counts as a cost-effective excuse) varies wildly across different relationships, communities, cultures, and eras, and they may often be the subject of dispute, but what's not in dispute is that sanctioning penalties may legitimately apply in interpersonal life with no need for any deep metaphysical support or any moral support beyond the fairness guiding the system.

This final point helps deliver some powerful benefits when we try to apply all of these lessons to responsible agency. Recall the **Motto** with which I began the book:

> To be a responsible agent is to be an apt candidate for responses such as blame and praise.

If true, then given what I've argued for, there are several new data points we now need to take seriously in our theorizing about responsible agency:

- The relevant responses (blame and praise) are all part of a unified system, whose function is norm maintenance (across all normative domains). The relevant norm-maintaining responses are stinging or buzzing costly signals of the respondent's commitment to both the norms and their maintenance.
- There are many different sub-parts to the blame/praise system. Some responses seek acknowledgment, some don't. Some are fundamentally expressive, some aren't. Some are primarily self-directed, some aren't. Some are emotional, some aren't.
- The purely attitudinal elements of the system are grounded entirely in terms of fittingness, although what renders any individual response fitting depends on the type of response in question. The same is true of all non-acknowledgment-seeking blame/praise treatments of others (e.g., mockery and compliments).
- To the extent that interpersonal sanctions are a legitimate part of the system, they need no normative grounding in desert; rather, they are penalties for rules or spirit violations rendered apt by the rules or spirit of the specific game being played (where the system of sanctions itself is governed by fairness in its application).

164 THE ARCHITECTURE OF BLAME AND PRAISE

These bullet points now correlate with some suggestions about how we might best investigate responsible agency going forward:

- Responsible agency is most generally about norm adherence, violation, and supersession, which blame and praise serve to patrol. This includes norms of all stripes. Responsible agency is thus something we have to investigate in all normative domains, not just the moral. We should thus prepare ourselves for the possibility that the nature of said agency may differ across different domains.
- Relatedly, adherence, violation, and supersession of norms all require specific agential capacities, and identifying what those are would seem to be a proper target of our investigation. Indeed, given all of the sub-parts of the blame/praise system, one natural method for theorizing about responsible agency would be to explore what capacities are required to make sense of the different sub-parts. In other words, an acknowledgment-seeking form of blame or praise makes sense only for targets who are capable of providing the sought response. An expressive form may require different capacities in the confronted agent, depending on the point of the expression (which sometimes may simply be to rally the troops or to stand in solidarity). Merely emotional forms may require no particular capacities in their targets for them to be sensible responses, but what those emotions respond *to* may require various capacities (and so see the next bullet point).
- If most of the responses in the blame/praise system get normative grounding only from their fittingness, and if different responses are rendered fitting by different agential properties, then investigation into the nature of responsible agency will require investigation into the different properties (e.g., capacities, normative orientation, reasons-responsiveness, manifestation of deep selves…?) that render different responses fitting. This will be the most arduous work, as there are many sub-parts to the system. So, for example, slighted-anger is rendered fitting by slights, and gratitude is rendered fitting by heights, but what agential capacities are required to slight or height people? Are they the same? Does an agent's history matter here? What renders something mockable or complimentable, precisely, or contemptible or admirable? How are these properties related, if at all, to those of slighted-anger or heighted-gratitude? (Recall that narcissists are fitting targets of mockery-blame but not slighted-anger-blame.) What do the differences in the fittingness conditions for other- and self-directed anger (which are,

recall, different types of anger) tell us about responsible agency? Are there differences in what it means (and what's required) to be responsible *to* others versus being responsible *to* oneself, given these differences in holding others and oneself to account? Are there differences between these two targets as well in terms of the role of backward-looking versus forward-looking considerations? How do these differences affect the relevant capacities required for fit in each case?

- Can we say something more substantial about what makes various sanctions/penalties within various interpersonal relationships apt? In particular, even if robust free will or desert aren't required for sanctions to fairly apply to someone, what are? If sanctions serve an incentivizing function within the system of norm maintenance, what agential properties are required to be responsive to them? Does this way of viewing matters bear on what counts as an excuse or justification (and can we sustain that distinction?)? And do different relationships or normative communities require different capacities for their members to be properly responsive in their sanctioning systems?

There are a lot of hard questions here. But they are at least now more accurately focused than questions about responsible agency have been in the past, I think. In particular, what's notable about this list is what's *not* on it, namely, any questions about desert, free will, the ability to do otherwise, ultimate sourcehood, determinism, and so forth. These are the questions that have long been part of what's known as the "traditional" investigation into the free will problem, and that have led, in contemporary theorizing, to several of what I have labeled "fault lines" (Shoemaker 2020), very different methods for investigating the nature of responsible agency that have generated a "dialectical stalemate" (Fischer 1994: 83–5), one that is deeply entrenched and seems to offer no way out. But once we recognize that we need no longer worry about that "traditional" question, we are finally free to make genuine progress together in our theorizing, to bridge those fault lines. Or at least that has been the optimistic hope of this book.

I conclude, then, with the fully filled-in Table C.2, which lays out the entire blame/praise system, in all of its complicated, messy, yet ultimately symmetrical, unified, and coherent glory. This is really just a first pass. I welcome any tweaks, corrections, additions, deletions, or general improvements to this architecture. This is and ought to be a group design, as it'll ultimately be a house we all have to live in.

166 THE ARCHITECTURE OF BLAME AND PRAISE

Table C.2 The complete architecture of blame and praise

		Blame	Praise
	Acknowledgment-Seeking	Paradigmatic Emotional Form: *Slighted-Anger* (demands emotionally pained empathic acknowledgment)	Paradigmatic Emotional Form: *Gratitude* (invites pleasurable gratification [empathic acknowledgment])
OTHER-DIRECTED		Paradigmatic Non-Emotional Forms: *Protest* or *Reproach* (seeks uptake, change of ways, may tap into proleptic mechanisms)	Paradigmatic Non-Emotional Forms: *Cheers, Honors*, or *Encouragement* (seeks uptake, preservation of ways, may tap into proleptic mechanisms)
	Non-Acknowledgment-Seeking	Paradigmatic Expressive Form: *Mockery*	Paradigmatic Expressive Form: *Complimenting*
		Paradigmatic Non-Expressive (Emotional) Forms: *Disdain, Contempt, Disappointment (in)*	Paradigmatic Non-Expressive (Emotional) Forms: *Admiration, Pride, Joy (in)*
	Nonmoral (Forward-Looking)	*Negative Self-Talk* (goal-frustrated anger)	*Positive Self-Talk* (encouragement)
SELF-DIRECTED	Moral (Backward-Looking)	*Slighting-Anger* (self-effacing in the psychologically healthy, transmogrifies into guilt/remorse)	*Heighting-Gratitude* (self-effacing in the psychologically healthy, transmogrifies into gratification)

The Architecture of Blame and Praise: An Interdisciplinary Investigation. David Shoemaker, Oxford University Press.
© David Shoemaker 2024. DOI: 10.1093/9780198915867.003.0010

References

Achs, Rachel. 2023. "In Defense of Guilt-Tripping." *Philosophy & Phenomenological Research*. DOI: 10.1111/phpr.13009.

Algoe, Sara B., and Haidt, Jonathan. 2009. "Witnessing Excellence in Action: The 'Other-Praising' Emotions of Elevation, Gratitude, and Admiration." *Journal of Positive Psychology* 4: 105–27.

Aristotle. 1954. *Aristotle: Rhetoric*. Trans. W. Rhys Roberts. New York: Modern Library.

Arpaly, Nomy, and Schroeder, Timothy. 2014. *In Praise of Desire*. Oxford: Oxford University Press.

Baker, Kevin. 2011. "The Myth of the Home Run that Drove an Angels Pitcher to Suicide." *The Atlantic* (October 27, 2011).

Basu, Rima. 2019a. "The Wrongs of Racist Beliefs." *Philosophical Studies* 176: 2497–515.

Basu, Rima. 2019b. "Radical Moral Encroachment: The Moral Stakes of Racist Beliefs." *Philosophical Issues*. https://doi.org/10.1111/phis.12137.

Basu, Rima. 2023a. "The Morality of Beliefs I: How Beliefs Wrong." *Philosophical Compass*. https://doi.org/10.1111/phc3.12934.

Basu, Rima. 2023b. "The Morality of Beliefs II: Three Challenges and an Extension." *Philosophical Compass*. https://doi.org/10.1111/phc3.12935.

Basu, Rima, and Schroeder, Mark. 2019. "Doxastic Wronging." In Brian Kim and Matthew McGrath, eds., *Pragmatic Encroachment in Epistemology* (London: Routledge), pp. 181–205.

Baumeister, Roy F. 1990. "Suicide as Escape from Self." *Psychological Review* 97: 90–113.

Bedau, Hugo Adam, and Kelly, Erin. 2010. "Punishment." In Edward N. Zalta, ed., *The Stanford Encyclopedia of Philosophy* (Spring 2010 Edition). http://plato.stanford.edu/archives/spr2010/entries/punishment/.

Beeghly, Erin. 2015. "What Is a Stereotype? What Is Stereotyping?" *Hypatia* 30: 675–91.

Beeghly, Erin. 2021. "Stereotyping as Discrimination: Why Thoughts Can Be Discriminatory." *Social Epistemology* 35: 547–63.

Bennett, Christopher. 2002. "The Varieties of Retributive Experience." *Philosophical Quarterly* 52: 145–63.

Berger, Fred. 1975. "Gratitude." *Ethics* 85: 298–309.

Bicchieri, Cristina. 2017. *Norms in the Wild*. Oxford: Oxford University Press.

Bingeman, Emily. Forthcoming. "The Ethics of Praise." *Oxford Studies in Agency & Responsibility* 8.

Bird, Rebecca Bliege, and Smith, Eric A. 2005a. "Costly Signaling and Cooperative Behavior." In Herbert Gintis et al., eds., *Moral Sentiments and Material Interests: On the Foundations of Cooperation in Economic Life* (Cambridge, MA: MIT Press), pp. 115–48.

Bird, Rebecca Bliege, and Smith, Eric A. 2005b. "Signaling Theory, Strategic Interaction, and Symbolic Capital." *Current Anthropology* 46: 221–48.

Björnsson, Gunnar. 2017. "Explaining away Epistemic Skepticism about Culpability." *Oxford Studies in Agency and Responsibility* 4: 141–64.

Björnsson, Gunnar, and Hess, Kendy. 2017. "Corporate Crocodile Tears? On the Reactive Attitudes of Corporate Agents." *Philosophy & Phenomenological Research* 94: 273–98.

Blanchfield, Anthony W., et al. 2014. "Talking Yourself out of Exhaustion: The Effects of Self-Talk on Endurance Performance." *Medicine & Science in Sports & Exercise* 46: 998–1007.

Boehm, Christopher. 1999. *Hierarchy in the Forest: The Evolution of Egalitarian Behavior*. Cambridge, MA: Harvard University Press.

Boorse, Christopher. 1976. "Wright on Functions." *The Philosophical Review* 85: 70–86.

168 REFERENCES

Bosman, R. A. J., and van Winden, F. A. A. M. 2002. "Emotional Hazard in a Power-to-Take Experiment." *Economic Journal* 112: 147–69.

Boxill, Bernard R. 1976. "Self-Respect and Protest." *Philosophy & Public Affairs* 6: 58–69.

Brink, David, and Nelkin, Dana. 2013. "Fairness and the Architecture of Responsibility." *Oxford Studies in Agency and Responsibility* 1: 284–313.

Brink, David, and Nelkin, Dana. 2022. "The Nature and Significance of Blame." In John Doris and Manuel Vargas, eds., *The Oxford Handbook of Moral Psychology* (Oxford: Oxford University Press), pp. 177–96.

Bryant, Richard A., and Guthrie, Rachel M. 2007. "Maladaptive Self-Appraisals before Trauma Exposure Predict Posttraumatic Stress Disorder." *Journal of Consulting and Clinical Psychology* 75: 812–15.

Calhoun, Cheshire. 1989. "Responsibility and Reproach." *Ethics* 99: 389–406.

Campbell, C. A. 1957. "Has the 'Self' Free Will?" In C. A. Campbell, ed., *On Selfhood and Godhood* (London: Routledge), pp. 157–79.

Card, Claudia. 1988. "Gratitude and Obligation." *American Philosophical Quarterly* 25: 115–27.

Carlsson, Andreas Brekke. 2017. "Blameworthiness as Deserved Guilt." *The Journal of Ethics* 21: 89–115.

Carlsson, Andreas Brekke. 2019. "Shame and Attributability." *Oxford Studies in Agency and Responsibility* 6: 112–39.

Carlsson, Andreas Brekke, ed. 2022. *Self-Blame and Moral Responsibility*. Cambridge: Cambridge University Press.

Caruso, Gregg D. 2016. "Free Will Skepticism and Criminal Behavior: A Public Health-Quarantine Model." *Southwest Philosophy Review* 32: 25–48.

Caruso, Gregg D. 2021. *Rejective Retributivism: Free Will, Punishment, and Criminal Justice.* Cambridge: Cambridge University Press.

Chadha, Monima. 2017. "No-Self and the Phenomenology of Agency." *Phenomenology and the Cognitive Sciences* 16: 187–205.

Chadha, Monima. 2018. "No-Self and the Phenomenology of Ownership." *Australasian Journal of Philosophy* 96: 14–27.

Chislenko, Eugene. 2020. "Scanlon's Theories of Blame." *The Journal of Value Inquiry* 54: 371–86.

Chislenko, Eugene. 2021. "Causal Blame." *American Philosophical Quarterly* 58: 347–58.

Clarke, Randolph. 2013. "Some Theses on Desert." *Philosophical Explorations* 16: 153–64.

Clarke, Randolph. 2014. *Omissions.* Oxford: Oxford University Press.

Clarke, Randolph. 2016. "Moral Responsibility, Guilt, and Retributivism." *The Journal of Ethics* 20: 121–37.

Clarke, Randolph. 2023. "Desert of Blame." *Philosophy and Phenomenological Research* 108: 62–80.

Clarke, Randolph, and Rawling, Piers. 2022. "Reason to Feel Guilty." In Carlsson 2022, pp. 237–52.

Coates, D. Justin, and Tognazzini, Neal A., eds. 2013. *Blame: Its Nature and Norms.* New York: Oxford University Press.

Coplan, Robert J., and Armer, Mandana. 2005. "Talking Yourself out of Being Shy: Shyness, Expressive Vocabulary, and Socioemotional Adjustment in Preschool." *Merrill-Palmer Quarterly* 51: 20–41.

Couch, Mark B. 2017. "Causal Role Theories of Functional Explanation." *The Internet Encyclopedia of Philosophy.* http://www.iep.utm.edu/func-exp/.

Craig, T. K. J., and Brown, George William. 1984. "Goal Frustration and Life Events in the Aetiology of Painful Gastrointestinal Disorder." *Journal of Psychosomatic Research* 28: 411–21.

Cummins, Robert. 1983. *The Nature of Psychological Explanation.* Cambridge, MA: MIT Press.

Czarna, Anna Z., Zajenkowski, Marcin, and Dufner, Michael. 2018. "How Does It Feel to Be a Narcissist? Narcissism and Emotions." In Anthony D. Hermann, Amy B. Brunell, and Joshua D. Foster, eds., *Handbook of Trait Narcissism* (Cham, Switzerland: Springer): 255–63.

D'Arms, Justin. 2013. "Value and the Regulation of the Sentiments." *Philosophical Studies* 163: 3–13.

D'Arms, Justin, and Jacobson, Daniel. 2000. "The Moralistic Fallacy: On the 'Appropriateness' of the Emotions." *Philosophy & Phenomenological Research* 61: 65–90.

D'Arms, Justin, and Jacobson, Daniel. 2003. "The Significance of Recalcitrant Emotion (or, Antiquasijudgmentalism)." *Royal Institute of Philosophy Supplements* 52: 127–45.

D'Arms, Justin, and Jacobson, Daniel. 2022. "The Motivational Theory of Guilt (and Its Implications for Responsibility)." In Carlsson 2022, pp. 11–27.

D'Arms, Justin, and Jacobson, Daniel. 2023. *Rational Sentimentalism*. Oxford: Oxford University Press.

Darby, B. W., and Schlenker, B. R. 1982. "Children's Reactions to Apologies." *Journal of Personality and Social Psychology* 43: 742–53.

Darwall, Stephen. 2005. *The Second-Personal Standpoint*. Cambridge, MA: Harvard University Press.

De Quervain, Dominique J. F., Fischbacher, Uris, Treyer, Valerie, Schellhammer, Melanie, Schnyder, Ulrich, Buck, Alfred, and Fehr, Ernst. 2004. "The Neural Basis of Altruistic Punishment." *Science* 305: 1254–8.

Dennett, Daniel. 1984. "I Could Not Have Done Otherwise—So What?" *Journal of Philosophy* 81: 553–65.

Dennett, Daniel C., and Caruso, Gregg D. 2021. *Just Deserts: Debating Free Will*. Cambridge, MA: Polity Press.

Doris, John. 2015. *Talking to Our Selves*. Oxford: Oxford University Press.

Doris, John, and Knobe, Joshua. 2010. "Strawsonian Variations: Folk Morality and the Search for a Unified Theory." In John Doris and the Moral Psychology Research Group, eds., *The Moral Psychology Handbook* (Oxford: Oxford University Press), pp. 321–54.

Dorsey, Dale. 2020. "Respecting the Game: Blame and Practice Failure." *Philosophy and Phenomenological Research* 101: 683–703.

Duggan, A. P. 2018. "Moral Responsibility as Guiltworthiness." *Ethical Theory and Moral Practice* 21: 291–309.

Ellsworth, Phoebe C., and Tong, Eddie M. W. 2006. "What Does It Mean to Be Angry at Yourself? Categories, Appraisals, and the Problem of Language." *Emotion* 6: 572–86.

Enoch, David. 2012. "Being Responsible, Taking Responsibility, and Penumbral Agency." In Ulrike Heuer and Geral Lang, eds., *Luck, Value, and Commitment: Themes from the Ethics of Bernard Williams* (Oxford: Oxford University Press), pp. 95–131.

Erzi, Seda. 2020. "Dark Triad and Schadenfreude: Mediating Role of Moral Disengagement and Relational Aggression." *Personality and Individual Differences* 157: 1–6.

Everts, Elisa. 2006. "Identifying a Particular Family Humor Style: A Sociolinguistic Discourse Analysis." *Humor* 16: 369–412.

Faraci, David, and Shoemaker, David. 2010. "Insanity, Deep Selves, and Moral Responsibility: The Case of JoJo." *Review of Philosophy and Psychology* 1: 319–32.

Faraci, David, and Shoemaker, David. 2014. "Huck vs. JoJo: Moral Ignorance and the (A) Symmetry of Praise and Blame." *Oxford Studies in Experimental Philosophy* 1: 7–27.

Faraci, David, and Shoemaker, David. 2019. "Good Selves, True Selves: Moral Ignorance, Responsibility, and the Presumption of Goodness." *Philosophy & Phenomenological Research* 98: 606–22.

Farrell, Daniel M. 1989. "On Threats and Punishments." *Social Theory and Practice* 15: 125–54.

Fehr, Ernst, and Fischbacher, Uris. 2004. "Third Party Punishment and Social Norms." *Evolution and Human Behavior* 25: 63–87.

Fehr, Ernst, and Gächter, Simon. 2000. "Cooperation and Punishment in Public Goods Experiments." *American Economic Review* 90: 980–94.

Fehr, Ernst, and Gächter, Simon. 2002. "Altruistic Punishment in Humans." *Nature* 415: 137–40.

Feinberg, Joel. 1970. "Justice and Personal Desert." *Rights and Reason: Essays in Honor of Carl Wellman*. (Dordrecht: Springer Netherlands), pp. 221–250.

Firestone, Lisa. 2013. "In a Relationship with a Narcissist? What You Need to Know about Narcissistic Relationships." *PsychAlive*. https://www.psychalive.org/narcissistic-relationships/.

170 REFERENCES

Fischer, John Martin. 1986. "Introduction: Responsibility and Freedom." In John Martin Fischer, ed., *Moral Responsibility* (Ithaca, NY: Cornell University Press), pp. 9–61.

Fischer, John Martin. 1994. *The Metaphysics of Free Will: An Essay on Control.* Cambridge: Blackwell.

Fischer, John Martin, and Ravizza, Mark. 1998. *Responsibility and Control.* Cambridge: Cambridge University Press.

Fischer, John Martin, and Tognazzini, Neal A. 2011. "The Physiognomy of Responsibility." *Philosophy & Phenomenological Research* 82: 381–417.

Flanagan, Owen. 2017. *The Geography of Morals.* New York: Oxford University Press.

Frank, Robert. 1988. *Passions within Reason.* New York: W. W. Norton and Company.

Frankfurt, Harry. 1988. *The Importance of What We Care About.* Cambridge: Cambridge University Press.

Franklin, Christopher Evan. 2013. "Valuing Blame." In Coates and Tognazzini 2013, pp. 207–23.

Fricker, Miranda. 2016. "What's the Point of Blame? A Paradigm Based Explanation." *Nous* 50: 165–83.

Frijda, Nico. 1986. *The Emotions.* Cambridge: Cambridge University Press.

Frijda, Nico. 1993. "Appraisal and Beyond." *Cognition & Emotion* 7: 225–31.

Frijda, Nico. 1994. "The *Lex Talionis*: On Vengeance." *Emotions: Essays on Emotion Theory* (New York: Psychology Press), pp. 263–89.

Frith, Chris D., and Frith, Uta. 2007. "Social Cognition in Humans." *Current Biology* 17: 724–32.

Fritz, Kyle G., and Miller, Daniel. 2018. "Hypocrisy and the Standing to Blame." *Pacific Philosophical Quarterly* 99: 118–39.

Fritz, Kyle G., and Miller, Daniel. 2019. "The Unique Badness of Hypocritical Blame." *Ergo* 6. http://dx.doi.org/10.3998/ergo.12405314.0006.019.

Girodo, Michel, and Wood, Douglas. 1979. "Talking Yourself out of Pain: The Importance of Believing That You Can." *Cognitive Therapy and Research* 3: 23–33.

Gollwitzer, Mario, and Denzler, Markus. 2009. "What Makes Revenge Sweet: Seeing the Offender Suffer or Delivering a Message?" *Journal of Experimental Social Psychology* 45: 840–4.

Gollwitzer, Mario, Meder, Milena, and Schmitt, Manfred. 2011. "What Gives Victims Satisfaction When They Seek Revenge?" *European Journal of Social Psychology* 41: 364–74.

Graham, Jesse, et al. 2013. "Moral Foundations Theory: The Pragmatic Validity of Moral Pluralism." *Advances in Experimental Social Psychology* 47: 55–130.

Graham, Jesse, Meindl, Peter, Koleva, Spassena, Iyer, Ravi, and Johnson, Kate M. 2015. "When Values and Behavior Conflict: Moral Pluralism and Intrapersonal Moral Hypocrisy." *Social and Personality Psychology Compass* 9: 158–70.

Graham, Peter. 2014. "A Sketch of a Theory of Blameworthiness." *Philosophy & Phenomenological Research* 88: 388–409.

Green, Ava, and Charles, Kathy. 2019. "Voicing the Victims of Narcissistic Partners: A Qualitative Analysis of Responses to Narcissistic Injury and Self-Esteem Regulation." *Sage open* 9. https://doi.org/10.1177/2158244019846693.

Greengross, Gil, and Miller, Geoffrey F. 2008. "Dissing Oneself versus Dissing Rivals: Effects of Status, Personality, and Sex on the Short-Term and Long-Term Attractiveness of Self-Deprecating and Other-Deprecating Humor." *Evolutionary Psychology* 6. https://doi.org/10.1177/147470490800600303. Greenspan, Patricia S. 1988. *Emotions and Reasons: An Inquiry into Emotional Justification.* London: Routledge & Kegan Paul.

Greenspan, Patricia S. 1992. "Subjective Guilt and Responsibility." *Mind* 101: 287–303.

Greggs, Tom. 2017. "In Gratitude for Grace: Praise, Worship and the Sanctified Life." *Scottish Journal of Theology* 70: 147–65.

Grice, H. P. 1957. "Meaning." *Philosophical Review* 66: 377–88.

Haidt, Jonathan. 2003. "The Moral Emotions." *Handbook of Affective Sciences* 11: 852–70.

Haidt, Jonathan, and Joseph, Craig. 2004. "Intuitive Ethics: How Innately Prepared Intuitions Generate Culturally Variable Virtues." *Daedalus* 133: 55–66.

Hardy, James. 2006. "Speaking Clearly: A Critical Review of the Self-Talk Literature." *Psychology of Sport and Exercise* 7: 81–97.

REFERENCES   171

Hardy, James, Hall, Craig R., and Alexander, Mike R. 2001. "Exploring Self-Talk and Affective States in Sport." *Journal of Sports Sciences* 7: 469–75.

Hatzigeorgiadis, Antonis, et al. 2008. "Investigating the Functions of Self-Talk: The Effects of Motivational Self-Talk on Self-Efficacy and Performance in Young Tennis Players." *The Sport Psychologist* 22: 458–71.

Hay, Jennifer. 2001. "The Pragmatics of Humor Support." *Humor* 14: 55–82.

Hieronymi, Pamela. 2001. "Articulating an Uncompromising Forgiveness." *Philosophy & Phenomenological Research* 62: 529–55.

Hieronymi, Pamela. 2004. "The Force and Fairness of Blame." *Philosophical Perspectives* 18: 115–48.

Hieronymi, Pamela. 2021. "Fairness, Sanction, and Condemnation." *Oxford Studies in Agency and Responsibility* 7: 229–58.

Holden, George W., et al. 2017. "Researchers Deserve a Better Critique: Response to Larzelere, Gunnoe, Roberts, and Ferguson." *Marriage and Family Review* 53: 465–90.

Hopfensitz, A., and Reuben, E. 2009. "The Importance of Emotions for the Effectiveness of Social Punishment." *Economic Journal* 119: 1534–59.

Howard, Christopher, and Rowland, R. A., eds. 2022. *Fittingness: Essays in the Philosophy of Normativity*. Oxford: Oxford University Press.

Hume, David. 1960. *A Treatise of Human Nature*. Ed. L. A. Selby-Bigge. Oxford: Oxford University Press.

Isserow, Jessica, and Klein, Colin. 2017. "Hypocrisy and Moral Authority." *Journal of Ethics & Social Policy* 12: 191–222.

Izard, Carroll E. 1993. "Four Systems for Emotion Activation: Cognitive and Noncognitive Processes." *Psychological Review* 100: 68–90.

Izard, Carroll E. 1997. "Emotions and Facial Expressions: A Perspective from Differential Emotions Theory." *The Psychology of Facial Expression* 2: 57–77.

Jackson, Frank, and Pettit, Philip. 1995. "Moral Functionalism and Moral Motivation." *Philosophical Quarterly* 45: 20–40.

Jacobson, Daniel. 2013. "Regret, Agency, and Error." *Oxford Studies in Agency and Responsibility* 1: 95–125.

James, Samantha, et al. 2014. "The Dark Triad, Schadenfreude, and Sensational Interests: Dark Personalities, Dark Emotions, and Dark Behaviors." *Personality and Individual Differences* 68: 211–16.

James, William. 1894. "Discussion: The Physical Basis of Emotion." *Psychological Review* 1: 516–29.

Janoff-Bulman, Ronnie. 1979. "Characterological versus Behavioral Self-Blame: Inquiries into Depression and Rape." *Journal of Personality and Social Psychology* 37: 1798–809.

Janoff-Bulman, Ronnie. 1982. "Esteem and Control Bases of Blame: 'Adaptive' Strategies for Victims versus Observers." *Personality* 50: 180–92.

Jauk, Emanuel, et al. 2017. "The Relationship between Grandiose and Vulnerable (Hypersensitive) Narcissism." *Frontiers in Psychology* 8: 1600.

Jeppsson, Sofia, and Brandenburg, Daphne. 2022. "Patronizing Praise." *The Journal of Ethics* 26: 663–82.

Jonason, Peter K., et al. 2013. "Different Routes to Limited Empathy in the Sexes: Examining the Links between the Dark Triad and Empathy." *Personality and Individual Differences* 54: 572–6.

Jonason, Peter K., and Krause, Laura. 2013. "The Emotional Deficits Associated with the Dark Triad Traits: Cognitive Empathy, Affective Empathy, and Alexithymia." *Personality and Individual Differences* 55: 532–7.

Kagan, Shelly. 2014. *The Geometry of Desert*. Oxford: Oxford University Press.

Kant, Immanuel. 1964. *The Doctrine of Virtue: Part II of the Metaphysic of Morals*. Trans. Mary J. Gregor (New York: Harper).

Kassinove, Howard, Sukhodolsky, D. G., Tsytsarev, S. V., and Solovyova, S. 1997. "Self-Reported Anger Episodes in Russia and America." *Journal of Social Behavior & Personality* 12: 301–24.

172 REFERENCES

Kincaid, Harold. 1990. "Assessing Functional Explanations in the Social Sciences." *Proceedings of the Biennial Meeting of the Philosophy of Science Association* 1: 341–54.

Lane, Andrew M., Thelwell, Richard C., Lowther, James, and Devonport, Tracey J. 2009. "Emotional Intelligence and Psychological Skills Use Among Athletes." *Social Behavior and Personality: An International Journal* 37: 195–201.

Larzelere, Robert E., et al. 2017. "Children and Parents Deserve Better Parental Discipline Research: Critiquing the Evidence for Exclusively 'Positive' Parenting." *Marriage & Family Review* 53: 24–35.

Lazarus, Richard. 1982. "Thoughts on the Relation between Emotion and Cognition." *American Psychologist* 37: 1019–24.

Lazarus, Richard. 1991. *Emotion and Adaptation*. New York and Oxford: Oxford University Press.

Lenman, James. 2006. "Compatibilism and Contractualism: The Possibility of Moral Responsibility." *Ethics* 117: 7–31.

Lerner, Jennifer S., and Keltner, Dacher. 2001. "Fear, Anger, and Risk." *Journal of Personality and Social Psychology* 81: 146–59.

Leung, Debbie W., and Slep, Amy M. Smith. 2006. "Predicting Inept Discipline: The Role of Parental Depressive Symptoms, Anger, and Attributions." *Journal of Consulting and Clinical Psychology* 74: 524–34.

Lewis, Michael. 1993. "The Development of Anger and Rage." In Robert A. Glick and Steven P. Roose, eds., *Rage, Power, and Aggression* (New Haven, CN: Yale University Press), pp. 148–68.

Lewis, Michael, Alessandri, Steven M., and Sullivan, Margaret W. 1990. "Violation of Expectancy, Loss of Control, and Anger Expressions in Young Infants." *Developmental Psychology* 26: 745–51.

Lippert-Rasmussen, Kasper. 2022. "Praising without Standing." *The Journal of Ethics* 26: 229–46.

List, Christian. 2006. "The Discursive Dilemma and Public Reason." *Ethics* 116: 362–402.

List, Christian, and Pettit, Philip. 2002. "Aggregating Sets of Judgments: An Impossibility Result." *Economics and Philosophy* 18: 89–110.

List, Christian, and Pettit, Philip. 2011. *Group Agency: The Possibility, Design, and Status of Corporate Agents*. Oxford: Oxford University Press.

Lubit, Roy. 2002. "The Long-Term Organizational Impact of Destructively Narcissistic Managers." *Academy of Management Perspectives* 16: 127–38.

Lutwak, Nita, Panish, Jacqueline, and Ferrari, Joseph. 2003. "Shame and Guilt: Characterological vs. Behavioral Self-Blame and Their Relationship to Fear of Intimacy." *Personality and Individual Differences* 35: 909–16.

Lynn, Michael. 2008. "Race Differences in Restaurant Tipping: A Literature Review and Discussion of Practical Implications." *Journal of Foodservice Business Research* 9: 99–113.

Macnamara, Coleen. 2013a. "'Screw You!' and 'Thank You.'" *Philosophical Studies* 165: 893–914.

Macnamara, Coleen. 2013b. "Taking Demands out of Blame." In Coates and Tognazzini 2013, pp. 141–61.

Macnamara, Coleen. 2015. "Reactive Attitudes as Communicative Entities." *Philosophy & Phenomenological Research* 90: 546–69.

Macnamara, Coleen. 2020. "Guilt, Desert, Fittingness, and the Good." *The Journal of Ethics* 24: 449–68.

March, Evita. 2019. "Psychopathy, Sadism, Empathy, and the Motivation to Cause Harm: New Evidence Confirms Malevolent Nature of the Internet Troll." *Personality and Individual Differences* 141: 133–7.

March, Evita, et al. 2020. "Somebody That I (Used to) Know: Gender and Dimensions of Dark Personality Traits as Predictors of Intimate Partner Cyberstalking." *Personality and Individual Differences* 163: 110084.

Martin, Rod A., et al. 2003. "Individual Differences in Uses of Humor and Their Relation to Psychological Well-Being: Development of the Humor Styles Questionnaire." *Journal of Research in Personality* 37: 48–75.

Martin, Rod A., et al. 2012. "Relationships between the Dark Triad and Humor Styles: A Replication and Extension." *Personality and Individual Differences* 52: 178–82.

REFERENCES 173

Marušić, Berislav, and White, Stephen. 2018. "How Can Beliefs Wrong?—A Strawsonian Epistemology." *Philosophical Topics* 46: 97–114.

Mason, Elinor. 2019a. "Between Strict Liability and Blameworthy Quality of Will." *Oxford Studies in Agency and Responsibility* 6: 241–64.

Mason, Elinor. 2019b. *Ways to Be Blameworthy*. Oxford: Oxford University Press.

Matheson, Benjamin, and Milam, Per-Erik. 2021. "The Case against Non-Moral Blame." *Oxford Studies in Normative Ethics* 11: 199–222.

McCloskey, H. J. 1957. "An Examination of Restricted Utilitarianism." *The Philosophical Review* 66: 466–85.

McCormick, Kelly. 2023. "Basic Desert and the Appropriateness of Blame." In Joseph Keim Campbell, Kristin A. Mickelson, and V. Alan White, eds., *A Companion to Free Will* (London: Blackwell): pp. 393–405.

McGeer, Victoria. 2013. "Civilizing Blame." In Coates and Tognazzini 2013: 162–88.

McGeer, Victoria. 2019. "Scaffolding Agency: A Proleptic Account of the Reactive Attitudes." *European Journal of Philosophy* 27: 301–23.

McKenna, Michael. 2006. "Collective Responsibility and Agent Meaning Theory." *Midwest Studies in Philosophy* 30: 16–34.

McKenna, Michael. 2012. *Conversation and Responsibility*. New York: Oxford University Press.

McKenna, Michael. 2013. "Directed Blame and Conversation." In Coates and Tognazzini 2013: 119–40.

McKenna, Michael. 2018. "Power, Social Inequities, and the Conversational Theory of Moral Responsibility." In Katrina Hutchison, Catriona Mackenzie, and Marina Oshana, eds., *Social Dimensions of Moral Responsibility* (New York: Oxford University Press), pp. 38–58.

McKenna, Michael. 2022. "Fittingness as an Intellectualist Trinket?" In Christopher Howard and R. A. Rowland, eds., *Fittingness: Essays in the Philosophy of Normativity* (Oxford: Oxford University Press), pp. 329–55.

McKenna, Michael. Manuscript. *Responsibility and Desert*.

McKenna, Michael, and Vadakin, Aron. 2008. "Review of George Sher, *In Praise of Blame*." *Ethics* 118: 751–56.

Mechanic, Kristen L., and Barry, Christopher T. 2015. "Adolescent Grandiose and Vulnerable Narcissism: Associations with Perceived Parenting Practices." *Journal of Child and Family Studies* 24: 1510–18.

Mele, Alfred. 1987. *Irrationality: An Essay on Akrasia, Self-Deception, and Self-Control*. New York: Oxford University Press.

Miller, Joshua D., and Maples, Jessica. 2011. "Trait Personality Models of Narcissistic Personality Disorder, Grandiose Narcissism, and Vulnerable Narcissism." In W. Keith Campbell and Joshue D. Miller, eds., *The Handbook of Narcissism and Narcissistic Personality Disorder: Theoretical Approaches, Empirical Findings, and Treatments* (Hoboken, NJ: John Wiley and Sons), pp. 71–88.

Moore, Michael. 1987. "The Moral Worth of Retribution." In F. Schoeman, ed., *Responsibility, Character, and the Emotions* (Cambridge: Cambridge University Press), pp. 179–219.

Morreall, John, ed. 1987. *The Philosophy of Laughter and Humor*. Albany, NY: State University of New York Press.

Nadelhoffer, Thomas, Heshmati, Saeideh, Kaplan, Deanna, and Nichols, Shaun 2013. "Folk Retributivism and the Communication Confound." *Economics and Philosophy* 29: 235–61.

Nelkin, Dana Kay. 2009. "Responsibility, Rational Abilities, and Two Kinds of Fairness Arguments." *Philosophical Explorations* 12: 151–65.

Nelkin, Dana Kay. 2011. *Making Sense of Freedom and Responsibility*. Oxford: Oxford University Press.

Nelkin, Dana Kay. 2013. "Desert, Fairness, and Resentment." *Philosophical Explorations* 16: 117–32.

Nelkin, Dana Kay. 2014. "Moral Responsibility, Conversation, and Desert: Comments on Michael McKenna's *Conversation and Responsibility*." *Philosophical Studies* 171: 63–72.

Nelkin, Dana Kay. 2016. "Accountability and Desert." *The Journal of Ethics* 20: 173–89.

Nelkin, Dana Kay. 2019a. "Desert, Free Will, and Our Moral Responsibility Practices." *The Journal of Ethics* 23: 265–75.

174 REFERENCES

Nelkin, Dana. 2019b. "Guilt, Grief, and the Good." *Social Philosophy and Policy* 36: 173–91.

Newman, George E., De Freitas, Julian, and Knobe, Joshua. 2015. "Beliefs about the True Self Explain Asymmetries Based on Moral Judgment." *Cognitive Science* 39: 96–125.

Nichols, Shaun. 2007. "After Incompatibilism: A Naturalistic Defense of the Reactive Attitudes." *Philosophical Perspectives* 21: 405–28.

Nichols, Shaun. 2013. "Brute Retributivism." In Thomas Nadelhoffer, ed., *The Future of Punishment* (Oxford: Oxford University Press), pp. 25–46.

Nichols, Shaun. 2015. *Bound*. Oxford: Oxford University Press.

Nihonmatsu, Naoto, Okuno, Masako, and Wakashima, Koubun. 2017. "Effects of Interpersonal Relations on the Cognition of Self-Deprecating Humor." *International Journal of Brief Therapy and Family Science* 7: 2–12.

Norrick, Neal R. 1993. *Conversational Joking: Humor in Everyday Talk*. Bloomington, IN: Indiana University Press.

Nowell-Smith, P. H. 1954. *Ethics*. Baltimore, MD: Penguin Books.

Nussbaum, Martha. 2004. "Emotions as Judgments of Value and Importance." In Robert Solomon, ed., *Thinking about Feelings: Contemporary Philosophers on Emotions* (New York: Oxford University Press), pp. 183–99.

Nussbaum, Martha C. 2015. "Transitional Anger." *Journal of the American Philosophical Association* 1: 41–56.

Ohmura, Yu, and Yamagishi, Toshio. 2005. "Why Do People Reject Unintended Inequity? Responders' Rejection in a Truncated Ultimatum Game." *Psychological Reports* 96: 533–41.

Pagel, Mark D., Becker, Joseph, and Coppel, David B. 1985. "Loss of Control, Self-Blame, and Depression: An Investigation of Spouse Caregivers of Alzheimer's Disease Patients." *Journal of Abnormal Psychology* 94: 169–82.

Parfit, Derek. 1984. *Reasons and Persons*. Oxford: Oxford University Press.

Pereboom, Derk. 2001. *Living without Free Will*. Cambridge: Cambridge University Press.

Pereboom, Derk. 2014. *Free Will, Agency, and Meaning in Life*. Oxford: Oxford University Press.

Pereboom, Derk. 2021a. *Wrongdoing and the Moral Emotions*. Oxford: Oxford University Press.

Pereboom, Derk. 2021b. "Undivided Forward-Looking Moral Responsibility." *The Monist* 104: 484–97.

Pereboom, Derk. 2022. "A Forward-Looking Account of Self-Blame." In Carlsson 2022, pp. 77–94.

Peterburs, Jutta, et al. 2017. "Processing of Fair and Unfair Offers in the Ultimatum Game under Social Observation." *Scientific Reports* 7: 1–12.

Peterson, Christopher, Schwartz, Stanley M., and Seligman, Martin E. 1981. "Self-Blame and Depressive Symptoms." *Journal of Personality and Social Psychology* 41: 253–9.

Pettit, Philip. 2000. "Groups with Minds of Their Own." Mimeo. Canberra, Australian National University.

Pettit, Philip. 2001. *A Theory of Freedom*. Cambridge: Polity Press.

Pettit, Philip. 2007. "Responsibility Incorporated." *Ethics* 117: 171–201.

Pettit, Philip, and Rabinowicz, Wlodek. 2001. "Deliberative Democracy and the Discursive Dilemma." *Philosophical Issues* 11: 268–99.

Pickard, Hanna. 2011. "Responsibility without Blame: Empathy and the Effective Treatment of Personality Disorder." *Philosophy, Psychiatry, and Psychology* 18: 209–23.

Pillutla, Madan M., and Murnighan, J. Keith 1996. "Unfairness, Anger, and Spite." *Organizational Behavior and Human Decision Processes* 68: 208–24.

Piopiunik, Marc, et al. 2020. "Skills, Signals, and Employability: An Experimental Investigation." *European Economic Review* 123: 103374.

Pizarro, David, Uhlmann, Eric, and Salovey, Peter. 2003. "Asymmetry in Judgments of Moral Blame and Praise: The Role of Perceived Metadesires." *Psychological Science* 14: 267–72.

Plato. 1992. *Republic*. Trans. G. M. A. Grube. Revised by C. D. C. Reeve. Indianapolis, IN: Hackett Publishing Co.

Plaufcan, Melissa R., Wamboldt, Frederick S., and Holm, Kristen E. 2012. "Behavioral and Characterological Self-Blame in Chronic Obstructive Pulmonary Disease." *Journal of Psychosomatic Research* 72: 78–83.

Porter, Stephen, et al. 2014. "Soldiers of Misfortune: An Examination of the Dark Triad and the Experience of Schadenfreude." *Personality and Individual Differences* 67: 64–8.

Portmore, Douglas W. 2022. "A Comprehensive Account of Blame: Self-Blame, Non-Moral Blame, and Blame for the Non-Voluntary." In Carlsson 2022, pp. 48–76.

Prinz, Jesse. 2005. "Are Emotions Feelings?" *Journal of Consciousness Studies* 12: 9–25.

Quinn, Warren. 1985. "The Right to Threaten and the Right to Punish." *Philosophy & Public Affairs* 14: 327–73.

Reis-Dennis, Samuel. 2018. "Anger: Scary Good." *Australasian Journal of Philosophy* 97: 451–64.

Roberts, Robert C. 1988. "What an Emotion Is: A Sketch." *The Philosophical Review* 97: 183–209.

Rohmann, Elke, Hanke, Stephanie, and Bierhoff, Hans-Werner. 2019. "Grandiose and Vulnerable Narcissism in Relation to Life Satisfaction, Self-Esteem, and Self-Construal." *Journal of Individual Differences* 40: 194–203.

Ronningstam, Elsa. 2010. "Narcissistic Personality Disorder: A Current Review." *Current Psychiatry Reports* 12: 68–75.

Rose, Paul, and Campbell, W. Keith. 2004. "Greatness Feels Good: A Telic Model of Narcissism and Subjective Well-Being." In Serge P. Shohov, ed., *Advances in Psychology Research* 31 (Nova Science Publishers): 3–27.

Roseman, Ira J., and Smith, Craig A. 2001. "Appraisal Theory." In Angela Schorr and Tom Johnstone, eds., *Appraisal Processes in Emotion: Theory, Methods, Research* (Oxford: Oxford University Press), pp. 3–19.

Rossi, Benjamin. 2018. "The Commitment Account of Hypocrisy." *Ethical Theory and Moral Practice* 21: 553–67.

Russell, Paul. 2004. "Responsibility and the Condition of Moral Sense." *Philosophical Topics* 32: 287–305.

Russell, Paul. 2017. *The Limits of Free Will*. New York: Oxford University Press.

Sars, Nicholas. 2022. "Strawson's Underappreciated Argumentative Structure." *European Journal of Philosophy*. https://doi.org/10.1111/ejop.12815.

Scanlon, T. M. 1986. "The Significance of Choice." In Sterling McMurrin, ed., *The Tanner Lectures on Human Values 8*. (Salt Lake City, UT: University of Utah Press), pp. 149–216.

Scanlon, T. M. 1998. *What We Owe to Each Other*. Cambridge, MA: Belknap Press of Harvard University Press.

Scanlon, T. M. 2008. *Moral Dimensions*. Cambridge, MA: Belknap Press of Harvard University Press.

Scanlon, T. M. 2015. "Forms and Conditions of Responsibility." In R. Clarke, M. McKenna, and A. Smith, eds., *The Nature of Moral Responsibility: New Essays*. (Oxford: Oxford University Press), pp. 89–111.

Scanlon, T. M. 2018. *Why Does Inequality Matter?* Oxford: Oxford University Press.

Scarantino, Andrea. 2014. "The Motivational Theory of Emotions." In Justin D'Arms and Daniel Jacobson, eds., *Moral Psychology and Human Agency* (Oxford: Oxford University Press), pp. 156–85.

Schacter, Hannah L., White, Samantha J., Chang, Vickie Y., and Juvonene, Jaana. 2014. "'Why Me?': Characterological Self-Blame and Continue Victimization in the First Year of Middle School." *Journal of Clinical Child & Adolescent Psychology* 44: 446–55.

Schlick, Moritz. 1966. "When Is a Man Responsible?" In Bernard Berofsky, ed., *Free Will and Determinism* (New York: Harper and Row), pp. 54–63.

Schneller, Gregory R., and Swenson, John Eric. 2013. "Talking to God: Psychological Correlates of Prayers of Praise and Gratitude." *Christian Psychology* 7: 39–50.

Schoenleber, Michelle, Sadeh, Naomi, and Verona, Edelyn. 2011. "Parallel Syndromes: Two Dimensions of Narcissism and the Facets of Psychopathic Personality in Criminally Involved Individuals." *Personality Disorders: Theory, Research, and Treatment* 2: 113–27.

Schroeder, Mark. 2018. "When Beliefs Wrong." *Philosophical Topics* 46: 115–28.

Segerstrom, Suzanne C., Taylor, Shelley E., Kemeny, Margaret E., Reed, Geoffrey F., and Visscher, Barbara R. 1996. "Causal Attributions Predict Rate of Immune Decline in HIV-Seropositive Gay Men." *Healthy Psychology* 15: 485–93.

176 REFERENCES

Sepinwall, Amy J. 2017. "Blame, Emotion, and the Corporation." In Eric W. Orts and N. Craig Smith, eds., *The Moral Responsibility of Firms* (Oxford: Oxford University Press), pp. 143–66.

Shaver, Phillip, Schwartz, Judith, Kirson, Donald, and O'Connor, Cary. 1987. "Emotion Knowledge: Further Exploration of a Prototype Approach." *Journal of Personality and Social Psychology* 52: 1061–86.

Sher, George. 2006a. "Out of Control." *Ethics* 116: 285–301.

Sher, George. 2006b. *In Praise of Blame*. Oxford: Oxford University Press.

Sher, George. 2021. *A Wild West of the Mind*. Oxford: Oxford University Press.

Shoemaker, David. 2007. "Moral Address, Moral Responsibility, and the Boundaries of the Moral Community." *Ethics* 118: 70–108.

Shoemaker, David. 2013. "Blame and Punishment." In D. Justin Coates and Neal A. Tognazzini, eds., *Blame: Its Nature and Norms* (Oxford: Oxford University Press), pp. 100–18.

Shoemaker, David. 2014. "Review of *Free Will, Agency, and Meaning in Life*, by Derk Pereboom," *Notre Dame Philosophical Reviews*. https://ndpr.nd.edu/reviews/free-will-agency-and-meaning-in-life/.

Shoemaker, David. 2015. *Responsibility from the Margins*. Oxford: Oxford University Press.

Shoemaker, David. 2017. "Response-Dependent Responsibility: or, A Funny Thing Happened on the Way to Blame." *The Philosophical Review* 126: 481–527.

Shoemaker, David. 2018a. "Cruel Jokes and Normative Competence." *Social Philosophy & Policy* 35: 173–95.

Shoemaker, David. 2018b. "You Oughta Know! Defending Angry Blame." In Myisha Cherry and Owen Flanagan, eds., *The Moral Psychology of Anger* (London: Rowman & Littlefield), pp. 67–88.

Shoemaker, David. 2019a. "Blameworthy but Unblamable: A Paradox of Corporate Responsibility." *The Georgetown Journal of Law & Public Policy* 17: 897–918.

Shoemaker, David. 2019b. "Hurt Feelings." *Journal of Philosophy* 116: 125–48.

Shoemaker, David. 2020. "Responsibility: The State of the Question—Fault Lines in the Foundations." *The Southern Journal of Philosophy* 58: 205–37.

Shoemaker, David. 2021. "The Forgiven." In Michael McKenna, Dana Nelkin, and Brandon Warmke, eds. *Forgiveness and its Moral Dimensions* (Oxford: Oxford University Press), pp. 29–56.

Shoemaker, David. 2022a. "Empathic Control?" *Humana.Mente*. https://www.humanamente.eu/index.php/HM/article/view/401.

Shoemaker, David. 2022b. "The Trials and Tribulations of Tom Brady: Self-Blame, Self-Talk, Self-Flagellation." In Carlsson 2022, pp. 28–47.

Shoemaker, David. 2023. "Threatening Quality of Will." *Journal of Moral Philosophy*. https://doi.org/10.1163/17455243-20234092.

Shoemaker, David. 2024. *Wisecracks: Humor and Morality in Everyday Life*. Chicago, IL: University of Chicago Press.

Shoemaker, David, and Vargas, Manuel. 2021. "Moral Torch Fishing: A Signaling Theory of Blame." *Nous* 55: 581–602.

Siderits, Mark. 2011. "Buddhist Non-Self: The No-Owner's Manual." In Shaun Gallagher, ed., *The Oxford Handbook of the Self* (Oxford: Oxford University Press), pp. 297–315.

Sinnott-Armstrong, Walter, and Wheatley, Thalia. 2012. "The Disunity of Morality and Why It Matters to Philosophy." *The Monist* 95: 355–77.

Sliwa, Pauline. 2019. "The Power of Excuses." *Philosophy & Public Affairs* 47: 37–71.

Smart, J. J. C. 1970. "Free Will, Praise, and Blame." In Gerald Dworkin, ed., *Determinism, Free Will, and Moral Responsibility* (Englewood Cliffs, NY: Prentice-Hall), pp. 196–213.

Smart, J. J. C. 1973. "An Outline of a System of Utilitarian Ethics." In J. J. C. Smart and Bernard Williams, *Utilitarianism: For and Against* (Cambridge: Cambridge University Press), pp. 1–74.

Smith, Angela M. 2012. "Accountability, Answerability, and Accountability: In Defense of a Unified Account." *Ethics* 122: 575–89.

Smith, Angela M. 2008. "Control, Responsibility, and Moral Assessment." *Philosophical Studies* 138: 367–92.

Smith, Angela M. 2011. "Guilty Thoughts." In Carla Bagnoli, ed., *Morality and the Emotions* (Oxford: Oxford University Press), pp. 235–56.

Smith, Angela M. 2005. "Responsibility for Attitudes: Activity and Passivity in Mental Life." *Ethics* 115: 236–71.

Smith, Angela M. 2007. "On Being and Holding Responsible." *The Journal of Ethics* 11: 465–84.

Smith, Angela M. 2013. "Moral Blame and Moral Protest." In Coates and Tognazzini 2013, pp. 27–48.

Solomon, Robert. 1988. "On Emotions as Judgments." *American Philosophical Quarterly* 25: 183–91.

Sosis, R. 2001. "Costly Signaling and Torch Fishing on Ifaluk Atoll." *Evolution and Human Behavior* 21: 223–44.

Stace, Walter T. 1952. *Religion and the Modern Mind* (New York: Harper Collins).

Stout, Nathan. 2020. "On the Significance of Praise." *American Philosophical Quarterly* 57: 215–26.

Stratton, Peter. 2003. "Causal Attributions during Therapy II: Reconstituted Families and Parental Blaming." *Journal of Family Therapy* 25: 161–80.

Strawson, Galen. 1994. "The Impossibility of Moral Responsibility." *Philosophical Studies* 75: 5–24.

Strawson, P. F. 1962. "Freedom and Resentment." *Proceedings of the British Academy* 48: 1–25; reprinted in (and cited page numbers from) Gary Watson, ed., *Free Will* (2nd edition) (Oxford: Oxford University Press, 2003), pp. 72–93.

Swannell, Sarah, Martin, Graham, Page, Andrew, Hasking, Penelope, Hazell, Philip, Taylore, Anne, and Protani, Melinda. 2012. "Child Maltreatment, Subsequent Non-Suicidal Self-Injury and the Mediating Roles of Dissociation, Alexithymia and Self-Blame." *Child Abuse & Neglect* 36: 572–84.

Szigeti, Andras. 2015. "Sentimentalism and Moral Dilemmas." *Dialectica* 69: 1–22.

Talbert, Matthew. 2008. "Blame and Responsiveness to Moral Reasons: Are Psychopaths Blameworthy?" *Pacific Philosophical Quarterly* 89: 516–35.

Talbert, Matthew. 2012. "Moral Competence, Moral Blame, and Protest." *The Journal of Ethics* 16: 89–109.

Talbert, Matthew. 2022. "The Attributionist Approach to Moral Luck." *Midwest Studies in Philosophy*. https://doi.org/10.1111/misp.12102.

Tappolet, Christine. 2016. *Emotions, Values, and Agency*. Oxford: Oxford University Press.

Telech, Daniel. 2021. "Praise as Moral Address." *Oxford Studies in Agency and Responsibility* 7: 154–81.

Telech, Daniel. 2022. "Praise." *Philosophical Compass*. https://doi.org/10.1111/phc3.12876.

Telech, Daniel, and Tierney, Hannah. 2019. "The Comparative Nonarbitrariness Norm of Blame." *Journal of Ethics and Social Philosophy* 16: 25–43.

Thomas, Alan. 1999. "Remorse and Reparation: A Philosophical Analysis." In Murray Cox, ed., *Remorse and Reparation* (London: Jessica Kingsley Publishers), pp. 127–45.

Tilghman-Osborne, Carlos, Cole, David A., Felton, Julia W., and Ciesla, Jeffrey Al. 2008. "Relation of Guilt, Shame, Behavioral and Characterological Self-Blame to Depressive Symptoms in Adolescents over Time." *Journal of Social Clinical Psychology* 27: 809–42.

Todd, Patrick. 2019. "A Unified Account of the Moral Standing to Blame." *Noûs* 53: 347–74.

Todd, Patrick, and Rabern, Brian. 2022. "The Paradox of Self-Blame." *American Philosophical Quarterly* 59: 111–25.

Tognazzini, Neal, and Coates, D. Justin. 2018. "Blame." Edward N. Zalta, ed. *The Stanford Encyclopedia of Philosophy*. https://plato.stanford.edu/archives/fall2018/entries/blame/.

Trost, Zina, et al. 2012. "Cognitive Dimensions of Anger in Chronic Pain." *Pain* 153: 515–17.

Tsai, George. 2017. "Respect and the Efficacy of Blame." *Oxford Studies in Agency and Responsibility* 4: 248–75.

REFERENCES

Ullman, Sarah E. 1996. "Social Reactions, Coping Strategies, and Self-Blame Attributions in Adjustment to Sexual Assault." *Psychology of Women Quarterly* 20: 505–26.

Van Kleef, Gerben A., De Dreu, Carsten K. W., and Manstead, Antony S. R. 2004. "The Interpersonal Effects of Anger and Happiness in Negotiations." *Journal of Personality and Social Psychology* 86: 57–76.

Van Raalte, Judy L., Brewer, Britten W., Rivera, Patricia M., and Petitpas, Albert J. 1994. "The Relationship between Observable Self-Talk and Competitive Junior Tennis Players' Match Performances." *Journal of Sport and Exercise Psychology* 16: 400–15.

Van Raalte, Judy L., Brewer, Britton W., Lewis, Brian P., and Linder, Darwyn E. 1995. "Cork! The Effects of Positive and Negative Self-Talk on Dart Throwing Performance." *Journal of Sport Behavior* 18: 50.

Vargas, Manuel. 2013. *Building Better Beings*. Oxford: Oxford University Press.

Vasudha, Sykam, and Prasad, Rajiv. 2017. "Narcissism, Happiness, and Self Actualization." *International Conference on Advances in Computing, Communications and Informatics (ICACCI)*. IEEE.

Veling, Harm, Ruys, Kristen, and Aarts, Henk. 2012. "Anger as a Hidden Motivator: Associating Attainable Objects with Anger Turns Them into Rewards." *Social Psychology and Personality Science* 3: 438–45.

Veselka, Livia, et al. 2010. "Relations between Humor Styles and the Dark Triad Traits of Personality." *Personality and Individual Differences* 48: 772–4.

Wai, Michael, and Tiliopoulos, Niko. 2012. "The Affective and Cognitive Empathic Nature of the Dark Triad of Personality." *Personality and Individual Differences* 52: 794–9.

Wallace, R. Jay. 1994. *Responsibility and the Moral Sentiments*. Cambridge, MA: Harvard University Press.

Wallace, R. Jay. 2010. "Hypocrisy, Moral Address, and the Equal Standing of Persons." *Philosophy & Public Affairs* 38: 307–41.

Watson, Gary. 1987. "Responsibility and the Limits of Evil: Variations on a Strawsonian Theme." In Ferdinand Schoeman, ed., *Responsibility, Character, and the Emotions* (Cambridge: Cambridge University Press), pp. 256–86.

Watson, Gary. 2004. *Agency and Answerability*. Oxford: Oxford University Press.

Watson, Gary. 2014. "Peter Strawson on Responsibility and Sociality." *Oxford Studies in Agency and Responsibility* 2: 15–32.

Wertheimer, Roger. 1998. "Constraining Condemning." *Ethics* 108: 489–501.

Williams, Bernard. 1995. "Internal Reasons and the Obscurity of Blame." In Bernard Williams, *Making Sense of Humanity* (Cambridge: Cambridge University Press), pp. 35–45.

Wolf, Susan. 2001. "The Moral of Moral Luck." *Philosophic Exchange* 31: 4–19.

Wolf, Susan. 2011. "Blame, Italian Style." In R. Jay Wallace, Rahul Kumar, and Samuel Freeman, eds., *Reasons and Recognition: Essays on the Philosophy of T. M. Scanlon* (New York: Oxford University Press), pp. 332–47.

Wright, Larry. 1976. *Teleological Explanations: An Etiological Analysis of Goals and Functions*. Berkeley, CA: University of California Press.

Zeigler-Hill, Virgil, et al. 2013. "The Status-Signaling Property of Self-Esteem: The Role of Self-Reported Self-Esteem and Perceived Self-Esteem in Personality Judgments." *Journal of Personality* 81: 209–20.

Zeigler-Hill, Virgil, and Besser, Avi. 2013. "A Glimpse behind the Mask: Facets of Narcissism and Feelings of Self-Worth." *Journal of Personality Assessment* 95: 249–60.

Zimmerman, Michael. 1988. *An Essay on Moral Responsibility*. Totowa, NJ: Rowman and Littlefield.

Index

ability to do otherwise 86, 87, 159, 166
accountability 9 n. 15, 10, 18 n. 4, 63, 102, 113,
      115, 157
  and capacity for empathy 69 n. 12
  and sanctions 157–159
  moral 126
accounting theory of blame, *see* blame and
      blaming, accounting theory of
acknowledgment xxiii, 5, 82, 162
  and being heighted, *see* heights, and
      acknowledgment
  empathic 57, 58, 63, 67, 68, 73, 110–111, 133,
      135, 137, 142, 143 n. 4
  failure of 68
  remorseful, *see* remorse
  seeking of 68–69, 72–73, 135, 160, 164
action-tendencies, *see* emotions,
     action-tendencies of
admiration xxi, 10, 23, 44, 63, 75–76, 81, 82 n. 3,
     98, 101, 102, 140, 161
  fitting (admirable) 84, 157, 158, 164
affective theory of blame, *see* blame and
     blaming, affective theory of
agency, collective 108
  ambiguous 114–115
  capacities of 162
  responsible, *see* responsible agency
amusement 61, 65, 85, 86, 90
  fitting 84
anger xxi, 16, 22, 63, 65, 107, 133, 134
  and babies or nonhuman animals 66
  and blame, *see* blame and blaming, angry
  and demands 52–53, 68, 110
  and harm 85, 87–88
  and slights xxiv, 67–68
  cognitively sharpened 124
  expressions of 87, 95
  fitting or unfitting 90, 135–136
  goal-frustration view of 66, 68, 131–132,
     133–134, 136, 138, 139, 162
  moral 41, 44
  non-agential 65–66
  pluralistic view of 66, 131
  positive counterpart of 71
  private 87, 88–92
  recalcitrant 137

slighted- 66–70, 73, 77, 81, 84, 91, 98, 101, 102,
     104, 105, 107, 110–112, 116, 120, 128,
     131–132, 133–134, 140–141, 143 n. 4, 145,
     156, 158, 161, 162, 164
  self-directed 135–137, 139, 162
  aims of 67–68
  and accountability 113
  and negative self-talk 133, 162
  as self-effacing 135–136, 162
answerability 102, 113, 157, 161
apology 4, 59, 69, 119–120, 136
appraisals 85, 90, 92
  hurtful 90
attributability xix n. 2, 9 n. 15, 18 n. 4, 82, 102,
     113 n. 17, 115, 157
Aristotle 65, 67
Arpaly and Schroeder 6, n. 9, 9 n. 14, 58 n. 5,
     59 n. 6

backward-looking reasons xxiv, xxvi, 7, 43,
     82–83, 85, 95, 133–134, 162, 164
Basu, Rima 90, 116–121
Basu and Schroeder 91 n. 17, 116, 117
Beeghly, Erin 116
Berger, Fred 70 n. 14
Bicchieri, Cristina 24–25
Bingeman, Emily 50
Björnsson and Hess 109–112
blame and blaming
  accounting theory of 13, 16
  acknowledgment- and non-acknowledgment
     seeking forms of 62, 68, 72, 157, 164
  aesthetic 40, 44, 45
  affective theory of 13, 15, 41–43
  and alienation 85
  and attitudes 5
  and confrontation 5, 52
  and danger 3, 8, 46–49
  and demands xx, 4–5, 85
  and excuses 6, *see also* excuses
  and generation of shame 85
  and harm 85–86, 87–88
  and moral ignorance 10
  and morality 6
  and punishment 140
  and slights 6, 65, 66

180 INDEX

blame and blaming (*cont.*)
  and standing 8, 73, 85
  and withdrawal of trust 85
  angry 5, 18 n. 4, 19 n. 7, 27, 44, 52–53, 57, 58,
      61, 66, 72, 90, 104, 107–109, 161
  as sanctions 156–158
  as scary 27
  athletic 44, 45
  backfire effect of 31 n. 15
  behavioral 47–48
  characteristic force of 27
  characterological 47–48
  communicative theory of 13–14, 15, 16 n. 3,
      43–45
  conversational theory of 43
  corporate 107–113, 161
  counterfactual 17, 37–38, 40, 45
  criminal xxvi, 141–143
  culinary 40, 44, 45
  disjunctive theory of 19–20
  emotional 124–125
  emotionless 37
  hypocritical 73, 129–132
  influence theory of 13, 16, 18
  minimal theory of 14–15, 16–19
  mockery- 56–58, 72, 81, 134, 140, 160,
      161, 162
    acknowledgment- and
        non-acknowledgment-seeking 75
    and attitudes 59
    and danger 61
    and demands 59
    and desert 59, 158
    and emotions 59
    and excuses 60
    and moral justification 60–61, 158
    and morality 60
    and quality of will 60
    and standing 61, 73
    hypocritical 73
    private 75
  moral 27, 40, 44
  moral justification for 158–159
  nonmoral 40, 44–45
  norms of 35
  of non-agents xvii n. 3
  over- 46–49
  private xxiv, 6, 16, 37, 43, 44, 88–92, 95
  proleptic 161
  protest theory of 14, 15, 39–41, 112–113
  relationship theory of 13, 15
  self-directed xxiii, 4, 15, 37, 48, 122–139
    and acknowledgment 123
    and hypocrisy 128–130, 162

  and poor quality of will 123
  and relationship damage 123
  athletic 122–123, 134, 162
  behavioral 138
  characterological 138
  moral 135–136, 162
  mutual entailment with
      other-blame 124–125
  sting of xxiv, 16, 27, 35, 38, 41, 45, 46, 56, 58,
      76, 81, 83, 128, 158, 160, 163
  stranger 16
  the dead 15, 16
  theories of 13–15
  third-party 16
  under- 49
  unfitting 104
  unity of xx, xxii
  ways of xx
  worthiness of xxv, 14, 17, 27, 81, 91, n. 16,
      104–105, 108, 112–114, 116–120, 125
blame and praise 72, 163
  acknowledgment-seeking or non-
      acknowledgment-seeking 72–75, 102,
      161, 163
    and emotions 75
  aptness of xxi, xxiv, 21, 38, 81ff, 96, 158 n. 28,
      161, 163, 164
  architecture of 63, 76–77, 160–166
  athletic 21–22, 38, 40, 44, 45
  attitudes and expressions of 22–23
  capacities for 11, 53
  constitutivist account(s) of xx, 36–38
  corporate 97, 107–113
  emotions forms of 63–77
  expressive and non-expressive forms
      of 77, 161
  functional account of xxii, 25–26, 160, 163
  normative domains of 160
  over- and under- xxiii, 50, 52
  seeming asymmetries of xx, xxii, 4–11,
      62, 72, 160
  self-directed 25, 96, 162
  symmetry of xxiii, 3, 58–61, 63, 72, 76–77
  system of xxii, 20–22, 28, 42, 43–44, 72, 73,
      76, 81, 102, 140, 158, 160, 163
  without signaling 36–37
  worthiness of, *see* aptness of; *see also* blame,
      worthiness of
Bloom, Paul 10
BP 107–108
Brink, David 106 n. 9
Brink and Nelkin 14–15, 17, 89
Brown, Eric 129 n. 16
buzzes, *see* praise and praising, buzzes of

INDEX 181

Carlsson, Andreas Brekke 123 n. 4, 125–127, 136 n. 24
Caruso, Gregg 141–142 n. 3
Cicero 56
Clarke, Randolph 86, 89–90, 123
communicative theory of blame, *see* blame and blaming, communicative theory of
compliments, *see* praise and praising, complimenting-
condemnation xxiii, 9 n. 14, 23, 24
confrontation 67
contempt xxiii, 10, 18 n. 4, 23, 63, 65, 75, 77, 81, 82 n. 3, 89, 102, 140, 155, 158, 160
  expressions of 87
  fitting (contemptible) 84, 158, 164
corporations, agency of 108–112
  blame and blamability of, *see* blame and blaming, corporate
  blame or praise, *see* blame and praise, corporate
  responsibility of, *see* responsibility, corporate
costly signaling 12, 160, 163
  and guilt 128
  and honesty 32, 38, 39
  and mockery 57
  in blame 31–34
  in praise 34
  long-term benefits of 33, 38
  types of costs of 30–31, 34
Costly Signaling Theory (CST) 28–31
criticism 23, 25, 44
cross-world comparisons 95

Dark Triad 51
  and empathy 69–70
  humor styles of 54–55
D'Arms and Jacobson 67 n. 10, 89 n. 15
deep selves 164
demands and demanding 23, 25, 68–69, 73, 111, 143
  and authority 143
Dennett, Daniel 71, 144 n. 11
depression 48, 50, 51, 102, 138
Descartes, Rene 93
desert xxiii, xxiv, 5, 7–8, 18 n. 5, 47, 84–87, 138, 140, 159, 163, 166
  and fairness or justice 86, 88, 149
  and fit, *see* fit and fittingness, and desert
  and free will 84, 86, 87, 162
  and mockery 93–95
  and moral justification 86–87, 140
  and punishment 140–141, 143
  and purely attitudinal blame 88–92, 140

and sanctions 147, 152–153, 163
  basic 86
  in games 146 n. 11, 155
determinism 83, 103, 106, 140, 166
  and indeterminism 86
disapproval 17
disappointment xxiii, 13, 17, 22, 25, 44, 63, 75–77, 81, 158, 161
  expressions of 87
disdain xxiii, 18 n. 4, 23, 44, 75–77, 97, 101, 155, 158, 161
  fitting 84, 157
disgust 17, 65
dismay 17
distrust 23
Doris, John 10
doxastic immorality 119–121
dread 17
Duggan, A.P. 123

economic games xxi, 44, 144–148
  and penalties 146–148
elevation 76
embarrassment 134–135
emotions
  acknowledgment- and non-acknowledgment-seeking 75
  action-tendencies of 64–65
  and appraisals 65, 83, 85
  and corporations 110–111
  appraisal theories of 64
  aptness of 65 n. 7
  basic or natural 83
  control precedence of 65
  expressions of 85
  feeling theories of 64
  fitting 85, 88, 156
  functional equivalents of 110–111
  motivational theories of 64–65
  pancultural 64
  perceptual theories of 64 n. 4
  recalcitrant 88, 91
  syndromes of 64
empathy 5, 51, 57
  capacity for 69–70
  demand for 68–69, 101
emulation 76
Enoch, David 113 n. 19
evolutionarily stable system 30
excuses 69, 72, 89, 100–101, 150, 152–157, 166
  and intent 154
expectations 25
expressive theory of blame, *see* blame and blaming, communicative theory of

182 INDEX

fairness 7, 86, 155, 159
  and desert, *see* desert and fairness or justice
  and mockery 93, 95
  and sanctions, *see* sanctions and fairness
fear 17, 64–65, 85, 86, 90, 133
  fitting 84
Feinberg, Joel 88
fit and fittingness xxiv–xxv, 83–92, 104, 140–141,
      157, 159, 163, 164
  and desert 88, 93–95, 161
  and expressions of emotions 85
  and *pro tanto* reasons 84
fitmakers 97–121, 161
flagrant fouls 154–155
Force Majeure 17–18, 37
forgiveness 111, 114
forward-looking reasons xxiv, 7, 43, 82–83, 86,
      133–135, 164
Four Case Argument 105
Frank, Robert 33 n. 17, 42
free will xxiv, 4, 81, 84, 85, 103, 106, 140, 158–159,
      162, 166
  and accountability 157–159
  and desert, *see* desert and free will
Fricker, Miranda 43, 44–45
frustration 17, 66 n. 8
functions and functionalism 20, 23–24
  and artifacts 26–27
  communicative 43–44
  found 24 n. 12
  in competitor theories of blame 39–45
  multiple realizability of 44
  teleological 20

Ginet, Carl 149 n. 15
goal-frustration view of anger, *see* anger,
      goal-frustration view of
Good True Self theory xxi
grading 148–149
  and bad luck 148–149
  and sanctions, *see* sanctions and grading
Graham, Peter 123
gratification xxiii, 9, 71, 73
gratitude xxiii, 21, 23, 44, 63, 70–72, 77, 100, 101,
      140, 156, 158, 161
  and complimenting-praise 71 n. 16
  and heights 72, 164
  and narcissists 70
  and praise, *see* praise and praising, and gratitude
  buzz of 72
  fittingness of 84
  hypocritical 73
  multiple types of 70–71

gratitude-praise, *see* praise and praising, and
      gratitude
Green, Draymond 154
grief 65, 85, 86, 90
  fitting 84
guilt xxv, 4, 7, 9, 23, 27, 50, 53, 59, 65, 69, 75 n. 20,
      94, 100, 109, 111 n. 15, 124, 134, 135–137,
      158 n. 27
  and remorse, *see* remorse and guilt
  and self-blame 124, 125–127, 162
  and stings 128, 143 n. 4
  corporate 110–111
  mongers of 125–128, 138
  phenomenology of 110
guilting 23, 85, 87, 127–128, 141, 143 n. 4

Harris, Robert Alton 46–47
heights 70–72, 98, 101, 161, 164
  and acknowledgment 70–71, 101
  and gratitude, *see* gratitude and heights
Hieronymi, Pamela 14, 27, 40, 144, 148
holding responsible 18, 66, 73, 82, 164
honoring 40
hopes 25
horror 17
Huck Finn 7, 10
humor styles 54–55
  affiliative 54, 55
  aggressive 54, 56
  self-defeating 54
  self-enhancing 54, 55
hurt feelings xxiii, 91, 119, 121 n. 25
  and desert 91
  fittingness of 91
Hutcheson, Frances 56
hypocrisy xx, xxv, 8, 61, 73, 128–130, 133, 135–136

inadvertence 98, 113–115
indignation 7, 9, 100, 124, 127, 158
  private 125
  corporate 110–111
influence theory of blame, *see* blame and
      blaming, influence theory of

judgment-sensitivity 101
justifications 69, 72

Kant, Immanuel 71
Knobe, Joshua 10
Kwiatek, Tim 6 n. 9
  joy 65, 75 n. 19
  justice 8, 86
    and mockery 93, 95

INDEX 183

libertarianism 141
List, Christian 108

Macnamara, Coleen 18 n. 6, 43–44, 63
manipulation 98, 103
"marginal" agents 102, 157–158
Mason, Elinor 113–116
McGeer, Victoria 41–43
McKenna, Michael 14 n. 1, 43, 88 n. 14, 108–109,
    112, 127 n. 11
Mele, Alfred 130
Midnight Cowboy 68
minimal theory of blame, *see* blame and
    blaming, minimal theory of
mockery 55–56, 77
    and blame, *see* blame and blaming, mockery
        as a form of
    and costly signaling, *see* costly signaling
        and mockery
    and desert, *see* desert and mockery
    and funniness 61
    and mockability (fittingness of) 93–95, 96,
        98–100, 164
    affiliative 55, 57
    aggressive 56
    -blame and complimenting-praise 58–61, 75
    hypocritical 73
    self- 56, 138–139
        and hypocrisy 138
        and standing 138
    self-enhancing 55, 57
    stings of 56–58, 93, 99
Moore, Donnie 48–49, 138
moral agency 109–110
moral approval 43
moral encroachment 88 n. 13, 91 n. 16, 98
moral foundations theory 126
moral ignorance, 104; *see also* blame and
    blaming, and moral ignorance;
    see also praise and praising, and moral
    ignorance
moral luck 98, 103–105

narcissism and narcissists 50–52, 56, 113
    and empathy 69–70
    and self-mockery 56
    as asymmetrical people 52–53, 55
    grandiose 50, 56
    vulnerable 50, 56
negligence 98, 103, 105–106
Nelkin, Dana 3–4
Newman, George 10
Nichols, Shaun 24 n. 13, 41, 144

norm(s) 24
    adherence to 163
    commitment to 25–26
    maintenance 25–26, 36–37, 160, 163, 164
    of blame, *see* blame and blaming, norms of
    of excellence 28
    of praise, *see* praise and praising, norms of
    performance 25
    social 24
    violations of 85
Norm Maintenance Theory (NMT) 26–28, 73,
        76 n. 21
    and gratitude 72
    defense of against competitor functionalist
        theories 39–45
    defense of against constitutivist critics 36–39
normative authority 72–73
Nussbaum, Martha 152 n. 17
normative balance 68–69, 73, 130

Obama, Barack 57

Pereboom, Derk 86, 99 n. 5, 104
personhood, corporate 108
Pettit, Philip 108
Pizarro, David 10
Piovarchy, Adam 33–34
Plato 129–130
Portmore, Douglas 15, 126–127
praise and praising 20–21
    and danger 8, 34, 46, 50–52
    and demands xx, 5, 10
    and emotions 5
    and excuses 7
    and moral ignorance 7, 10
    and morality 6, 45
    and standing 8
    buzz(es) of 28, 34, 36, 38, 41, 45, 46, 58, 83,
        160, 163
    complimenting- 4, 21, 44, 58, 63, 72–73, 81,
        92, 96, 138, 140, 161
        acknowledgment and
            non-acknowledgment-seeking 75
        and attitudes 59
        and buzzes of 99
        and complimentability 99–100, 164
        and danger 61
        and demands 59
        and desert 59
        and emotions 59
        and excuses 60
        and moral justification 60–61, 92
        and morality 60

184 INDEX

praise and praising (*cont.*)
  and quality of will 60
  and standing 61, 73
    hypocritical 73
    private 75
  costliness of 34–36
  disproportional 34
  gratitude- 71–72, 81, 102
  hypocritical 61
  moral justification of 158
  nonmoral 45
  norms of 35
  over- and grandiose narcissism 50–51,
    158 n. 28
  private 6
  self- 133 n. 21
  self-directed xxv, 4, 37
  under- and vulnerable narcissism 51
  worthiness of, *see* blame and praise, aptness of
pride xxi, 63, 75–77, 81, 98, 101, 157, 158, 161
protest 23, 42–43
  and answerability 113
  and demands 112
  and threat 41
  theory of blame, *see* blame and blaming,
    protest theory of
psychopathy and psychopaths 102, 113, 137
punishment xxvi, 22, 24, 85, 140, 141–143,
    151, 162
  and desert, *see* desert and punishment;
    see also sanctions and punishment
  and harm 140
  asymmetrical authority relation required
    for 142–143, 162
  non-state 142
  quarantine model of 141–142 n. 3
  self-directed 137
purity 17

quality of will xxv, 7, 40, 69, 73, 92, 98, 100–101,
    103–121, 133, 155, 156–157
  and character 101–102, 121
  and evaluative judgments 101–102, 113, 121
  and regard 101–102, 112, 113, 121, 161
  as fitmaker of emotional blame or
    praise 97–98, 121, 161
  pluralism of 98, 101–102, 106, 112–113, 121

rage 22
reactive attitudes 43 n. 23, 44
reasons-responsiveness 101, 113, 164
recalcitrance, *see* emotions, recalcitrant
regret 23, 27, 75 n. 20, 84, 98, 101, 109, 126–127,
    157, 158 n. 27

Reis-Dennis, Sam 27 n. 14
relationship modification 10, 21, 33, 59
  theory of blame, *see* blame and blaming,
    relationship theory of
remorse 4, 27, 44, 45, 53, 59, 69, 110–112, 114,
    126–127, 135, 137
  and guilt 69 n. 10, 143 n. 4
repentance 82
resentment 7, 9, 22, 43, 92, 100, 124, 127, 158
  expressions of 95
  private 125
responsibility, taking on 97, 113–116
  corporate 107–113, 161
  gaps 106, 113
  tripartite theory of 102, 112–113, 157, 161
responsibility responses 72, 85
responsible
  agency xxi–xxiii, 11, 62, 63, 68, 160,
    163–164, 166
  being vs. being held xix, 3
retribution or retaliation xxi, 43, 44, 65, 67, 140,
    142–145, 150, 152
  secret 68
rewards xxi, 77, 85, 157 n. 25
Russell, Paul 106 n. 10, 109

sadness 65, 75 n. 19, 158
sanctions xxi, xxvi, 22, 24, 44, 73, 77, 85, 126,
    140–159, 164–165
  and desert, *see* desert and sanctions
  and fairness 148–149, 151, 153, 157, 159, 162,
    163, 164–165
  and grading 148
  and incentives 28, 148, 162, 166
  and moral justification 141, 145–146, 148
  and moral rights 149, 151
  and penalties 150–152, 155–156, 162–165
  and punishment 87, 95, 141, 144, 162
  for faultless conduct 150–151, 163
Sars, Nick 124 n. 6
Scanlon, T. M. 9–10, 13, 14, 72 n. 17, 90, 104
scapegoating 82, 86, 120
Scarantino, Andrea 64–65
schadenfreude 54, 92
Schroeder, Mark 116
self-blame, *see* blame and blaming, self-directed
self-control 129–130
self-deception 130
self-deprecation 138–139
self-praise, *see* praise and praising, self-directed
self-talk xxv, 132–135
  and goal-frustration 133
  forward-looking nature of 133
  negative 132–133

INDEX 185

nonmoral 134–135
  positive 132–133
shame 23, 50, 65, 75 n. 20, 134
shaming 23
Sher, George 4, 14, 16–17, 19 n. 8, 88 n. 13, 105
Sherriff in a Small Town case 86
shunning 23
signaling 111
  and gratitude 72
  blame and praise 37, 76
  costly, *see* costly signaling
  virtue 35
  without costs 33–34, 36
silent treatment 23, 139, 143, 149, 155
slighted-anger, *see* anger, slighted-
slights 98, 101, 120, 135, 161, 164; *see also* blame
        and blaming, and slights, or anger
        and slights, or anger, slighted-
Smith, Adam 130
Smith, Angela 14, 40
standing, *see* blame and blaming, and
        standing; praise and praising, and
        standing
stings, *see* blame and blaming, stings of

Strawson, P. F. 13–14, 43 n. 23, 46, 100, 124
strict liability 153, 155, 157

Talbert, Matthew 103–105
Telech, Daniel 71
Todd and Rabern 129 n. 17
torch fishing 12–13, 32
Trump, Donald J. 53 n. 6, 57

ultimatum game xxi, 44, 145
utilitarianism 82, 86

Vargas, Manuel 12–13, 15–16, 19 n. 8, 24 n. 12,
        82 n. 2
Velichkov, Alexander 134 n. 22

Wallace, R. Jay 7–8, 9–10, 127 n. 11
warm feelings xxiii, 13, 21
Watson, Gary 46–47, 72–73
Williams, Bernard 115
Wolf, Susan 113 n. 19
wrong kinds of reasons 84, 104, 114–115,
        120, 138
wronging beliefs 116–121